Sutherland and Sylvester demystify the magic of advertising in their thoughtful and practical explanation of what makes good ads work. They integrate advertising craft with cognitive learning and psychological theory to elucidate the elements of persuasive communication.

At every turn, deep respect is expressed for the audience of advertising. At the same time, agency teams are portrayed as up to the intellectual and creative challenge of designing 'feathers of advantage' for their clients.

Sara Lipson, Director of Consumer Sciences, AT&T

Puts the psyche of advertising on the analyst's couch to reveal the sometimes surprising mind of commercial persuasion.

Jim Spaeth, President, Advertising Research Foundation

This is a well-informed and engagingly written description of the processes involved in the communication of advertising. It does not share the problems of advertising text books, which are generally superficial as well as being invariably out-of-date. Nor is it one of those populist works that receive a wide sale by propagating over-simple theories. It is the work of two seasoned practitioners and it carries the authority of their experience in the real world.

John Philip Jones, author of When Ads Work *and
Professor of Marketing, Syracuse University*

I learned a lot from the book, while thoroughly enjoying it. It has much to offer for both the novice and the experienced advertising person. Insights about the advertising process are backed up with many examples of real advertising, research monitoring hundreds of advertising campaigns around the world, and a wide variety of academic research. Amazingly, all this is combined in a delightful writing style that entertains while it teaches.

Alan Sawyer, Professor of Marketing, University of Florida

A thought-provoking and practical book on how ads work and how advertising campaigns can be most effectively managed that also contains many useful ideas for achieving more effective advertising campaigns.

John Rossiter, Research Professor of Marketing and co-author of
Advertising Communications & Promotions Management

Consumer Communication Effectiveness is the first and last goal of all advertising, the authors' unique perspective gives you an added insight into developing a winning communication edge—a must-read for marketers!!

Paul Kennedy, Vice President Marketing, Fosters Brewing Group and President,
Australian Association of National Advertisers

If you have to read one business book this year, let this be the one. This book is a gem because it reveals the secrets of effective advertising gleaned from years of sophisticated advertising research. It should be on every manager's bookshelf.

Lawrence Ang, Senior Lecturer in Management,
Macquarie Graduate School of Management

Essential reading for all practitioners and everyone interested in how advertising works. In a new knowledge world, no one can afford to ignore the assets contained in these pages.

John Zeigler, Director of Digital Strategy,
DDB Worldwide

Max and Alice make sense. In a time when the gloss of new media often detracts from the importance of the message, they have successfully and succinctly refocussed our attention on the core issue—how to create effective communications.

Pat Williams, Williams Media Audits

Advertising and the Mind of the Consumer strips away the mystery that surrounds the black art of advertising in a sensible and readily comprehensible way.

Stan Glaser, former Professor of Management,
Macquarie University

Advertising
and the mind of the consumer

what works, what doesn't, and why

SECOND EDITION

MAX SUTHERLAND
AND ALICE K. SYLVESTER

ALLEN&UNWIN

Allen & Unwin
83 Alexander Street
Crows Nest NSW 2065
Australia
Phone: (61 2) 8425 0100
Fax: (61 2) 9906 2218
E-mail: info@allenandunwin.com
Web: http://www.allenandunwin.com

National Library of Australia
Cataloguing-in-Publication entry:

Sutherland, Max.
    Advertising and the mind of the consumer.
    what works, what doesn't and why.

    2nd ed.
    Includes index.
    ISBN 1 86508 231 7.

    1. Advertising — Psychological aspects. 2. Consumer
    behaviour. I. Sylvester, Alice K. II. Title.

659.1019

Internal design by Simon Paterson
Set in 11/13pt Berkeley by Bookhouse Digital, Sydney
Printed by Griffin Press, South Australia

10 9 8 7 6 5 4 3

Contents

132410

Contents

Figures

Tables

Acknowledgments

So many people have contributed to this book that it is impossible to cite everyone by name.

The opportunity to work with the many valued MarketMind clients, to track their and their competitors' advertising over time, has provided much raw material from which to discover how advertising really does work as opposed to how folklore or pure theory says it works. We thank them sincerely and the co-founder of MarketMind, Bruce Smith, for his constant support and encouragement in the writing of this book.

It is through the communicating and sharing of ideas and case-study observations over many years that a body of knowledge such as this emerges. Therefore many of the NFO MarketMind staff contributed either directly or indirectly to this book.

Special thanks for the contribution made to this revised edition goes to Stephen Holden of Bond University, whose international experience provided many valuable, international ad examples, as well as Professor Andy Gross and Mary Van De Walle for their continued assistance throughout the process. Thanks also to John Wigzell (Consultant) and Jon Stayt (Geronomo Business & Financial Marketing) for their invaluable advice on European case examples. On the production side, in this edition, Neil Francis assisted in the preparation of various case-study graphs, a task that in the original edition was carried out by Effie Damaskopoulos, Tony Westerlo and Elick Teitelbaum. The job of scanning images and word processing for this edition

Acknowledgments

was expertly done by the ever-reliable Peggy Duell, who took over the role from Kate Dundon.

Mel Sutherland suffered through many iterations of the proofreading of the original edition in addition to a somewhat impoverished social and family life while this book was being written. To our families, Mel, Keli, Julia and Kent Sutherland along with Michael, Max and Alice Amelia Stepanek, go our thanks for the time to do this book. It came from you.

Many valued academic colleagues and friends have influenced our thinking over the years. In particular we want to mention Professor John Rossiter (Wollongong University), Dr John Galloway (NetMap), Larry Percy (Consultant), Professors Joe Danks and David Riccio (Kent State University), Dr Rob Donovan (University of Western Australia), Geoff Alford (Alford Research), Stephen Holden (Bond University), Shelby McIntyre (Santa Clara University), Bob Warrens and the Chicago Media Research Department of J. Walter Thompson, Josh McQueen (Leo Burnett), Kary McIlwain (Young & Rubicam) and, from the 'earlier years', Drs Bob March, Stan Glaser and Graham Pont. All these and many others have influenced the thinking and hence, indirectly, the content of this book. Of course that does not imply that they will all agree with everything that is written here. The ultimate responsibility for the content, together with any omissions or errors, must remain ours.

Lastly, we are indebted to Larry Gold for bringing the two of us together to write this international edition, as well as to the three people who constantly urged the writing of the original book until it finally happened: Malcolm Cameron, Mike Hanlon and Tom Valenta.

About the authors

Max Sutherland

Max Sutherland is former Chairman and Creative Director of NFO Market-Mind, a subsidiary of NFO Worldwide. He is also Professor of Marketing at Monash University and Swinburne University of Technology in Australia, and Visiting Professor at Santa Clara University in California, USA.

Professor Sutherland is a registered psychologist with three degrees: a PhD in Psychology from Kent State University (USA), a Master of Arts degree in psychology from Sydney University and a Bachelor of Commerce (Marketing) from the University of New South Wales.

After failing and leaving secondary school he started a career in retail sales (major appliances and insurance) and resumed study later as a mature-age student. He held positions in market research with the Coca-Cola Export Corporation and the Overseas Telecommunications Commission. He has held full-time lectureships in market research and consumer behavior at the University of NSW and the David Syme Business School (now Monash University) as well as Visiting Professor at Kent State University in the USA.

The company he co-founded has specialized in tracking the effects of advertising for many of the leading advertisers in over 20 countries including Gillette, Merck, Kodak, McDonald's, Miller, Qantas, McCain, AT&T, Nestlé, Pfizer, as well as various utility and telecom organizations.

He is a former editor of the *Australian Marketing Researcher*, a former Chairman of the Market Research Society of Australia, and a Fellow of the Market Research Society of Australia and the Australian Marketing Institute. Max can be contacted at msutherland@compuserve.com.

Alice K. Sylvester

Alice K. Sylvester is a veteran American ad agency researcher and currently Vice-President, Account Planning Director, Foote, Cone & Belding in Chicago. She has worked for various ad agencies including Young & Rubicam Inc., Leo Burnett, J. Walter Thompson and Tatham-Laird & Kudner (now Euro Tatham RSCG).

She is a past Chairman of the Board of the Advertising Research Foundation, and a member of the Editorial Review Board of the *Journal of Advertising Research*. She also chairs the 'David Ogilvy Awards for Research Excellence' committee of the ARF.

M/s Sylvester has a diverse interdisciplinary background in media research and account planning as well as brand research. A winner of the Thompson Innovation Award for a new approach to planning, 'Sales Effective Media Planning and Budgeting', she has also judged the American Marketing Association's EFFIE Competition for advertising that produces marketplace results.

Over the years, M/s Sylvester has consulted to many of the United States' largest advertisers. She is widely published and a frequent speaker on advertising at US and global conferences. She now specializes in brand health, advertising budgeting and marketplace effects.

M/s Sylvester has a Masters of Science degree in Administration and a Bachelor of Arts degree in English Communications, both from DePaul University. She lives in Arlington Heights, Illinois, with her husband Michael, a commercial illustrator, and their school-age children, Max and Alice Amelia.

PART A

Why advertising
has remained a mystery
for so long

Introduction

The subject of advertising seems to be riddled with mystique and apparent contradictions. This book resolves some of those contradictions. It had its beginnings in regular columns for various trade publications and journals; Part B brings together some of those articles. This book is aimed at advertisers and their ad agencies but also at the people to whom they advertise. As David Ogilvy, a leading advertising expert, said (in the chauvinistic 1960s): 'The consumer is not a moron. She is your wife!'[1] Our wives, our husbands, our partners, our children are all consumers. The consumer is not an idiot. The consumer is you and me.

Many years ago the advertiser's dilemma was expressed in this way: 'I know that half my advertising is wasted—but I don't know which half!'[2] But developments in market research are beginning to change all that by better enabling advertisers to identify what works and what doesn't.[3] This book draws on the experience of tracking week by week the effects of hundreds of advertising campaigns over a period of more than ten years.

Almost everybody is interested in advertising. Approximately $US400 billion is spent on advertising each year in the world (over $US200 billion in the USA alone).[4] The average consumer is exposed to hundreds of ads every day.[5] By the time we die we will have spent an estimated one and a half years watching TV commercials.[6] Yet advertising continues to be something of a mystery.

The response 'Gee, I didn't know that' to an advertisement tends to be the exception. A round trip to New York for $400 is news. Ads that announce the release of a new product like Viagra, DVD or voice-operated computing

3

are news. And if we are someone who is compulsive about germs maybe Mr. Clean with a new disinfectant that kills germs 50 per cent better than the old Mr. Clean might also be news. With news advertising we can easily recognize the potential of the advertising to affect us.

But most advertising is not 'news' advertising. Much of the advertising we encounter doesn't impart news and it is difficult for us to see how it works on us. As consumers we generally believe it does not really affect us personally. Despite this, advertisers keep on advertising. So something must be working—but on whom, and exactly how?

This book demystifies the effects of advertising and describes some of the psychological mechanisms underlying them. It is written primarily for those who foot the bill for advertising and those who produce advertising. In other words, for those many organizations involved with advertising—the marketing directors, marketing managers, product managers, advertising managers, account execs, media people and creatives. However, we hope that it will also be read by interested consumers who wonder how advertising works and why advertisers keep on advertising. Understanding the mechanisms and their limitations tends to lessen the anxieties we may have about wholesale, unconscious manipulation by advertising.

It may come as a surprise to many consumers that those who foot the bill for advertising are often frustrated by knowing little more than the consumers themselves about how, why or when their advertising works. Advertising agencies, the makers of advertising, also know less about these things than we might think. They are seen as wizards at selling, but an agency's most important pitch is to organizations that *want* to advertise—companies that will engage the agency's services to design and arrange placement of their advertising on an ongoing basis. To keep clients coming back, advertising agencies need to sell the effectiveness of their advertising to those clients and to the world. Inevitably, some agencies become much more accomplished at selling their clients and the world on the great job the advertising is doing than they do at creating advertising that is truly effective.

Like the skills of tribal healers, ad agencies' powers and methods are seen to be all the greater because of the mystery that surrounds advertising. Books like Vance Packard's *The Hidden Persuaders*[7] enhance this image of the power of advertising agencies because they portray them as having witch-doctor-like powers. So in a way the mystique and aura of advertising works in favor of its makers—the advertising agencies—by boosting their image, status and perceived power.

In 1978 Alec Benn, an advertising agency principal in the United States, claimed in his book *The 27 Most Common Mistakes in Advertising*: 'There is a great conspiracy participated in by advertising agencies, radio and television stations and networks, advertising consultants, newspapers, magazines and others to mislead corporate management about the effectiveness of advertising.'[8] Benn was pointing out that advertising failed more often than it succeeded, usually because its effects 'are not measured objectively'.

Since then, advertising has begun to be measured more objectively and more often, indeed continuously, and this has highlighted the hard fact that many ads still fail. Part of the reason is that advertising agencies get too little in the way of 'news' to work with—there aren't the breakthrough things to say about existing brands to cause immediate impacts. But the other part of it is a historical overreliance on intuition and introspection.[9] When these qualities are used instead of objective measurement as the basis for deciding what works and what doesn't, there are more ads that fail than ads that are outstandingly successful. Sustained effects occur less than half the time.[10] Until recently these failures stood a good chance of going unrecognized because the majority of campaigns were not tracked in a formal way.[11]

In the general population there are those who believe that advertising is all powerful and that the mechanism of advertising must be unconscious and subliminal, because its effects do not seem open to introspection. Such views are associated with the 'dark and manipulative' view of advertising. This book reveals a much more benign interpretation of advertising's so-called 'unconscious' effects. In elaborating on some of the subtler mechanisms of advertising, it dispels many myths and exaggerated claims. At the same time it reveals just how subtle advertising's influence can be and how much impact it can have on the success or failure of one brand over another.

This book will help advertising agencies to diagnose the *why* of what works, and what doesn't. It shows advertisers how to get better results from their advertising budget and their agency. And it reveals to consumers how advertising works to influence which brands we choose—especially if the choice doesn't matter to us personally—and why it is that we find it difficult to introspect on advertising's effect.

1

Influencing people: myths and mechanisms

Why is it so difficult to introspect on advertising and how it influences us? Because we look for major effects, that's why! Too often, we look for the ability of an ad to persuade us. We look for a major effect rather than more subtle, minor effects. Big and immediate effects of advertising do occur when the advertiser has something new to say. Then it is easy for us to introspect on its effect.

But most effects of advertising fall well short of persuasion. These minor effects are not obvious but they are more characteristic of the way advertising works. To understand advertising we have to understand and measure these effects. When our kids are growing up we don't notice their physical growth each day but from time to time we become aware that they have grown. Determining how much a child has grown in the last 24 hours is like evaluating the effect of being exposed to a single commercial. In both cases, the changes are too small for us to notice. But even small effects of advertising can influence which brand we choose, especially when all other factors are equal and when alternative brands are much the same.

Weighing the alternatives: evaluation

It is easiest to understand this with low-involvement buying situations (Figure 1.1). The situation is like a beam-balance in which each brand weighs the same. With one brand on each side, the scale is balanced. However, it takes only a feather added to one side of the balance to tip it in favor of the brand on that side. The brands consumers have to choose from are often very similar. Which way will the buying balance tip? When we look for advertising effects we are looking for feathers rather than heavy weights.[1]

Figure 1.1
Low involvement: deciding between two virtually identical alternatives

The buying of cars, appliances, vacations and other high-priced items are examples of high-involvement decision-making. This high level of involvement contrasts with the low level brought to bear on the purchase of products like shampoo or soft drink or margarine. For most of us, the buying of these smaller items is no big deal. We have better things to do with our time than agonize over which brand to choose every time we buy something.

The fact is that in many low-involvement product categories, the alternative brands are extremely similar and in some cases almost identical. Most consumers don't really care which one they buy and could substitute easily if their brand ceased to exist. It is in these low-involvement categories that the effects of advertising can be greatest and yet hardest to introspect upon.

Even with high-involvement products the beam balance analogy is relevant because very different alternatives can weigh-up equal (Figure1.2). We often have to weigh up complex things like 'average quality at a moderate price' against 'premium quality at a higher price'. Often we find ourselves in a state of indecision between the alternatives. When the choice weighs equal in our mind, whether it be low involvement products or high-involvement products, it can take just a feather to swing that balance.

With high-involvement decisions we are more concerned about the outcome of the weighing-up process, so we think more about how much weight to give to each feature (quality, size or power). How many extra dollars is it worth paying for a feature? Automotive writers, for example, can reach very different opinions. The

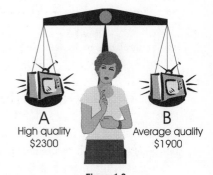

A
High quality
$2300

B
Average quality
$1900

Figure 1.2
High-involvement decision: very different alternatives can weigh equal

more complex a product's features the more complex the assessment because there are usually both positive and negative perspectives. For example, a compact car is positive in regard to fuel economy and manoeuverability but negative in regard to leg room and comfort.

So which way should we see it? What weight *should* we give to a particular feature in our minds? When advertising emphasizes points that favor a brand, it doesn't have to *persuade* us—merely raise our awareness of the positive perspectives. Chances are we will notice *confirmatory* evidence more easily as a result. When we subsequently read a newspaper or consumer report or talk with friends, research shows that we are prone to interpret such information slightly more favorably.[2] This effect is a long way from heavyweight persuasion. Rather it is a gentle, mental biasing of our subsequent perceptions, and we see in Chapter 2 how perspective can influence our interpretation. It is not so much persuasion as a shifting of the mental spotlight…playing the focal beam of attention on one perspective rather than another…

Repetition

Figure 1.3
Small cumulative increments: we don't notice a child's growth in 24 hours

As with the amount by which our kids grow in a day, we are just not aware of the small differences advertising can make (see Figure 1.3). Even though these imperceptibly small changes in time add up to significant effects, individual increments are too small for us to notice. They are below the just noticeable difference (JND). Through the process of repetition, these small increments can produce major perceived differences between brands, but we are rarely aware of the process taking place.

The cumulative effects of changes in brand image become starkly noticeable only in rare cases: for instance, when we return home after a long absence and find that an old brand is now seen by people in a different light—that in the intervening period the brand has acquired a different image.

Registering an advertising claim in our minds (e.g. 'taste the difference' or 'good to the last drop') does not necessarily mean we believe it. However, it makes us aware that there *are* claimed differences between brands. This is a proposition (a 'feather', if you will) that, when everything else is equal, may tip the balance of brand selection, even if only to prompt us to find out if it is true.

Repetition increases our familiarity with a claim. In the absence of evidence to the contrary, a feeling of greater likelihood that the claim *is* true begins to accompany the growing familiarity. This effect of repetition is known as 'the truth effect'.[3]

We tend to think that if something is not true it would somehow be challenged. If it is repeated constantly and not challenged, our minds seem to regard this as prima facie evidence that perhaps it is true. The effect of repetition is to produce small but cumulative increments in this 'truth' inference. It is hardly rational but we don't really think about it. We don't go out of our way to think about it because low involvement, by definition, means that we don't care much anyway. Such claims are 'feathers'.

In summary, the reasons we are unable to introspect on advertising's effects, especially in low-involvement situations, are:

- the effect of each single ad exposure is small;[4]
- with repetition, even imperceptibly small effects can build into larger perceived differences between brands;[5]
- if something gets repeated constantly without challenge, our minds seem to regard this as prima facie evidence that maybe, just maybe, it *is* true (the truth effect);
- often it is no big deal to us which of the alternative brands we choose, anyway.

If you have ever wondered why advertisers seem to persist in repeating the same ad—if you have ever wondered why they think this could possibly influence sane people like us—then here is the answer. Much of advertising creates only marginal differences, but small differences can build into larger differences. Even small differences can tip the balance in favor of the advertised brand. This is especially true of 'image advertising'.

Image advertising

The effect of image advertising is easier to see in relation to high-involvement products, so let us start with a high-involvement example—Volvo cars.

Between 1970 and 1990 Volvo focused its image advertising on safety. Through repetition, it built up a strong image for the Volvo as a safe car. On a scale of 1 to 10 for safety, most people would rate Volvo higher than almost any other car. Safety is now an integral part of our perception of this brand. (The fact that the car actually delivers on this promise has of course been a very important ingredient in the success of the safety campaign—but that is another story.)

One effect of image advertising, then, is to produce gradual shifts in our perception of a brand with regard to a particular attribute—in Volvo's case, safety (in other words, to effect marginal changes in our mental rating of the brand on that attribute). This is often not perceptible after just one exposure because the change, if it occurs, is too small for us to notice.

Now let's take a low-involvement product category—hairspray—and examine its history of brand image advertising.

The first brands of hairspray originally fought for market share on the basis of the attribute of 'hair-holding'. That is, each brand claimed to hold hair. To the extent that they all claimed the same thing, they were what we call 'me-too' brands.

To break out of this, one brand began to claim that it 'holds hair longer'. Just as Volvo claimed that it was safer, and thereby moved Volvo higher up the perceived safety scale, so this brand of hairspray made people aware that some brands of hairspray might hold hair longer than others. It then attempted to shift perception of itself on this attribute and so marginally increase the mental rating consumers would give it on 'length of hold'.

The next brand of hairspray to enter the market, instead of tackling that brand head-on, cleverly avoided doing battle on 'length of hold'. The new brand claimed that it was 'long-holding', but also that it 'brushes out easier'—a dual benefit. In doing so it successfully capitalized on the fact that hairsprays that hold longer are harder to brush out (or were until then). Many years later came the attribute of 'flexible hold' (Figure 1.4).

These examples of image advertising for hairspray and cars illustrate how one effect of advertising is to alter our perceptions of a brand. Advertising can marginally change our image of a brand by leading us to associate it with a particular attribute (like 'longer holding' or 'brushes out easily'), and to associate the brands in our minds with that attribute more than we associate it with any other competitive brand.

Gauging the effects that image advertising has on us is made even more complex

Figure 1.4
Vidal Sassoon hairspray ad claiming 'flexible hold'

because these effects may not operate directly on the image of the brand itself. Image advertising may produce small, incremental differences in the image of a brand, as in the case of Volvo—but sometimes it is aimed at changing not so much the image of the brand itself but of who we see in our mind's eye as the typical user of that brand.

User image

In advertising for Levi's, Revlon, Coca-Cola, Calvin Klein, Dior or Gap, the focus is often on people who use the brand (Figure 1.5). What changes is not so much our perception, or image, of the product as our perception of the user-stereotype—the kind of person who typically uses the brand, or the situation in which the brand is typically used.

When these brands are advertised, the focus is very much on image but often with this important, subtle difference. The advertising aims to change not how we see the brand itself—the brand image—but how we see:

- the stereotypical user of the brand—the user image; and
- the stereotypical situation in which the brand is used.

Figure 1.5
Jim Beam ad reinforcing the stereotypical user image as young, single males

If the user image of a brand resembles us, or the type of person we aspire to be, what happens when we come to buy that product category? The user image acts as a feather on one side of the beam-balance. If everything else is equal it can tip the scale (but, note, only if everything else is about equal).

User, or situational, image changes usually fall short of the kinds of rational, heavyweight reasons that make perfect sense of any choice. But they can still tilt the balance in favor of one brand. Minor effects like these constitute much of the impact of advertising. Yet they are usually much more difficult for us as consumers to analyze introspectively, and we tend to discount them because they clearly fall well short of persuasion.

Persuasion is the exception

We have been told so often that the role of advertising is to persuade that we seem to have come to believe it.

How often do we hear the comment, 'It wouldn't make me run out and buy it'? This is common in market research when participants are asked to analyze introspectively how they react to an ad, especially if it is an image ad. It demonstrates the myth of how advertising is supposed to have its influence. No one really believes that any ad will make them run out and buy the advertised product. Nothing has that kind of persuasive or coercive power. So why do people say, 'It wouldn't make me run out and buy it'? Because they can't think of any other way the ad could work. The effect of advertising is not to make us 'run out and buy'. This is especially true with low-involvement products and especially true with image advertising. It is beam-balance stuff.

High involvement

High-involvement buying contrasts with low-involvement, low-cost purchases. When people are parting with substantial sums of money to buy a TV, a car or a vacation, they do not take the decision lightly. These are high-involvement decisions for most consumers. Before making them, we actively hunt down information, talk with friends and generally find out all we can about our prospective purchase.

Furthermore, the alternative brands available will usually have many more differences. They are unlikely to be almost identical, as is the case with many low-involvement products.

Advertising is one influence in high-involvement buying decisions, but it is only one among many. Often it is a relatively weak influence, especially in comparison with other influences like word-of-mouth, previous experience and recommendations by 'experts'. In the case of high-involvement products, much of advertising's effect is not so much on the final decision as on whether a brand gets considered—whether we include it in the set of alternatives that we are prepared to spend time weighing up. This is one of the ways that advertising influences our thinking indirectly. For example, there are hundreds of brands and types of cars, far too many for us to consider individually in the same detail. We seriously consider only those that make it onto our short list. But what determines which cars make it onto our short list? This is where advertising comes into play.[6]

Influencing people: myths and mechanisms

If we are unlikely to be in the market for a new car, refrigerator or wall unit for several years, the advertising we see and hear for these products falls on low-involved ears. However, if our old car or appliance unexpectedly breaks down today, we may find ourselves propelled into the market for a new one. Suddenly, the ads we saw yesterday or last week or last month under low-involvement conditions become more relevant. One test of their effectiveness will be whether they have left enough impact to get their brand onto our short list.

A lot of advertising, even for high-priced items, thus has its effect in a low-involvement way. Again we see that, in looking for the effects of advertising, we need to look for subtle effects. It is a case of 'feathers' rather than persuasion—feathers that influence what alternatives get weighed up as well as feathers that add their weight to one side of the weighing-up process.

Two mental processes in decision making

There are two fundamentally different mental processes at work in choice decisions. We have already considered the most obvious one, the weighing up of alternatives. But there is another process that consumers and advertisers tend to be less conscious of. *Weighing up the alternatives is one thing. Which alternatives get weighed up is another!*

Which alternatives get weighed up?

What determines the alternatives that are actually considered?

Think about a consumer decision that you probably make every day. It's getting on for noon, you are feeling hungry and you ask yourself, 'What am I going to have for lunch today?' Your mind starts to generate alternatives and evaluate each alternative as you think of it. The process goes something like this:

'Will I have a salad?'
'No, I had a salad yesterday.'
'A sandwich?'
'No, the sandwich store is too far away and, besides, it's raining.'
'I could drive to McDonald's.'
'Yes...I'll do that.'

There are two things to note here. First, what the mind does is to produce alternatives, one at a time. This 'mental agenda' of alternatives is ordered like this:

What's the choice for lunch?
1. Salad
2. Sandwich
3. McDonald's
4. TGI Friday
5. Pizza Hut

Second, the order in which the alternatives are arranged is the order in which they are elicited by the mind. This order can influence your final choice. You may enjoy Pizza Hut more than McDonald's. But in the example you didn't go to Pizza Hut, you went to McDonald's.

Had you continued your thought process instead of stopping at the third alternative (McDonald's), you would probably have gone to Pizza Hut. But if Pizza Hut is only fifth on your mental agenda of lunch alternatives, it is unlikely to get much of your business. You didn't get to Pizza Hut because you didn't think of it before you hit on a satisfactory solution—McDonald's. You didn't get there *physically* because you never got there *mentally*. Even if we like or prefer something, if it is not reasonably high on our mental agenda it is likely to miss out.

How many times have you found yourself doing something and realised too late that there was something else you would rather have been doing but didn't think about in time? The most preferred alternatives are not necessarily the ones you think of first. (Anyone who has ever left an important person off an invitation list will appreciate this.) Next time you go out for dinner and are trying to decide which restaurant to go to, observe your thought pattern. There are two separate processes at work. One is generation of alternatives. The other is evaluation of the alternatives.

To affect the outcome of buying decisions, advertisers can try to influence:

- the order in which the alternatives are evoked;
- the evaluation of a particular alternative; or
- both.

When we think of advertising's effects we almost invariably think of how advertising influences our evaluation of a brand. Yet much of advertising's influence is not on our evaluations of a brand but on the order in which alternative brands are evoked.

Influencing people: myths and mechanisms

Agenda-setting effect

Influencing the order of alternatives has its basis in what is known as the agenda-setting theory of mass communications. This says: The mass media don't tell us what to think. But they do tell us what to think about! They set the mental agenda.

The agenda-setting theory was originally developed to explain the influence of the mass media in determining which political issues become important in elections. Adroit committee members and politicians claim that if you can control the agenda you can control the meeting. It was not until 1981 that the relevance of this to advertising was recognized.[7]

We can produce mental agendas for lots of things.

What's news?	*What's the choice for lunch?*
1. Presidential allegations	1. Salad
2. State of the economy	2. Sandwich
3. Youth suicide rate	3. McDonald's
4. A child abducted	4. TGI Friday
5. The Olympics	5. Pizza Hut

We can discover our mental agenda by pulling out what is in our minds under a particular category and examining the order (in which it emerges). The category may be 'What's the choice for lunch?', 'What's news?' or what brand of soft drink to buy.

When we reach into our minds to generate any of these agendas, the items do not all come to mind at once. They are elicited one at a time and in an order. The items on top of the mental agenda are the most salient and the ones we are most likely to remember first. It's the same with choosing which restaurant to go to or which department store to visit or which supermarket to shop at this week. It is the same with the decision about which cars or refrigerators to short-list and which dealers to visit. The order in which we retrieve the items from our memories seems almost inconsequential to us but may be critically important in determining the chances of our going to a McDonald's versus Pizza Hut.

This effect also occurs if we have a list of the alternatives or a display of them such as in the supermarket. Even here, where the brands are all set out in front of us, all of them do not get noticed simultaneously. In fact, they do not all get noticed.

Think about the process. We stand there at the display. We notice first one brand, then another and then another. It happens rapidly, but in sequence. So, despite the fact that the brands are all displayed, they are not necessarily all equal in terms of the probability that they will come to mind or be noticed. Supermarkets today carry more than 30 000 items, up from 17 500 a decade ago.[8] This raises a question. At supermarket displays, what makes a brand stand out? To use the marketing term, what makes it 'break through the clutter' of all the alternative packs and get noticed? What makes one brand get noticed more quickly than others at the supermarket display?

This introduces the concept of *salience*, which is formally defined in the next section. In this context we ask how a brand can be moved up from fifth, to fourth to third, to second, to become the first one noticed. The higher up it is in this order, the better chance it has of being considered and, consequently, the better chance of its being purchased.

The brand's physical prominence, the amount of shelf space it occupies and its position in the display are very important. But advertising can influence choice when other factors (like shelf space or position) are otherwise equal. Advertising can help tip the balance.

Asking what makes one brand more salient—more likely to come to mind or get noticed—than another is like asking what influences Pizza Hut's position on our mental lunch agenda. In the supermarket, instead of having to recall all the alternatives by ourselves, we are prompted by the display. However, the brands we notice and the order in which we notice them can be influenced by more than just the display.

Salience

We think much more often about people and things that are important to us than about those that are not. The psychological term for this prominence in our thoughts is *salience*. Advertisers would like us to think of their brands as 'more important' but they will settle for 'more often'.[9] In other words, they would like their brands to be more salient for us.

Our definition of salience is the probability that something will be in the conscious mind at any given moment. One way advertising can increase this probability is through repetition. We have all had the experience of being unable to rid our minds of a song we have heard a lot. The repetition of the song has increased its salience; it has increased its probability of being in the conscious mind at any moment. Repetition of an advertisement, especially a jingle, can have a similar effect. Through repetition of the ad, the salience of the brand—the star of the ad—is increased in our minds.

Another way that advertising influences what we think about and notice is through 'cueing'. To explain this, answer a few questions.

- What's the first thing you think of when you see: *'Just Do It.'*
- What's the first thing you think of when someone says: *'Don't leave home without it.'*
- What comes to mind if you are asked: *'Where do you want to go today?'*
- What's the first thing you think of when someone says: *'Cross your heart'*?
- When you see the word *'Always...'*, what do you think of?
- What's the first thing you think of when someone asks *'Where's the beef?'* in America or *'Which bank?'* in Australia.

Words or expressions such as these come up naturally in everyday conversation. When a brand is linked to them through repetition, they become cues that help increase the salience of the brand.

An actor in a play takes his cue from a line or some other happening or event. The human mind takes its cue from its intentions and its immediate environment. Such cues can influence what we think about next. That's how we go to sleep at night. We turn off the cues. We turn off the light and the radio. We try to reduce distractions or cues so that things won't keep popping into our minds.

One way advertising can use cues is by tying a brand to something that frequently recurs in the ordinary environment. There are many common words, expressions, symbols or tunes that can be developed by means of repetition into mnemonic devices that trigger recollection of the brand (Table 1.1).

If the cue recurs in the circumstances under which the product is likely to be consumed, such as at lunch time, all the better. The ideal mnemonic cue is not just frequently recurring but occurs at these strategic times.

This cueing effect is so much a part of the way we respond to our environment that we are largely oblivious to it. As someone once said, fish are probably unaware of water because it is all round them.

However, most people are aware of cueing to some degree. Almost everybody has had the experience of a particular smell evoking special memories. Pipe tobacco perhaps reminds you of your grandfather; the smell of new carpet may trigger a vivid memory of the first day you moved into your new house. When these memories pop into our minds we are prone to reminisce about past days.

If you have ever had trouble getting to sleep at night because your mind can't switch off, you can relate to how involuntary this process usually is. In other words, what pops into our minds at any point in time is not totally under voluntary control.

When you hear the words 'Don't leave home without...' the speaker may be referring to your keys or your coat, but your mind is involuntarily

Table 1.1
Mnemonic devices that trigger recollection of the brand

Cue (Mnemonic)	Brand/Product	Country
Gimme a break	*Have a Kit Kat*	USA
Have a break...	*Have a Kit Kat*	UK & Australia
Mmmmmmmm...	Big M flavored milk	Australia
MmmmmMmmmmm Good	Campbell's Soup	USA
Don't leave home without it...	American Express	Global
Do you know me?	American Express	Global
Just do it.	Nike	Global
Where do you want to go today?	Microsoft	Global
The real thing...	Coca-Cola	Global
Always...	Coca-Cola	Global
Think different.	Apple	Global
Because you're worth it...	L'Oreal	Global
Reach out and touch someone	AT&T	USA
Thanks! I needed that!	Mennen Skin Bracer	USA
Have a good weekend...	(& don't forget the Aerogard) insect repellant	Australia
Good weekend...	*good VSD* VSD Magazine	France
Which bank?	Commonwealth Bank	Australia
Wednesday...	*is Prince Spaghetti night*	USA
Good on you mum...	*Tip Top's the one.* Bread	Australia
Where's the beef?	Wendys Restaurants	USA
The car in front is...	(a Toyota)	UK
Oh what a feeling...	(Toyota)	USA, Australia
Ring around the collar.	Wisk detergent	USA
Anyhow*...	*Have a Winfield* Cigarettes	Australia
I feel like...	*a Toohey* Tooheys Beer	Australia
Who cares?	Boots Pharmacies	UK
You deserve a break today	McDonald's	USA, UK, Aust.
Thank you for your support	Bartles and Jaymes wine	USA
All because...	*the lady loves...Milk Tray*	UK
Cross your heart...	Playtex Bra	UK, USA, Aust.

reminded of American Express. When a friend asks 'Where do you want to go today?' can your mind help but be reminded of Microsoft? When someone says 'Just do it' can you help but think of Nike?

Celebrities, expressions and music extracts can come to be so 'owned' by a brand that they automatically prompt our thoughts in that direction. In the USA Paul Hogan (Crocodile Dundee) is linked to the Subaru brand. In Australia he was traditionally linked to Winfield cigarettes (Figure 1.6). The word 'Anyhow*' still makes older Australians think of Paul Hogan and Winfield cigarettes because it was uttered by Hogan as part of the commercial ('anyhow*...have a Winfield'). Like Joe Camel in the USA, Hogan and the expression 'Anyhow*' came to stand for the brand and automatically trigger it in people's minds. Even the classical theme music behind the Winfield campaign came to be thought of as 'the Winfield music' and would recall the brand in people's memories. The Marlboro brand did the same thing globally with the theme music from *The Magnificent Seven* which came to be thought of as 'the Marlboro music'.

Figure 1.6
In Australia, Paul Hogan
triggered instant recall of the
brand, Winfield

Our minds are in a sense a 'stream of consciousness'—an inexorable flow that is frequently diverted, sometimes paused, but never stopped. Environmental cues can influence what enters the flow and what direction it takes. One type of advertising focuses on tying a brand to one or more such cues, so that whenever we hear, see or think of the cue there is a high probability that we will think of the brand or notice its presence. It pulls it into our 'slipstream of thought'.[10]

Product category as a cue

Advertisers want us to think of their brand, but they particularly want us to think of their brand when we are making a decision involving the product category. One important cue is therefore the category itself. When we say 'soft drink', what do you think of? When we say 'lunch', what do you think of? If our conscious mind is in the process of being cued by a product category (e.g. it is noon and we are thinking 'lunch'), then what is likely to flit into our head is not a brand of hairspray or a car—we are much more likely to see in our mind's eye the first item on the mental agenda we have for the category 'lunch'.

When our mind is cued in to a particular product category, we almost automatically begin to think of the 'top-of-mind' members of that category. In the case of the category 'lunch', we will think of Pizza Hut or McDonald's or some other food alternative rather than hairspray or cars or anything else.

The technical term for this is *category-cued salience*, or the probability that the brand will come to mind whenever its product category does.

It is possible to measure category-cued salience and assess the influence of advertising on it. This is done by asking people what is the first brand that comes to mind when they hear or see the product category name, and then the next brand and the next.[11] In this way the agenda of brands can be elicited. The rank of a given brand in the product category agenda indicates its category-cued salience. It is a rough index of the probability that it will come to our mind when in the normal course of events we are prompted by the product category name.

If this questioning procedure is carried out with a different random sample of consumers every week, the agenda and the salience of each brand can be tracked, week by week, over time. Market research can detect any improvements resulting from advertising by the order in which the advertised brand is elicited. Advertising a brand generally improves its salience.

Point-of-sale advertising: how to upset the agenda

Many people wonder why Coca-Cola, which is so well known, needs to advertise so much and why it needs to 'waste all that money' on signs in grocery stores. The answer is that if it did not have its signs in these places, Pepsi or some other competitor certainly would. These other brands would try to upset consumers' mental agendas by 'jumping the queue'—by inducing us, at the point of sale, to consider them as well as Coke.

Both point-of-sale reminder advertising and our own mental agenda of brands can prompt us with alternatives to consider, before we ask for what we want. Advertisers therefore try to influence a brand's salience at the point of sale by not leaving it to our mental agendas alone. They erect signs in an attempt to visually cue us into their brand.

When we walk into a convenience store to buy a soft drink, we are already in a category-cued state. We are already thinking about soft drink and which one we will have. If Coke is not already top of our mind when we enter it almost inescapably will be once we have been inside for a moment, because Coke as a brand is likely to be prompted in our minds by (a) the product category cue and (b) the numerous Coca-Cola signs in the store.

Coke may be on top of most people's minds but if they are confronted with a Pepsi sign they may consider both brands. So Coke tries to dominate the clutter of mental alternatives as well as the clutter of point-of-sale advertising. This makes it difficult for other brands to cut through into people's minds at the point of sale. It protects Coke's category salience—something that it has invested a lot of money in building up through years of advertising.

Supermarket shopping: mental agendas versus brand displays

In the supermarket it may be thought that, because all the brands are displayed, they are all equally likely to be noticed—and considered. If this were so, then our mental agenda of brands would be irrelevant to supermarket shopping. However, this is not the case.

On average people take no more than 12 seconds to select a brand and in 85 per cent of purchases only the chosen brand is handled.[12] Observation studies of supermarket shoppers indicate that more than half of all buying is just 'simple locating behavior'.[13,14] That is, most people are simply locating the brand they bought last time, or the one that they came in to buy. They put it into their shopping cart with little or no attention to evaluating the alternatives.

For an alternative brand or pack to be noticed, let alone considered, it would have to cut through the display clutter and stand out in some way. In order to be considered it first has to cut through into conscious attention.

In low-involvement situations many people tend to do what they did last time unless there is something to interrupt the routine. Thus a brand or pack has to cut through the display clutter just as an ad has to cut through the clutter of other ads. And the two, the pack and the advertising, can work together.

The importance of being noticed was demonstrated in another study when regular buyers of a product category were asked if they had seen a particular new brand on the supermarket shelves. They were shown color photographs of the new brand's packs so that it was a task of recognition rather than recall. Only 45 per cent said they had seen the brand, yet it had been in virtually every supermarket for over five weeks.[15]

Just because something is present does not mean we necessarily notice it or consider it. The more cluttered the environment, the more alternatives there are in the product category, the greater this problem is for the advertiser. Advertising signs at the point of purchase can help considerably here, especially when they tie in with advertising that we have already seen. They are then more likely to 'connect' with us and get us to notice the brand.

In the supermarket, it is not signs but usually the brands themselves that are displayed. Potentially we are able to be reminded of every brand in the display by its physical presence. So is our mental agenda of brands still relevant? Yes, though it is now one influence among several. In particular, it orients us by determining which brands we notice in the display.

To illustrate this, imagine you are in a supermarket doing the shopping. As you approach the detergent section, what is in your mind? The category 'detergents'. Why? Because the layout of the supermarket is familiar to you, or because when you approach that section the category is prompted by the display in front of you?

Even in the supermarket, then, the product category as a cue is likely to be triggered in our minds at a particular point and to trigger in turn expectations of the brands we are likely to see in that category. What we see first in the display is likely to be influenced not only by a brand's position and shelf space but also by our expectations of seeing the brand there. All other things being equal, we tend to notice first the brands we are familiar with. This is of course especially true when our mindset is that of looking to locate the one that we bought last time.

When something is heavily advertised, it is more likely to come to mind and, other things being equal, to be noticed faster in a display. We know from the psychological literature that people recognize the familiar more quickly, so it will come as no surprise that familiar brands will be very salient and be noticed more quickly. Advertising exposure of the brand and the pack helps to make the brand more familiar and increase its salience. Repeated exposure of the pack in advertising makes it more familiar and hence gives it a better chance of being noticed earlier or faster than its competitor.

The importance of this marginal effect is seen in the finding mentioned above—that more than half of all purchases in the supermarket are made by simply locating what is wanted. Shoppers hardly pause at the display but simply reach out and pick up the item they are after. So in the supermarket a brand or pack has to cut through the clutter—to stop people walking at more than 1 mile per hour (2 km/h)—and get itself noticed.

Shelf displays, shelf 'talkers' and off-location displays are all ways to help a brand 'pop out' and get our attention. Advertising that we have been exposed to previously, however, also plays an important part in increasing the visual salience of a particular brand. The aim is to modify the degree to which the brand 'pops out' in the display and engages the shopper's notice earlier than other brands.

Measuring visual salience

Advertisers can quantify the visual salience of a pack or brand through market research in much the same way as they uncover the mental agenda. They give each brand in a supermarket display equal shelf space and then take a photograph of the display. They show the photo to a random sample of consumers and ask them to name the brands they see. The order and speed with which the brands are noticed provide a measure of their visual salience. (Actually, researchers use several photographs and control for position in the display by randomly changing the position of each brand.)

Figure 1.7
Visual salience—the 'pop-out' effect.
Inclined letters 'pop out' more than
upside down letters[16]

Summary

One reason we find it difficult to analyze advertising's effects introspectively and why advertising has remained a mystery for so long is that these effects are often so simple and so small that they fall short of outright persuasion. Advertising influences the order in which we evoke or notice the alternatives we consider. This does not feel like persuasion and it is not. It is nevertheless effective. Instead of persuasion and other major effects we should look for 'feathers', or minor effects. These can tip the balance when alternative brands are otherwise equal and, through repetition, can grow imperceptibly by small increments over time.

2

Image and reality: seeing things in different ways

In Chapter 1 we considered the ways in which advertising can influence our decisions by influencing the order in which we evoke or notice the options. Now let us turn to advertising and focus on how it influences our *evaluation* of brand alternatives.

Human beings have a remarkable capacity for seeing things in different ways. The same physical stimulus, the same product or service, can be seen in more than one way. Look at Figure 2.1…is it a rabbit or a duck? It can be seen either way.

Figure 2.1
Is it a rabbit or a duck?[1]

Look at the next figure, 2.2. Think of it as a brand. You should be able to see it in two different ways. When you see a vase in the figure your mind is seeing 'white figure on black background'. When you see two faces, your mind is seeing 'black figure on white background'. This white-on-black or black-on-white that you are using to make sense of what you see is called the *frame of reference*. You overlay a frame of reference on a stimulus to generate a perception.

Figure 2.2
A vase or two faces?

A brand, company or service can also be perceived in different ways depending on the frame of reference that people bring to it. Frame of reference is a psychological term that refers to a mindset or previous experience.

Evaluating a brand

When we evaluate brands we try to do so by evaluating their attributes or features. This is not always a straightforward task, for two reasons. First, there is the problem of what attributes the brand has. Second, there is the problem of how to interpret these attributes.

For example, with the brand Volvo you might think of heavy construction, safety, conservative styling and so on. Heavy construction is closely related to safety, which you rate positively. But you may also associate it with poorer fuel economy, a negative feature. Thus the same attribute, heavy construction, can be rated positively or negatively depending on how you look at it. Similarly, large size may suggest either comfort (a positive) or poor fuel economy (a negative). And cloth seat coverings are more comfortable than vinyl and look better, but are harder to keep clean.

Our minds can interpret any attribute positively or negatively. For example, Levin and Gaeth have shown that our attitudes towards ground beef vary markedly depending on whether it is labeled '75 per cent lean' or '25 per cent fat'.[2] There are upsides and downsides to almost anything in life and a brand's features are no exception.

Positively or negatively charged features

Attribute associations can greatly influence the way we feel about something. 'Cars are imaged variously as shields against accidents, reliable companions, virile athletes or purveyors of fun.'[3] Similar variations occur in our images of other types of categories. Think, for example, of the image you associate with these:

- professions (lawyers, advertisers, doctors, car salespeople)
- countries (France, USA, Australia)
- cities (Sydney, London, New York)
- organizations (International Monetary Fund, United Nations, OPEC)
- corporations (IBM, AT&T, Microsoft, Neiman Marcus, Sears, DuPont)
- brands (Toshiba, Apple, Hewlett Packard)
- services (Speedy Mufflers, Qantas, Virgin Air, DHL)
- product categories (pearls, wine, motor cycles)

Consider the product category 'pearls'. Most people think of pearls as beautiful jewelry, whose salient associations are with gift-giving, attractive women, high fashion and expensiveness (Figure 2.3). But, like any product, pearls also have non-salient features, aspects most people tend not to think of unless their attention is drawn to them for some reason.

To pursue the example, a competitor of Mikimoto (perhaps De Beers) may seek to remind us of these other attributes because it wants us to buy diamonds instead of pearls. It may point out that a pearl is 'more easily damaged than a diamond (a small 'feather'). Or it could point out that a pearl is an oyster tumor. Ugh! What unpleasant associations that statement triggers (a much bigger feather).

Figure 2.3
Advertising pearls

Under normal circumstances we would never have cause to think about these aspects of pearls. Nevertheless, we would have to agree that both are true. The information that a pearl is more easily damaged than a diamond and that a pearl is an oyster tumor is now there in our heads. But these attributes usually occur so far down on our mental attribute agenda that we would rarely, in the normal course of thinking about pearls, bring them to mind. Neither of them is a salient feature.

Calling a pearl 'an oyster tumor' plays the focal beam of our attention on an unpleasant aspect of pearls. This is a 'feather' but in this case a potentially large one and if it were repeated often enough its salience would be likely to increase. (In a sense, this is what the conservationists have done with the product category of furs.) It may not make us stop buying pearls but it might take some of the shine off our perception of them.

Under normal circumstances the focal beam of our attention is only wide enough to encompass a few of the attributes of a brand or product. By shifting the spotlight and playing the focal beam of attention on other attributes, it is possible to marginally change our perceptions. This is what the graffiti artists are trying to do when they write 'Meat is murder' on walls and bridges. Most of us eat meat. We also know where it comes from. But we don't want to think about it too much. If we did, we would probably consider becoming vegetarians. The killing of animals in order to eat their flesh is hardly an association that we want to be reminded of.

Advertising influence on our brand attribute agenda

When you think of Volvo you perhaps think 'safe', 'reliable', 'heavy'. You could consider many other attributes, but your mind has only time to touch on a few. The advertiser wants safety to be high on the Volvo attribute agenda. So its advertising uses words and pictures to highlight the brand's association with that attribute.

A confectionery brand could focus on attributes like fun, popularity, self-indulgence, color, taste, shape or texture. M&M, for example, plays the focal beam of our attention on one specific attribute—'melts in your mouth not in your hand'. Lifesavers focuses on shape—'the candy with the hole'.

With drinks, too, there are all sorts of attributes on which an advertiser can play the focal beam of attention. Some that will be familiar are:

* Taste: *Just for the taste of it—Diet Coke*
* Unpretentious: *Image is nothing. Taste is everything—Sprite*
* Pretentious/exclusivity: *Stella Artois—reassuringly expensive*
* Sport: *Life is a sport. Drink it up—Gatorade*
* Modern/up-to-date: *Pepsi—The taste of a new generation; Generation Next*
* Thirst-quenching: *Heineken—refreshes the parts other beers can't reach*
* Flavor... *7UP, the Uncola*
* Ubiquity... *Always Coca-Cola*
* Quality/flavor: *Good to the last drop... Maxwell House*
* Origin: *Fosters—Australian for beer; Columbia Coffee—100% pure Columbian coffee beans*
* Health: *Another day, another chance to feel healthy—*Evian mineral water

The chain of associations (visual or verbal) that a brand automatically triggers in our mind can be ranked in the order in which they are triggered, with the most salient ones at the top. This is the attribute agenda.

One of the most important aspects of advertising, then, is to play the focal beam of attention on a particular attribute and make that attribute more salient for us when we think of the brand.[4,5] In other words, advertising influences the attribute agenda for a brand by rearranging the order in which we think of its attributes.

Using positively charged features: positioning

Words and images can be used to make the positive attributes of an advertiser's brand or product more salient; to increase the probability that when we think of that brand we will think of those positive attributes; to place them higher on the brand's attribute agenda.

What do you think of when we say 'Colgate'? Your stream-of-thought perhaps went something like this:

- Toothpaste
- Cleans teeth
- Whitens teeth
- Kids
- Prevents decay
- The fluoride gets in

Now, what do you think of when we say 'Close-Up' toothpaste? Your stream-of-thought is likely to be heavily influenced by the advertising for Close-Up, which features scenes of couples kissing. It plays the focal beam of our attention on quite different attributes from those we associate with Colgate. It puts the brand's major selling point, the attributes associated with kissing—'fresh breath' and 'sex appeal'—high on our agenda of associations. This attribute agenda is quite different from Colgate's.

Using negatively charged features: repositioning the opposition

Advertisers usually try to highlight the positive attributes of their own brand. An alternative strategy is to highlight the negative features of the opposition's product. We saw how this works with product categories when we discussed the examples of pearls and meat. Highlighting the negatives in the opposition brand is referred to as 'repositioning the opposition'—repositioning the opposition brand in people's minds.

The best known example of this was the famous Avis rental car advertising campaign which used the line: 'Avis. We're Number Two, so why should you rent from us? We try harder!'

In this campaign Avis acknowledged that it was not the market leader and scored points and credibility for its honesty. At the same time it indirectly and subtly highlighted a negative attribute often associated with strong market leaders and monopolies—that they can be complacent and give poor service, that they don't try hard enough. The proposition that Avis as number two in the market would be trying harder to deliver better service was the positive flip-side of this. It was given more credibility by the company's apparent honesty in admitting it was not Number One.

Thus, words and images can be used to make particular negative attributes of an opposition brand or product more salient: to increase the probability that when we think of the brand we will think of that negative attribute. It is a matter of advertising influencing which attributes our minds focus on when we think of the brand. When we think of pearls or brand leaders we don't usually think of the negative attributes, and this leaves them looking attractive.

The Sprite campaign: 'Image is nothing. Taste is everything' was another attempt at highlighting a negative attribute of opposition soft drink brands. Sprite positioned itself as 'unpretentious', focused on taste, not needing to play the focal beam of attention on image hype like other soft drink brands.

It is the fact that our minds are usually focused on the positive attributes (like 'jewelry', 'good-looking', 'valuable', 'great gift') that makes a brand attractive. Just as there is a mental agenda of brands that we free-associate to the product category, so there is a mental agenda of attributes that we free-associate to entities like meat or pearls, or brands like Volvo or Pepsi. Advertising can make certain attributes more salient and therefore higher on a product's attribute agenda. As a consequence, when we think of the product we think of the advertised features before, and perhaps instead of, other negative but less salient attributes.

Point-of-sale advertising: attribute cueing

Just as ads or signs at the point of sale can remind us of a brand, so too can they remind us of a particular attribute of the brand.

- Just for the taste of it! Diet Coke
- BA...The world's favorite airline...British Airways
- M&M. Melts in your mouth not in your hand

The words and pictures used to label and describe a brand can direct our attention to quite different aspects of the same thing; they can help us to see it in different ways.

To illustrate: What do you think of when I say 'Ted Turner'? A biography of Ted Turner could conceivably carry any of the following subtitles: ...the man, ...the adventurer, ...the media mogul, ...the husband, ...the philanthropist, ...the sailor...

Ted Turner is one person but he has all these attributes. Depending on which subtitle was chosen, the book would attract a slightly different audience and have slightly different appeals. The same man is being described but what we expect to see in the book would be very much influenced by which title or description was used. Whether people bought it would be influenced by a combination of their own attribute agenda for Ted Turner and how much they are interested in 'adventurers' or 'media moguls' or 'philanthropists' or 'sailing' or whatever cue is used in the subtitle of the book. Each description of Ted Turner plays the focal beam of our attention and our expectations on a different attribute of the same person. It consequently influences our perceptions and our expectations and does not leave them solely to our own mental agenda.

Figure 2.4
Ted Turner

Point-of-sale advertising does the same thing. It influences us by playing the beam of our attention on the brand and the featured attribute at the same time.

Influenced by the brand name

Advertisers frequently choose the name of a brand so the name itself can help direct attention, dictate people's expectations and determine the brand's most salient features. Names like Safe and Sound (baby seats), Posturepedic (mattress), BeautyRest (mattress), Revlon ColorStay (makeup), Head & Shoulders (shampoo), Chips Ahoy (cookies) and I Can't Believe It's Not Butter (margarine). These not only name the product but also make an implicit statement about its salient attributes. So we expect baby seats with the name 'Safe and Sound' to have features like quality and safety. We expect beds called 'Posturepedic' not to damage our back, and so on.

This has a very long history. 'Erik the Red named the country he had discovered Greenland, for he said that people would be more tempted to go there if it had an attractive name.'[6] Erik the Red obviously had an intuitive feel for what influences people's expectations even though he did not think of it in terms of a product's attribute agenda.

Another example from history: before the Civil War, in areas of the USA known as temperance regions, alcoholic beverages had no market because of the social taboo. Interestingly, however, the marketers of patent medicines found these regions were a big market for their products—especially those containing up to 44 per cent of the preservative alcohol![7]

Summary

How we evaluate a brand, a service or a product depends on how we perceive it. This, in turn, depends on the frame of reference we overlay on it. The frame of reference comes largely from our experience. Just as there is a mental agenda of brands that we associate with a given product category, so there is a mental agenda of attributes that we free-associate to a given brand.

Under normal circumstances the focal beam of our attention is only wide enough to focus on a limited number of the possible attributes of a brand or product. By shifting the spotlight and playing the focal beam of our attention on other attributes, it is possible to change our perceptions of the product. Words and images can be used to make its positive attributes more salient, to increase the probability that when we think of the brand we will think of those attributes.

Again, these may be 'feathers', but they may nevertheless be enough to tip the scales in favor of a particular brand, especially when all other factors are equal.

3

Subliminal advertising: the biggest myth of all

Advertising is in an odd position. Its extreme protagonists claim it has extra-ordinary powers and its severest critics believe them.

Andrew Ehrenberg[1]

There are those who believe that advertising is all powerful, with a mechanism that is unconscious and subliminal, and that is why its effects are not open to introspection. This chapter points to *subtlety*, not subliminality, as the important factor, and dispels the subliminal advertising myth. We also examine the reasons why 'embeds' which fan people's fears—continue to appear in advertising from time to time.

The never-ending story

When the Lion King movie was released Disney found itself under attack from accusers who said the word s-e-x could be discerned in the dust as the lions were playing.

More recently in the USA, in print ads for Camel cigarettes, the image of a camel was barely discernible, embedded in the patterns of exhaled smoke and in the arrangement of iced water droplets (Figure 3.1).

And in a number of visual ads with no apparent message the Mercedes three-point star appeared embedded in a variety of obscure places (see Figure 3.2).

Figure 3.1
The image of a camel appeared in
the smoke

Figure 3.2
Only the word 'Speed' appeared on
this ad. Note the Mercedes three-point
star in the sole of the shoe

Not surprisingly, these things make consumers very uneasy. Things that
we don't understand make us more fearful. The natural fear is that somehow these images are seducing us in some way without our knowledge.

There has been so much nonsense talked about 'subliminal advertising'
there is always risk that writing about it will fuel the uninformed hype. But
by understanding its mythical origins we will see how subtlety, not subliminality, is what is important in advertising and how the fears of subliminal
advertising effects have been grossly overblown.

The original scare was caused by a cinema owner in the USA in the
1950s who flashed 'Drink Coca-Cola' and 'Eat popcorn' on the screen during
a movie so fast that no one was supposed to be aware it was happening.
He reported that sales of Coca-Cola and popcorn increased dramatically.
There was such an uproar that legislation was quickly prepared to ban subliminal advertising.

If subliminal advertising did indeed have this kind of effect on our behavior, and without our knowledge, then clearly we would need protection
from it. It is still widely believed that in the 1950s subliminal advertising
was made illegal in the USA. In fact, no such legislation was passed either

federally or in any state. Laws were enacted in a number of other countries including the UK and Australia, but, as we will see, this was unnecessary.

That was more than a quarter of a century ago. Since then there have been numerous attempts—all unsuccessful—to replicate the effect claimed by the cinema owner, and more than 200 scientific papers have been published on the subject. Pratkanis and Aronson, after exhaustively researching the literature, concluded that 'no study has demonstrated motivational and behavioral effects similar to those claimed by the advocates of subliminal seduction'.[2] Then in 1984, when confronted with the overwhelming evidence against subliminal advertising, the cinema owner, James Vicary, was reported in *Advertising Age* magazine as admitting that his original claim had been a fabrication.[3] So subliminal advertising was just a myth all along.

Self-help tapes

If that is so, you may ask, what about those self-help tapes? The ones that are supposed to contain subliminal messages to help you give up smoking or improve your self-esteem? Are they also nonsense?

In the same way that a sugar pill will relieve pain in about one-third of sufferers if they think it is aspirin, so too will such tapes work on a proportion of the people who use them—because they expect them to. Pratkanis and Aronson convincingly demonstrated this several times by giving experimental subjects tapes of classical music marked 'Subliminally improve your memory' or 'Subliminally improve your self-esteem'. A significant proportion of the subjects reported improvements in their memory or self-esteem, depending on how their tape was labeled, but the proportion was the same whether the tapes actually had subliminal messages embedded in them or not.[4]

The practical jokesters: embedded words and images

What about the images and words like 'sex' that have been shown to be embedded in some advertisements? Don't they prove that subliminal advertising is being practiced and that it must be working? They prove nothing of the kind! Despite the furor and paranoia created by such books as *Subliminal Seduction* by Wilson Bryan Key,[5] we believe this is nothing but visual graffiti and practical joke playing by those who design the advertising.

It is rather like Hershfeld, the cartoonist for the *New Yorker*, who puts his daugher's name, 'Nina', in every one of his cartoons. You really have to look for it but it's there just the same.

Most of Key's examples are in print advertising. It is very easy for an art director to put something in an ad—a caricature of his boss, for example—without his boss being aware that it is there. An art director friend once pointed out a figure in a poster he had designed and which his boss must have seen hundreds of times. There, right in the middle of the crowd scene in the poster, was a caricature of his boss. Like the Waldo character in the children's books, he was virtually invisible—until you looked. After a hearty laugh this art director swore us all to silence. These things are rarely discovered. The infamous Robert Maxwell's own London *Daily Mirror* once ran a cartoon in which the cartoonist inserted the words 'Fuck Maxwell' in tiny letters among the squiggles.[6]

When the word 'sex' is found disguised in the shadows of ice cubes in a Gilbey's gin ad, as likely as not it is an art director playing a joke on his client or his boss, or just seeing if he can get away with it without anybody noticing.

This kind of thing, however, gives ammunition to the conspiracy theorists who interpret words or images as proof that subliminal advertising is practiced and must therefore be seducing us without our knowledge.

Why did the subliminal myth take hold?

If subliminal advertising is just a myth, how could the myth have been perpetuated for so long?

One reason is to be found in the fact that legislators in some countries moved so quickly to ban it. In doing so they lent a kind of legitimacy to unfounded beliefs about the power of subliminal advertising. The need to prepare legislation to ban it provided history with prima facie evidence that subliminal advertising was a real threat. This helped to enshrine and perpetuate the myth.

Another reason is that the myth fits the image of advertising that is perpetuated by the advertising industry. As we saw in Chapter 1, people believe that advertising has much greater powers to influence us than it really does. Once we started imputing witch-doctor-like powers to ad agencies, it was a small step to believing that they had the modern equivalent: the power to persuade us subliminally.

The media have also done their bit to foster this belief. Mystique makes for good copy and greater reader interest. Subliminal advertising taps into the same mystique as TV programs like *The X Files* and *Ripley's Believe It or Not*.

But is that all there is to it? Just myth, hype and mistake? No. There is another important reason why the belief in subliminal advertising has persisted for so long. A high-jumper can leap six feet (two metres) but this doesn't mean that humans can fly. There are limits to how high we can go, unassisted. Similarly, as the earlier chapters of this book have shown, we are able to learn without full conscious awareness—but only up to a point. There is no doubt that we can be influenced without awareness, but there is nothing necessarily unique or evil or manipulative about this. It is a quantum leap from here to believing in wholesale manipulation of people's minds through subliminal advertising. Just because we can learn without full awareness does not mean that advertising practices mass manipulation on us. People can jump six feet—but flying is something else.

Claims about subconscious learning held a kernel of truth. Claims about subliminal advertising were wildly exaggerated and distorted this truth. Advertising often works without our being able to keep track of the process. There is no need for subliminal exposures on TV and cinema screens. The process happens naturally. It is what low-involvement communication is all about.

Thirty years of research later

So let's look at the claims—more than 35 years later—in light of the substantial body of scientific research in cognitive psychology that has accumulated since then.

The notion of subliminal advertising was based on the belief that awareness was an all-or-nothing thing. That is, we are either aware of something or we are not. This is demonstrably untrue. Research in cognitive psychology over the past 35 years has shown that *conscious awareness is a dimension and not a dichotomy. It is a matter of degree.*

By way of illustration, let us draw your attention to the sounds around you right now. What can you hear? Were you aware of the sounds before we mentioned them? Probably not. The reason is a matter of degree of consciousness. You were not paying attention to the sounds but that does not mean they were 'subliminal' in the sense that they were unable to be heard.

A more useful way of thinking about this issue is in terms of depth of mental processing. Instead of 'subliminal' we could use the term 'shallow processing'.

The logic and illogic of subliminal advertising

The concept of subliminal advertising was based on the notion of a threshold. Subliminal meant 'below the limen, or threshold'. This was thought to be a fixed point below which awareness does not extend. This 'limen' was just another name for the threshold.

We know that, for some sounds, dogs have a much lower threshold than humans. They can hear sounds that we can't. This is the principle of the dog-whistle.

When we have a hearing test, the loudness of a tone is gradually increased until we indicate to the doctor that we can hear it. This is the threshold at which sound enters our consciousness. The same applies to sight. If a word is flashed on a screen for 50 milliseconds we will not be aware of it. If the time of the exposure is increased, at a certain point the word crosses the threshold and enters our conscious awareness.

Subliminal advertising was supposed to be pitched just barely below the threshold of awareness. If it was too far below it would not work. The theory was that the exposure should be sufficiently long for people to register the message unconsciously but not long enough for them to become aware of it. Research has since shown that there is no absolute threshold below which we are always unconscious of something and above which we are always conscious of it. (For example, when we are hungry we recognize food words at much shorter exposures than non-food words. The threshold is lower for these words when we are hungry and higher if we have just eaten.)

Thresholds therefore turn out to vary in the same person from day to day and even from hour to hour. This is partly because sometimes we are more alert than at other times. Thresholds also vary as a result of tiredness, lack of sleep or drugs like alcohol or caffeine. And they vary from person to person.

For an advertiser always to pitch his message precisely at or just under the threshold would therefore seem impossible. Psychologists have now redefined the threshold of awareness—in probabilistic rather than absolute terms—as the exposure level that enables a subject in repeated trials to detect a word 50 per cent of the time. To reach everyone, a message would have to be exposed for a relatively long period. But since this would put it above many people's threshold, the message could no longer be termed subliminal. Subliminal advertising as originally defined is therefore a myth.

Awareness and attention: limits to our capacity

Attention is not an all-or-nothing thing. Even though some people seem to be able to attend to more than one thing at a time, there are limits. Psychological studies show that the more things we allocate our attention to, the shallower the mental processing of any one of them.

Psychology experiments on shared attention show that there are real limits to our attention capacity when other things in the environment are competing for our attention. We have only a limited amount of mental processing capacity at any one time, so some things are given shallow mental processing. Others are given deep attentional processing. There are just too many things around to process them all in the same depth.

Interestingly, the more attention that is paid to something, the easier it is for us to recall it later.[7]

So what happens when some of our attention is directed away from the ad on the radio or TV? What happens when we are barely aware of the advertising around us? To answer, let me take you into the fascinating world of the experimental psychologist and introduce you to what is known as the 'divided attention' experiment.

Divided attention

At first glance divided listening experiments seem akin to a slow form of torture. Psychologists get subjects to listen through headphones to two different stories (or ads) simultaneously—one in the left ear and one in the right ear. (Experimental psychologists use stories while marketing psychologists might use radio ads.)

The subjects are tested immediately afterwards for what they remember. Not surprisingly, they recall only part of what they heard and there is often a lot of confusion between what they heard in the right ear and what they heard in the left ear. Compared with subjects who are exposed to only one ad at a time, these people recall substantially less and their recollections are more confused. That is, the competition between simultaneous stimuli reduces the degree of recall.

This is not surprising. It is why many of us didn't do as well as we could have at school. And it's why television ads also have to be intrusive and interesting—to cut through and hold our attention, especially for low-involvement product categories.

Choosing what we attend to: selective processing

We can choose what we attend to and process deeply. The more interesting the stimulus the more we are likely to pay attention to it and the more of it we recall—in other words, the more impact it has.

What happens if the experimenter asks subjects to listen to the messages in both ears while 'shadowing' (repeating aloud) what they hear in one ear?

In this way the experimenter can get the subject to direct more attention to (process more deeply) the message coming into one ear. What happens when the experimenter tests for recall? It is no surprise that for the shadowed ear the degree of recall is very high. This illustrates that the greater the attention, and the deeper the processing, the greater the recall will be.

But when the experimenter tests for recall of the message heard in the unshadowed ear, the result is zero. The subjects remember nothing—indeed, it is almost as if they had not been exposed to the other ad at all. (Poor recall of radio advertising is reflective of this phenomenon.) But if the subjects can't recall the message, does it mean it had no effect on them? Not necessarily.

The fact that some, albeit minimal, processing can occur at a very low level of consciousness is revealed by a further refinement of the divided attention experiment. In this version, the experimenter interrupts a subject while he is shadowing the ad in one ear and asks what he heard in the last second or two in the unattended ear. Lo and behold, the subject recalls the previous two seconds of the unshadowed message perfectly! This is amazing, is it not? Especially since we know from the previous experiment that 30 seconds after the experiment the subject will remember nothing of that ad.

Thus the ad, even though it may not be recalled after the event, may nevertheless be processed, albeit at some very low level of attention.

Choosing what not to attend to: shallow processing

The problem is that the unattended message is not processed deeply enough. Its content is not retrievable after more than a few seconds unless we are induced to process it further by having our attention directed to it or by repetition.

It seems that a minimum level of attention is necessary for conscious awareness and recall to be retained. When glancing at ads as we skim through a magazine or newspaper, unless we spend at least three-quarters of a second with the ad, we will not even be able to recognize it later.[8] The more stimuli we are exposed to the less attention is left over for processing other stimuli. Advertising that receives only shallow processing, far from being frighteningly powerful, is likely to be very inefficient, and almost certainly has less impact than advertising that is processed at a more conscious level.

This is not to say that such advertising has no effect—just that its effects seem to be marginal, and the shallower our processing of the ad the weaker these effects are likely to be. What are these effects?

There is some evidence that shallowly processed or so-called 'subliminal advertising' can cue a primary drive (e.g. remind us that we are hungry or thirsty or arouse us to feel sexy). This is no different from ordinary advertising. Even at a low level of conscious processing we can be reminded that we are hungry or thirsty. The implication of this is that a theatre owner may be able to increase drink or food sales, but could not direct the extra demand towards specific items such as Coke or popcorn—unless these items were the only things immediately available.

Anita Roddick reportedly put strawberry essence on the pavement outside her first Body Shop store.[9] A well known producer of freshly baked biscuits is said to pump out baking smells from its stores in shopping centers.[10] Anyone who has ever walked past a Body Shop or a hot-bread shop knows that aromas can tweak our senses. There is nothing subliminal about it. Similarly, it would be much more sensible for a theatre owner to use popcorn smells, or regular Coca-Cola advertising, to remind people that they are hungry or thirsty than to rely on less efficient stimuli such as so-called 'subliminal' messages flashed on the screen.

Shallow processing: effects on behavior and brand image

What about the impact of shallowly processed advertising on brand image, brand salience and brand choice? Can it produce small brand-image shifts, or increase brand salience and thereby affect choice when everything else is equal?

The scientific evidence is mixed at this stage. Two experiments seemed to show it could,[11,12] but another which attempted to replicate one of the earlier ones failed to find the same effect.[13] The problem seems to be that, in the experiments, subjects were exposed to only one or two repetitions of an ad. In the real world, the effect of one or two exposures may be too small to observe or measure.

Tracking many advertising campaigns continuously over weeks, months and sometimes years gives a better picture. The influence of low-involvement messages on the image and salience of particular brands seems to be much the same as, but less efficient than, advertising that is attended to more closely and processed more deeply. Over time, advertising appears to be able to produce small but cumulative image shifts and salience increments. Often, the advertising needs to be continued to maintain these effects. When it stops, the gains are eroded.

These small changes are like the 'feathers' we talked about in Chapter 1. With repetition, they can eventually tip the balance—assuming everything else is equal.

Nike and Mercedes may draw comfort from their brand being triggered by just a Swoosh (see Figure 20.4) or a three-point star in the ad. This meager cue can be an effective supplementary branding device and certainly means a brand has achieved presence.[14] A recognizable presence has more to do with successful advertising than any claims for subliminal effect.

When everything else is equal is when advertising is most effective

There is no evidence that low-involvement messages can directly influence or manipulate our conscious choices by *overriding* consciously received input or reasoning.

Whether it is processed at a shallow or a deep level, however, advertising of a particular product or brand is likely to have greatest impact when the alternatives weigh in equally and we don't care too much about the outcome. So its influence is in situations where we don't care much anyway. Or, in situations where we do care, it might help to remind us of a favorable alternative or a nice thing to do that we might not have thought about otherwise.

As the story of subliminal advertising shows, we need to be very careful that we don't jump to the wrong conclusion in evaluating advertising's effects.

Summary

Subliminal advertising, which began as a hoax in the 1950s, became enshrined in myth. Legislators in some countries reacting so quickly to ban it lent a kind of legitimacy to beliefs about its power.

Human beings can learn without full conscious awareness, but there are real limitations to this. We have only a certain amount of mental processing capacity at any one time. Some stimuli receive only shallow mental processing, while others receive deep processing. So conscious awareness is a dimension, not a dichotomy. It is a matter of degree.

The more attention we pay to a message, and the more consciously we process it, the more aware we are of it and the easier it is for us to recall it later. Advertising that receives shallow processing, far from being frighteningly powerful, is likely to be very inefficient and is almost certainly weaker than advertising that engages us at a more conscious level.

4

Conformity: the popular thing to do

In our society a celebrity is a person who is famous for being well known.

Lee Iacocca[1]

The same is true of brands. And companies!

Seeing things as others see them

We noted earlier that there are a number of different ways of seeing the same thing. What we perceive as 'reality' is very much influenced by how other people see it—the popular consensus. In making choices people are influenced by two things:

- what they think; and
- what they think other people think.

Let us illustrate this with an experiment (see Figure 4.1). Look at Card 1. Imagine that the line there is a brand. Call it Brand A. Brands have images and this one is no exception. We are going to ask you to compare this brand with others. The 'image characteristic' we want you to judge it on is its length.

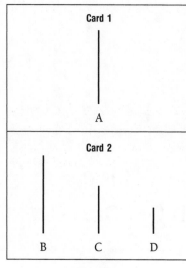

Figure 4.1
Cards 1 and 2

Its competitors are the three lines below it on Card 2. Which one (of Brand B, Brand C and Brand D) is most similar to the one at the top, Brand A? Before reading any further, look at the card. Which one is closest in length to Brand A? Brand B is the correct answer, of course. It's so obvious that nobody is likely to give any other answer, right? Wrong!

What happens if we get several people together in the same room? Unbeknown to our subject, all of them except that person are stooges who are going to say what we have told them to say—that Brand C is the same length as Brand A. Imagine yourself as the subject. Everyone who answers before you has given what you believe is the wrong answer. Now comes your turn. Imagine your dilemma. You break out in a sweat. Your senses are telling you that B is the right answer but all these other people seem so certain that C is correct.

How can this be? you ask yourself. What is wrong with me? Or them? What do you say? Can you resist conforming to the consensus?

This is a classic psychological experiment first performed by Solomon Asch many years ago. He showed that 75 per cent of people in this situation go against their own perception and give the popular response.

The thought process behind this will be familiar to anyone who has ever attended a business meeting. When we see things differently from others, do we always back our own perception and go public? Or do we play safe and go along with the popular opinion? Very often we play safe. We conform. But how does the conformity so vividly illustrated in Asch's experiment operate outside the laboratory? Advertisers can't organize stooges or enforce conformity in everyday situations. So what relevance does this have for advertising?

To answer this, let's vary the experiment. We have demonstrated that when people make choice decisions, they do so on the basis of two types of information:

• objective evidence; and
• what they think other people think.

Popular opinion can influence not only compliance and conformity, but how we perceive reality.

When everything else is equal

In our experiment there was a real and noticeable difference between the brands (the lengths of the lines). When the difference is this obvious it takes a lot of peer pressure to get people to go against their own judgment and conform to the popular view. What happens if we reduce the differences? After all, in the real world, brands are often virtually identical.

We repeat the experiment, but this time we have our subject compare the original Brand A with three brands that are closer to it in length: Brands E, F and G (see Figure 4.2). Which brand (line) on Card 3 is the same length as Brand A on Card 1?

In fact, all of them are identical to Brand A. But you have to choose, just as you do in the real world when faced with three identical brands (assuming you want to buy the product).

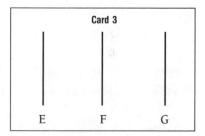

Figure 4.2
Card 3

Imagine your surprise when everybody before you picks E (as they have been instructed to do). All the brands look the same to you. You must be missing something, you think. E looks about the same length as A—but so do the other lines. How is everybody else so sure the answer is E and not F or G, or all of them?

In this situation people tend not only to conform by giving E as the answer but also to doubt the evidence of their own senses. This is the beginning of the belief in differences between brands.

It makes sense that in this situation the subjects will naturally have less conviction about the conclusion coming from their own senses. When there is less evidence to go on, or the evidence is ambiguous, people are less sure of their perceptions. The less sure they are, the more readily they will go along with other people's 'perceptions'. As the real differences between brands diminish, people rely more and more on outside cues to help them make judgments and decisions. This is when advertising seems to be most effective. When everything else is equal, it takes only a 'feather' to tip the balance and influence the choice.

The bandwagon effect: indicators of the norm

Conformity—being with the 'in group', not being out of step—is a powerful human motivator. It can make the crucial difference in many brand choice decisions. When there is no real difference between brands or when the choice is not really important to a person, it takes much less than full consensus to influence their judgment. People will go with what they think the majority of other people perceive—the popular view.

This is known as the *bandwagon effect*. It occurs in situations as diverse as voting in elections and backing favorites in horse races.

Canned laughter, opinion polls and the Billboard Top 100 are all indicators of the norm. They tell us how others are reacting and thereby influence how we are likely to react. They provide signals about what to laugh at, what to think about and what to listen to.

Figure 4.3
Savin ad appealing to
popularity (fastest growing)

How else do people form their impressions of what is popular or what is the norm? This is where marketing comes into play. TV and radio stations, newspapers and magazines frequently claim to be Number One. There is no doubt that this influences where media buyers and advertisers place their advertising. Other indicators are even more subtle but nevertheless very powerful (Figure 4.3).

In the 1950s and 1960s the Billy Graham Crusades made a global name for this most powerful of evangelical preachers. How did Graham manage to get all these people to 'come forward for God'? Arizona State University researchers infiltrated the Billy Graham organization and revealed that: 'By the time Graham arrives in town and makes his altar call, an army of six thousand wait with instructions on when to come forth at varying intervals to create the impression of a spontaneous mass outpouring.'[2]

In the USA, bartenders often 'salt' their tip jars with a few dollar bills at the beginning of the evening. This gives customers the impression that tipping with paper money is the norm.[3]

On telethons, inordinate amounts of time are spent reading out the names of people who have donated money. The message is clear: everybody else has donated—what are you doing?

As real differences between choices diminish, people rely more and more on outside cues to help them make decisions. One such cue is what other people are thought to be choosing. The beam-balance effect, therefore, is another reason why product positioning works. When everything else is equal, conformity may be the feather that tips the balance.

Insecurity: a motivator for conformity

People seem to have a natural aversion to being seen to be out of step with others, or different from the norm. This often leads us to take the safe course. We try to anticipate what others would do and then do the same. This can spare us embarrassment and it can sometimes save us from thinking too hard.

Management in bureaucratic organizations is notoriously motivated by this. If a decision maker does what everybody else would do, and it turns out to be wrong, she won't be blamed. The personal risk is minimized. As the saying goes: 'Nobody ever got fired for buying an IBM.'

People conform most when they are insecure. Adolescence is a time of great insecurity and uncertainty. It is no surprise, then, that teenagers are highly conformist. While rebelling against the outmoded values of their parents, they are at the same time the ultimate slaves to conformity within their own peer group. This characteristic determines and maintains success in the advertising of products such as jeans, soft drinks, T-shirts, sporting footwear, CDs and radio stations.

Perceived popularity

How popular a brand is thought to be, or how familiar a company is thought to be, is an important dimension of image.

Popularity is a magnet. It attracts. And advertising can enhance its power to attract. Try to think of a single product of which the most popular brand is not advertised. Difficult, isn't it? Does this mean that advertising *causes* popularity? Not exactly. Advertising makes the brand *appear* popular. It influences its perceived popularity. The more a brand is advertised, the more popular and familiar it is perceived to be.

Advertising usually delivers specific messages that associate the company or brand with an image dimension or target attribute, such as 'reliability', 'environment-consciousness', 'value for money', 'good taste', 'ease of use'.

Figure 4.4
America Online
advertising its
position as No. 1

Figure 4.5
Nivea claiming to be No. 1
in the world

Sometimes the attribute is 'popularity'. The advertiser may tell us explicitly that the brand in question is popular. For example:

- 'British Airways—the world's favorite airline'
- 'Budweiser…the most popular beer the world has ever known'
- 'Nickelodeon…the #1 network for kids'
- 'Quicken…the world's #1 selling financial software'.[4]

Or the popularity may merely be implied (e.g. 'America spells cheese K-R-A-F-T).

The interesting thing about communicating popularity, however, is that the advertiser doesn't necessarily have to do so in so many words. We as consumers somehow infer that a product is popular simply because it is advertised.[5] The psychological mechanism behind this is known as the *'false fame' effect.*[6]

A supportive study

Some years ago one of the authors conducted a study in which people were asked which brand in various product categories they thought was the most popular.[7] Irrespective of which brand they named, they were then asked why they thought it was the most popular. Thirty-six per cent of the responses took the form 'It must be popular...because it is advertised so much'. (Others included...'because it has so much shelf space in the supermarket'.) This was compelling evidence that presence,[8] and especially a sustained advertising presence, translates into an image of popularity. It leaves a perception of popularity in our minds.

Advertising side effect

Unlike other image dimensions (such as reliability, taste or price) this perception of popularity is largely independent of the specific advertising message. In other words, it is a side effect.

The graph in Figure 4.6 shows a brand which positioned itself largely on the attributes of taste and suitability. Note, however, the effect of advertising on people's perceptions of its popularity. The mere fact of its being advertised significantly increased the proportion of people who associated it with the attribute 'everybody seems to be drinking it'.

So, whether advertising is designed to communicate the image of taste, style, reliability or whatever, it is also likely to increase the perceived popularity and the salience of the brand. This is a side effect of the advertisement that influences which brands come to mind, which brands we think are popular and which brands we include in our consideration set.[9]

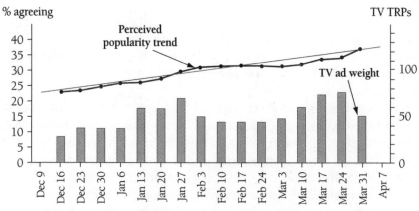

Note: The mere fact of something being advertised can increase its perceived popularity.

Figure 4.6
Image of increasing popularity—everybody seems to be drinking it.
Source: NFO MarketMind

Agenda setting

The mechanism behind this side effect is one we have already met. It is 'agenda setting'. The amount of media weight that an issue is given in newspapers, magazines or on TV indicates to people the degree of importance that the issue should have in their thinking. It sets their mental agenda. In marketing, the agenda that is set is not made up of political issues, but of the brands that are thought to be popular. For 'popular' read 'important'. Our agenda-setting mechanism is not necessarily logical or rational. After all, is a brand advertised because it is important? Or is it important because it is advertised? There is a circularity here that is difficult for logic and rationality to come to grips with. But logic and rationality do not reign here.

Is perceived popularity a plus?

If a brand seems to be popular, are people more likely to buy it? Yes.[10]

Advertising and media weight affect the perceived popularity image of a brand. They affect people's feelings of familiarity with the brand as well as their perceptions of the popularity of the brand. And that, in turn, can affect their buying of the brand.[11]

There is clear evidence that advertising can impact on the perceived popularity of a brand, and there are strong indications that perceived popularity also lends 'legitimacy' to the continued purchasing of a brand—in most circumstances. To understand why, we need to explore what 'having popularity' conveys about a brand.

Perceived popularity conveys notions such as 'a million people can't be wrong', that the brand is tried and trusted, that we are choosing the best. We have no reason to doubt or question our choice of a popular brand. We are reassured by the knowledge that others use it, that we are swimming with the tide.

So popularity is a positive reinforcer. It helps to reinforce our continued, unquestioning buying of the brand. It makes us less likely to question ourselves about why we continue to buy that brand. It is a feather on the scales of repeat buying. For advertisers, therefore, it can provide a basis for developing a kind of defense shield, to try to protect the established market share. Promotion of a brand as popular does not rely on persuasion; rather it represents a pre-emptive effort to fend off the inevitable competitors who will try to take over the brand's established mental territory. Used in this 'defensive' role, the popularity image of a brand is more akin to inoculation than to persuasion.

Popularity and the bandwagon effect

As we have seen, people tend to climb on the bandwagon of anything that seems to be gaining in popularity. If a new brand begins to acquire 'high visibility' and is seen as something that 'everyone is talking about' or that 'more and more people are using', this can be an attraction, a 'come-on', a temptation for us to try it too. The creation of high visibility is the basis for marketing many fads such as Batman, 101 Dalmations, Teenie Beanie Babies, Tomagatchi virtual pets, Power Rangers and so on, not to mention pop stars and politicians.[12] People are tempted to try 'the latest'—the one that everybody is talking about.

Overpopularity

The expression 'fast up…fast down' is particularly relevant in this context of creating popularity. If pushed too quickly, or to extremes, perceived popularity can go 'over the top'. The pole of the magnet can reverse and repel us rather than attract us. Advertisers have to guard against creating overpopularity, which can suddenly become a liability for their brand.

This is more often a danger when perceived popularity is used in an offensive role, to get us to try a brand initially, than when it is used defensively, as simply a reinforcer reminding us to buy the brand again. It is no accident that this type of marketing is often associated with products with short lifespans such as movies, children's toys and, perhaps, politicians. As the saying goes, 'One day a rooster, the next a feather duster'.

Using high visibility to persuade us to try a brand is very different from using it to maintain the brand's position. High visibility can help persuade us to try a brand but the success of such a strategy risks being very short-lived. For the brand, it may well be a case of 'fast up and fast down' and it may go the way of things like the Macarena dance craze, Pogs and Jennifer Aniston haircuts.

Why popularity can become a turn-off

Perceived popularity is not always positive. When too many people use a brand, it risks becoming perceived as common unless its image is carefully managed. It is not just a case of familiarity breeds contempt. Overpopularity can degrade the currency.

Peter De Vries, an American novelist, once said in another context: 'Everyone hates me because I am so universally liked.' Astute advertisers have learned to guard against this type of reversal. They know that simply giving a brand as much 'hype' as possible in as short a time as possible is not necessarily a good idea. Instead, they try to manage the perceived popularity of the brand as part of a long-term process of image development and ensure that they consolidate a lasting market share.

In 'social' product categories like wine and beer, if a brand becomes the most popular it risks becoming less and less acceptable for taking to other people's places or serving to guests. Why? Since everybody drinks it, it begins to take on an image of commonplace. It becomes too successful. To take a bottle of it to a dinner party can become unthinkable because of what this signals about your regard for your host and the occasion. A gift of Absolut brand vodka says something different from giving a gift of the more popular brand Smirnoff.

Gifts and special occasions

We mark special occasions by the use of things out of the ordinary: a very old bottle of red wine, hiring a stretch-limousine, eating out at a fine restaurant. Such symbols mark the specialness of the occasion. Similarly, when we want to express our caring and esteem for others, we give or do something special.

Hallmark cards, for example, reinforce us by using the tag line 'When you care enough to send the very best' and in more recent years have urged us to 'Turn the card over and make sure it's a Hallmark'. Once specialness for a brand is achieved it requires careful nurturing and reinforcement to maintain it in the face of mass popularity.

Positioning a brand or product as suitable for gift-giving or special occasions can therefore be a successful strategy, but if the product proves too successful it has within it the seeds of its own destruction. Overpopularity can 'devalue the currency'.

Price, exclusivity and popularity

Unless a prestige brand's image is maintained through high price or other image-lifting devices it risks gradual degradation from too much popularity (as seems to have happened to Pierre Cardin and Reebok).

International wine aficionados know that Veuve Clicquot champagne, and Grange Hermitage (the premier Australian red wine) are 'popular' in a very different sense from brands like Gallo or Smirnoff. Because of their high price, Grange and Veuve Clicquot are most acceptable, but not very affordable—and this is the point. Like Mercedes they have traditionally used price to try to protect the brand from the commonness that would otherwise go with great popularity. The high price and relative unattainability confers a degree of exclusivity, which in effect makes the well known brand more an aspirational symbol.

Advertising examples

Many advertising themes have tapped into the desire to conform.

- 'Fosters. Famous in Australia. Famous around the world.'
- 'Why go with the number two when you can go with the number one in rental cars?'
- 'The leader in digital audio...Sony.'
- 'Nashua—number one in photocopiers.'
- 'The world's favorite airline...British Airways.'
- 'America's largest discount broker...Charles Schwab.'
- 'America's number one nail protection...Hard-As-Nails.'

These are some of the more obvious examples. Others that are more subtle but work on the same principle include:

- 'Wouldn't you like to be a Pepper too?' (Dr Pepper)
- 'The word is getting around...Mitsubishi.'
- 'The one to watch...Renault.'
- 'Lifesavers...a part of living.'
- 'Chevrolet...Heartbeat of America.'
- 'Join the "regulars"...Kellogg's All-Bran.'
- 'Tylenol...first choice for patients in pain.'
- 'Going Ford is the going thing.'

Summary

As some wit once said, 'Conformity is something you can practice without making a spectacle of yourself.' In making choices we are influenced by two things:

- what we think; and
- what we think other people think.

Conformity is a powerful human motivator. Especially when everything else is equal, it can tip the balance in many brand choice decisions. We are more likely to go against our judgment and conform to the popular view if there are few real differences between brands. As the real differences become negligible, we rely more and more on outside cues to help us make our decisions. The more insecure we feel, the more likely we are to be influenced by others.

The more a brand is advertised the more popular and familiar it is perceived to be. Popularity is like a magnet, and advertising can enhance its power to attract. As consumers, we somehow infer that something is popular simply because it is advertised. If pushed too quickly or to extremes, perceived popularity can go 'over the top'. The pole of the magnet can reverse and repel rather than attract us. Overpopularity tends to 'devalue the currency'.

5

The advertising message: oblique and indirect

42.7% of all statistics are made up on the spot.

Anonymous graffiti

Like graffiti, advertising has moved a long way from simply imparting direct information messages. Advertising and graffiti often have succinct, clever messages that are not direct statements of information. Consider how much more powerful the quotation above is compared with a statement that urges us to 'Be careful of quoted statistics because they can be easily fabricated'. The message that we take away from it is the same thing even though the words don't contain that literal message. Indirect forms of communication sometimes register a point with more impact. For example, an ad for Boost nutritional energy bar simple shows the partly eaten bar still in the wrapper, with the line 'It's like taking candy from a doctor'. Or consider the print ad in Figure 5.1 for Jewelry.com, which was used in the Valentine's Day buying season. The advertising messages in both are oblique and indirect.

In management boardrooms advertisers traditionally ask their advertising agencies questions like: 'Are we getting our message across?' or 'What message are buyers taking out of our ad?' This is based on the assumption that advertising is meant to be informational.

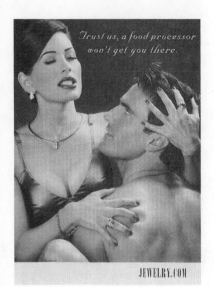

Trust us, a food processor won't get you there.

JEWELRY.COM

Figure 5.1
Valentine's Day ad for Jewelry.com.
Oblique communication can
sometimes register a point with more
impact. *By Robert Chandler &
Partners of Los Angeles*

Usually consumers are asked something like: 'What was the ad trying to say to you?' or 'What was the message that the advertiser intended?' Even with the above type of indirect message, this process can provide valuable feedback to advertisers and quickly tell them if their commercial is communicating what they want it to communicate—if the commercial is an informational one, that is. However, the more that the advertising moves away from *direct* message communication towards oblique message communication the less this makes sense. Entertainment commercials, which include image, musical and drama commercials, are often oblique communications and very different from lecture-style commercials.

We mentally process 'image' ads such as those for Pepsi, Nike, beer or perfume quite differently from informational ads, such as those announcing this week's special at Macy's or Walker's Valentine's Day sale. Indeed, it is difficult with many ads (image ads especially) to work out what message they intend to convey. Advertisers themselves find these ads the most difficult to evaluate, largely because there is little point in asking people what message they get from them.

There is a very real difference between advertising that has a clear, spoken, unambiguous message and advertising that is oblique, especially when it is more akin to drama or entertainment. We mentally process different types of ads in very different ways.

If you think of current advertising for various image-advertised brands, you may find that the ad or the message, or both, is difficult to recall. What is missing from some of these ads is the sense that someone is trying to tell you something directly. This does not mean that they are ineffective—just that they do not work by way of clearly elaborated messages.

Australians have a brand of non-alcoholic drink known as Claytons which was traditionally positioned successfully with the tagline 'Claytons…the drink you have when you're not having a drink'. Claytons has entered the vocabulary as a name for a 'social lubricant' substitute for alcohol acceptable for drinking on occasions when others are consuming alcohol. Multitudes of other acceptable substitutes have overtaken it today (like mineral water or lime and bitters) but the word Claytons remains linguistically generic among Australians to mean the one you are having when you are not having one. Many image ads could be said to have 'a Claytons message'—that is, the message you're having when you're not having a message.

What is a message?

Image ads do not usually lecture us. Instead, they present an experience of life or of being entertained—but in the process information gets in. If you tell us: 'Evander Hollyfield is tough', that is a message. But what if, instead of telling us that Evander Hollyfield is tough, you show a video clip of Hollyfield beating the hell out of someone? Answer: We get the same message! Yet if you asked, 'What was that clip trying to communicate to you?', we would probably think the question quite odd. It is not obvious that the film clip is trying to communicate anything to us. Even so, after seeing it we would definitely be inclined to agree with the statement 'Evander Hollyfield is tough'.

In other words we get the same message. But it doesn't seem like a message. It's a Claytons message…the message you're getting when you're not getting a message. Yet the impression that Hollyfield is tough is communicated just the same.

So, while advertisers frequently use 'message take-away' (or message 'take-out') as a measure of an ad's success, it is not necessary for consumers to be able to parrot back the message for an ad to be working. Communication of impressions can be just as effective as communication of facts.

Window on the mind

Let me ask you a question: How many windows are there in your home? Answer before you read on.

Now think about the mental process you went through to retrieve this information. Did you visualize each room in turn and add up all the windows? If you did, you are now more aware of one way in which our minds arrive at information other than by simple memory retrieval: by reprocessing other information that we have mentally filed away.

The stored information may be verbal or visual. We put these previously unconnected bits and pieces together in our minds and arrive at something new. Sometimes the 'something new' is another piece of information (like the number of windows there are in your home). At other times, however, it may be a new attitude or a new feeling about something.

As consumers we often construct our attitudes to brands out of stored information in this way. The attributes or images that have become associated with the brand may have lodged in memory without ever having been part of a verbal message. They may have originated in visual images from advertising, or experiential learning, or input from other people. It is therefore a mistake to think about advertising communication solely in terms of conscious message take-away.

Ask yourself who you think is the typical user of Pepsi, of Harley Davidson or of Volvo? While you don't have a complete answer, you are not without impressions either. For example, do you think the typical owner of a Volvo would be more or less conservative than the owner of a Ford? More or less affluent? Most people would agree that the Volvo owner is likely to be more conservative and more affluent than the Ford owner. Yet they have not acquired those pieces of information through any direct message.

Advertising for many product categories, such as soft drink, beer, confectionery, perfume, is dominated by ads that appear to have very little message. Image ads convey associations and are totally different from informational ads that communicate 'news' (such as one that communicates the existence of a new product, or one that announces what's on special this week at Safeway supermarkets). Associations are like individual windows. Images are like the number of windows. The number of windows in your home is not a piece of information that someone has communicated to you in a message. It is not directly stored in your memory. But you have the bits and pieces to generate it, nevertheless. In this way we can learn things or know things or develop attitudes without being very aware of the process. There is nothing necessarily manipulative or devious about this. It happens all the time. It is part of life.

Learning without awareness

What is missing from some communications is the sense of someone trying to tell us something or trying to communicate a message. As we saw earlier this does not mean that they are ineffective—it is just that the learning does not happen by way of someone sending a clearly elaborated message.

Some psychologists have labeled this type of indirect learning 'learning without involvement'.[1] Others have called it 'implicit memory'[2] and still others have called it 'incidental learning' or 'learning without awareness'.[3] Strictly speaking, this last term is inaccurate. It is not that people are unaware but rather that the 'focus of processing' is on something else in the communication. Our attention is focused on something other than the message per se.

In the TV series *Sesame Street*, messages were embedded in entertainment. Messages such as 'cooperation' and 'sharing' were communicated by drama and song. Learning the alphabet or learning to count is not a chore for *Sesame Street* viewers, but an experience. These skills are effectively conveyed in an entertaining kaleidoscope of sounds and visuals.

We can learn skills, information, image associations or almost anything by this incidental learning, provided it is not inconsistent with what we already know or believe. (Just as, under hypnosis, we will not accept a directive that conflicts with our own values, so too do our minds reject things that are inconsistent with our existing belief structures.[4] Communications that violate this principle risk being ineffective because they tend to invite rejection.)

We have thus discovered yet another reason why people find it hard to analyze introspectively the effects advertising has on them. Sometimes advertisements do not obviously impart information to us. (While this can be true of any type of commercial, it is more especially true of ads based on image, emotion or drama.) The important point is that there is a lessened sense of someone transmitting information—indeed, if there is any sense of it at all. Such ads may communicate mood more than message, feelings rather than words.

When psychologists study the effects of this type of incidental learning, they compare people's learning of the same material or skills in two situations: with and without intent to recall. They have concluded that incidental learning does not differ qualitatively from intentional learning. The difference is quantitative—that is, in the amount that is retained under different conditions.[5]

Memory and association

As we saw earlier in the chapter, the number of windows in your home is not a message or a piece of information that someone has communicated to you. It was not directly stored as a piece of information in your memory. But you had the bits and pieces to generate it, nevertheless. Once again: How many windows are there in your home? That was quick! You didn't have to think about it this time; you already had the answer, because it is now stored in its own 'slot' in your memory in a more readily accessible form. Having put the component bits and pieces together, you can now access that piece of information much more quickly and efficiently at any time by accessing it directly. You don't have to go through the process. You have enhanced its 'availability'.

Just like a commercial, this chapter first helped to evoke in you the necessary images or pieces of information to enable you to go through the process of arriving at that summary piece of information—the number of windows in your home. Having arrived at it, you stored it yourself as a new piece of information in a memory slot of its own.

In the consumer world, what gets stored in memory slots like this is not just information. It may be an attitude, a judgment, a position or a conclusion. But once formed and stored, these things are more readily accessible and hence more available to influence future buying decisions—especially those types of decisions that tend to be made 'on the fly'.[6]

The all important effect of a relatively subtle ad may rest on its ability to build the right visual or mood associations for a brand and lock them into memory, to put those associations on the brand's attribute agenda. Rather than communicating directly by a specific verbal message, the ad may be communicating indirectly, by associational imagery.

It is worth repeating that, strictly speaking, this is not learning without awareness. It is not that people are unaware but rather that the 'focus of processing' is on something else in the communication rather than the 'message'.

Learning by association

You visit a city for the first time, say Paris, and go to the top of the Eiffel Tower. What an experience! What a view! What is the view trying to tell you? What sort of a silly question is that? It is not trying to communicate anything. Views, just like some commercials, come across as an experience rather than an articulated message. Nevertheless, after just one or two exposures you may come to permanently associate a city with a wonderful visual experience. This splendid view is now higher up on the agenda of attributes that you associate with that city. An image can be built without any specific message. The process is not necessarily logical but it is real and natural, nevertheless.

In a sense it could be said that you have learned much the same information as if you had simply been told 'Paris is a beautiful city'. In that case you would have received a clear verbal message. However, two things are different.

- You have learned the information experientially instead of verbally. And this means that you probably have a much richer or deeper sense of it.
- You have learned the information 'without awareness'—that is, without

awareness of being taught something. There is no sense of any intended message.

This is not new. Years ago, the psychologist Charles Osgood demonstrated that when a given adjective is repeatedly paired with a given noun, the 'meaning' of the noun, as measured by a scale called 'the semantic differential', undergoes change in the direction of the adjective.[7] For example, when the noun 'snake' is repetitively paired with the adjective 'slimy', we begin to think of snakes as slimy creatures (even though they aren't). Little is made of such findings today but the phenomenon seems to underlie much of the process by which image advertising works.

Image advertising's effects

To 'play back' the message from an ad we need to be able to articulate our experience, to describe what we see as the message. As an index of an ad's effectiveness, this playback (or 'message take-away') is more appropriate for ads that are designed to communicate 'news' about a brand.

For the more subtle types of ads our inability to play back much in the way of a message does not, in itself, mean that the ad is not working (though it may not be). How then, you may ask, does anyone detect these more subtle effects? How do advertisers know that any such effects are happening? How can the invisible be made visible?

The answer is, by inference—by looking at how the ad has influenced our image of the brand, our attitude to it or behavior regarding it. We would be unable to see an invisible man but if he put on visible clothes we would know he was there. In the same way we cannot observe these invisible advertising effects directly but we can infer their existence by observing other things, such as:

- Changes in brand image dimensions, as measured by such questions as 'Which brand do you most associate with...(safety/best taste/most popular, etc)?'
- Changes in brand attitudes, as measured by such questions as 'How do you feel about brand X overall?' 'How much do you like it?'
- Changes in behavior, as measured by changes in sales and market share.

With image commercials, the invisible can be made visible by measuring the degree of association with image attributes, the degree to which the image features in the brand's attribute agenda and how high up it is on that agenda. These measurements are often taken indirectly and calibrated in the form of belief statements about the brand (e.g. 'liked by everyone', 'best quality', etc).

A fairly typical image-building strategy is to make an ad (like those for Coke or Fosters) that features the brand in a range of enjoyable situations. Blend in a musical sound track with appropriate lyrics and serve with generous quantities of exposure. Again, the important point to note about this type of advertising is that there is a lessened sense of someone transmitting information—indeed if there is any sense of it at all.

Communication by association

In the 1990s a new brand was launched into a frequently purchased snack food category. The TV ad was musically based with a very catchy jingle. The words made musical reference to the glowing attributes of the new brand. Message take-away was measured by asking a random sample of people what the message was. They responded with the attributes that were verbalized in the jingle. These were: 'better/best brand' and 'this brand is good for you'.

A subsidiary objective of the ad was to have the brand seen as 'modern and up-to-date' and 'a brand of today'. This was not expressed in words but was to be inferred from other pieces of information as well as the ad's tone, pace and fast-cut visuals. There was very little playback of this attribute. While some people said the ad was trying to communicate newness, almost no one mentioned 'modern', 'up-to-date' or 'a brand of today'.

However, as Figure 5.2 shows, a growing number of people were positioning the brand in their minds in association with this attribute. When they were asked: 'Which brand or brands do you most associate with the

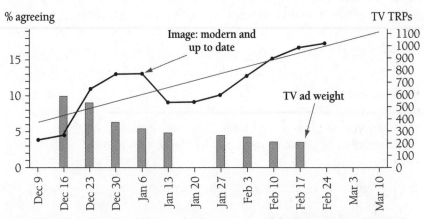

Note: Even though 'modern and up to date' was not part of the audio message that people 'took out', the association with this attribute is clearly affected by the advertising.

Figure 5.2
Image effects revealed—snack food product. *Source*: NFO MarketMind

description "a modern, up-to-date brand"?', the associative linkages created by the ad became visible. The effect was more evident the longer the ad continued to be aired.[8]

The increased association of the brand with this attribute was also linked with a significant improvement in overall attitude towards the brand and, to a lesser extent, increases in market share. Any advertiser who relied only on conscious message take-away as a measure of this ad's effectiveness would be severely misled. People could articulate that the ad was trying to communicate 'better/best brand' and 'good for you'—the message of the jingle—but the 'modern and up-to-date' message was simply inferred. It was a Claytons message. Yet it was in no way hidden. It was simply communicated visually rather than verbally.

Do you think in words or pictures?

When we are asked what message an ad is trying to communicate to us, the result is an index more than anything else of the success of the verbal communication in the ad. However, words are not the only way that we experience ads.

What does a television commercial communicate to you? Pictures, words or feelings? When you listen to a radio commercial, what goes on inside your head? Do you experience pictures or words? Or do you just experience the overall *feeling* of the commercial message?

Clearly, the answer depends to some extent on the type of commercial. An ad for Hawaii is vastly different from an ad for this week's specials at Safeway. But we now know from psychological research that different people tend to favor different modes of thinking. In other words, we differ in the way we mentally process information.[9]

You can start to get a feel for this by answering these questions:

- Do you think in words or pictures?
- Do you recall names better than faces?
- When you can't decide which way a word is spelled, does it help to write it down both ways and then choose the right one?
- When you hear a radio commercial, what do you experience? Pictures or words?
- When you remember a TV commercial, what do you remember first? Is it visual or verbal?

Compare your answers with those of a spouse or close friend. Most people are surprised to learn that the other person's answers are not the same as their own. We assume, without any real basis, that other people think the same way we do. Even advertisers tend to base their strategies on this assumption.

Individual differences

Over the years one of the authors has asked many groups of people the question: 'Do you think in pictures or words?' About a third say unequivocally that they think in pictures. Usually, somewhat less than a third say unhesitatingly that they think in words. And the rest say either that they think both ways, or that they can't answer the question.

The proportions vary from group to group but the really interesting thing is the reaction of the 'word thinkers' to the 'picture thinkers' and vice versa. The strict 'picture thinkers' are positively astounded by those who say they think in words and not pictures. 'How can you think in words?' they ask disbelievingly. 'How can you possibly think in pictures?' some of the 'word thinkers' throw back at them, not so much as a retort but in equal puzzlement and disbelief.

So even in an informal research exercise like this, it becomes readily apparent that people are not in agreement about the way in which their basic mental processes work. There are very definitely those who believe they are primarily visualizers (picture thinkers) and those who believe they are primarily verbalizers (word thinkers).

The significance of whether we think in words or pictures comes when we retrieve the commercial or its message from memory—say, at the point of sale when we recall that we have seen a commercial for the brand. Do we hear the ad in our mind? Do we see in words what it said? Or do we retrieve the visual images or impressions that are associated with it?

The cues that advertisers use at the point of sale, such as pack design, shelf talkers, slogans and so on, are designed to remind us of the verbal messages or to retrigger the visual associations that have been communicated by the ad.[10]

Summary

What is missing from some ads is the sense of someone trying to tell you something or communicate a message. This does not mean that such ads are ineffective—just that they do not work by way of clearly elaborated messages.

We mentally process image ads and visual experiences quite differently from informational ads or messages. We can learn or know things without being much aware of the process or the result. There is nothing necessarily manipulative or devious about this. It happens all the time. It is not that we are unaware of this in any subliminal sense but rather that our 'focus of processing' is often on something else in the communication rather than a verbal 'message'. We can learn skills, information, image associations, almost anything by this incidental learning, provided it is not inconsistent with what we already know or believe.

This is yet another reason why we find it hard to analyze the effects advertising has on us. As consumers we use the many bits and pieces that we receive from advertising, experiential learning and other people. They are put together as information, attitudes, judgments, positions and conclusions. Once stored in their own memory slots, these are more readily accessible to us and more available to influence other related decision making. They have the potential to influence our future buying decisions, especially those that tend to be made 'on the fly'.

6

Silent symbols and badges of identity

Everybody repeat after me…'We are all individuals'.

Anonymous

In America wearing a Miami Dolphins sweater or a Green Bay Packers T-shirt makes a statement. In England the teams have very different names, like Arsenal, Newcastle and Manchester United, while in Australia the teams that fans identify with have names like Sydney Swans or Brisbane Broncos. Such names are brand symbols. Wearing these names on T-shirts lets us, as individuals, make a statement about *our* association and *our* identification with that team.

Similarly, when we choose to consume a Pepsi or pull on a pair of Calvin Klein jeans, whether we are aware of it or not we are making a statement about ourselves, though in a much more subtle way. In the brands that we choose, our consumption behavior goes beyond the simple 'quenching of thirst' or selecting 'something to wear'. Football supporters don't wear the team cap and sweater just to keep them warm and nor do people wear designer clothes simply to keep warm. There is much more to it. Our choice of brands can become an expression of self-identity.

We have become accustomed to idols such as Michael Jordon, Cindy Crawford and Jerry Seinfeld being used to endorse brands like Nike, Pepsi and American Express. When a brand is seen being consumed by these people, it becomes more than a brand— it can become a symbol of association with that person and with an 'in group' (see Figures 6.1 and 6.2).

By consuming and displaying brand symbols that are associated with these entities we:

- reinforce in our minds our identification and closeness with the person or group they stand for;
- make an expression of our own identity, a subtle statement or symbol to the outside world about ourselves.

In this way the act of consuming a brand can become a way for us to express our identity—who we are, what we are like, what our concerns are, what we enjoy doing, what we value, who our friends are and so on.

Look closely at the advertising slogans. Consider the subtle but unmistakable allusions to how the brand reflects your identity, as part of a group, and how consuming that brand expresses something about you:

- *'Join the first team...reach for Winston.'*
- *'It's More you.'* (More cigarettes)
- *'Players go places.'* (Players cigarettes)
- *'You've come a long way baby.'* (Virginia Slim cigarettes)
- *'The best a man can get...Gillette.'*
- *'Canada Dry Ginger Ale...for when your tastes grow up.'*
- *'Coke is it!'*
- *'Pepsi...Generation Next.'*
- *'Wheaties...Breakfast of champions.'*
- *'The most unforgettable women in the world wear Revlon.'*
- *'Wouldn't you like to be a Pepper too?'* (Dr Pepper soft drink)

Figure 6.1
Omega ad with Martina Hingis

Figure 6.2
Michael Schumacher for Omega

Above all, consuming a particular brand becomes a way of sharing, of participating, of representing or identifying with something. There is something about being part of a group. Even mental membership has its privileges!

Expression and self-presentation

We can identify privately with someone or something without needing to tell anybody else. In this sense identification can be a very private thing.

The other side of it, however, is that very often we *want* to signal our feeling of identification—who we are and what we stand for—to the outside world. We do this non-verbally in our self-presentation and self-expression. We use symbols, mannerisms, gestures, idioms, and flags to communicate non-verbal messages to the outside world. We display symbols (wear Levi's, Lee or Calvin Klein; drive a Mercedes or a Land Cruiser or a VW Beetle), or use products that are symbolically associated with our favorite entities (Omega, Nike, Reebok).

In the USA, more students wear their college T-shirts on the Monday following a football game when the college team wins (especially after a big victory) than when it loses.[1] The motivation is not simply the desire to bask in reflected glory. It is related to the reasons people wear branded jeans (e.g. Lee, Levi's, Hilfiger), designer clothes (Hugo Boss, Calvin Klein, Polo) and branded sportswear (Esprit, Nike, Reebok). The broader, underlying motivation is one of personal identity and participation in (or association with) a larger, symbolic group.

Identification and conformity

As a motivator, identification is to be distinguished from conformity. Conformity is the need to avoid standing out from the crowd. It is based partly on the fear of being different; on the need to go along with the ideas or choices of others for fear of the consequences.

Identification is the flip-side to this. It is very similar to conformity, but at the same time very different. Most humans enjoy feeling part of something greater than themselves—their family, their school, their nation, their church, their football team. This is more than just trying to avoid being different. It is a positive desire to be like something, to be part of it, to find identification with it. It is a desire for the secure feeling of knowing we are not isolated—that we are not alone. There is a warm feeling in sharing common values, common symbols, common ideas with others.

In valuing with others the same things they do, we reinforce for ourselves the degree to which we value our identity as part of 'the group', and we make a statement to others about it. Teenagers, for example, find a great deal of camaraderie in worshipping the same pop idols and movie stars as their friends.

Such identification and bonding becomes even stronger when we share the same emotions or experiences with others. The more powerful the common emotions or experiences, the greater the feeling of mutual closeness. As teenagers most of us shared feelings of insecurity, of not knowing where we were going, and this brought us closer to those of our own age.

Pratkanis and Aronson adopted the term 'granfalloons', originally coined by American novelist Kurt Vonnegut, to refer to the entities we identify with.[2]

Granfalloons

Some granfalloons we are born into. The most important of these is our family. Most of us identify with our family and express this in our buying behavior at Christmas, on Mother's Day and so on.

Other granfalloons we *choose* to identify with. Our choice here, however, is frequently influenced, if not determined, by the groups we already identify with. Many of us passionately support what we call 'our football team', but this often turns out to be the same team our family supported. Thus, identifying with one granfalloon such as our family can lead us to identify with other related granfalloons such as a particular football team. The reason we consume certain products or display certain brand symbols (such as sweaters in the team's colors) can often be traced back through a chain of associations to the people and entities we identify with.

The stronger this feeling of identification, the more we defend the group and display its symbols. The more the granfalloon is attacked by outsiders, the stronger the feeling of comradeship within it. (This is why the promotion of nationalism, and even war, is sometimes used by politicians. It functions as a very powerful cohesive mechanism.)

Even when our assignment to a group is random, such as in schools that have interhouse sporting competitions, identification takes place. When complete strangers are formed into groups on the basis of something as trivial as the toss of a coin, this same thing happens.[3] Though our reasons for belonging are unclear or meaningless, we nevertheless identify with the group. Any brand or product that associates itself symbolically with our group, family, team or values taps into this motivation.

This happens even with groups such as Amnesty International, in which most members never meet, and it also happens with individuals. Our behavior can be influenced by observing what other people do, or imagining what they would do in the same situation. We identify with them and model ourselves on them. The closer our identification, the more likely it is that our behavior will be affected. In other words, the more similar we feel the other person is to us the more likely this modeling or copying influence will take place.

Children who are terrified of dogs can be greatly affected by watching another child play happily with a dog for 20 minutes a day. In one experiment, after only four days of observation, 67 per cent of previously phobic children were willing to climb into a playpen with a dog and stay there alone petting the dog.[4]

The for and against position

Football team supporters often wear badges that say 'I support the New York Jets' or whatever team they identify with. They also wear badges that say 'I hate the Dallas Cowboys' or the team they most love to hate in their country. Whether the hated team is called the Cowboys, Arsenal or Broncos doesn't matter. It illustrates the fact that people can find identity not only in being *for* something but also in being *against* something else. Our identification with something can be expressed either way.

Teenagers show their identification with their peer group by looking and acting like them but also by denigrating the tastes and preferences of the 'out group'—often their parents.

At its extremes this 'anti'-motivation manifests itself in the form of jingoism or religious zealotry. In the super-strength, concentrated form it is a motivation sufficiently powerful for people to fight and die to preserve the integrity of the group and its values and symbols. Some people will even die in defense of the symbols alone (e.g. a country's flag).

At the opposite end of the scale the influence of this motivation is much more subtle and more difficult, though not impossible, to measure.

Reaction to symbols

Advertising has created some of the most recognized symbols in the world—symbols such as the golden arches (McDonald's), the Swoosh (Nike), the apple with the bite out of it (Apple), the cowboy (Marlboro) and the Nutrasweet swirl. Advertisers use symbols as shorthand communication and reap the benefits of investing for years in making the symbols mean something.

We react to symbols. At a red light we react by stopping. At a green light we go. When we see a swastika we feel revulsion. The 'man' symbol on a public toilet affects half the population one way and the other half the other way.

Whether our reaction to a symbol is external (stop, go) or internal (revulsion) it is a learned reaction. It is learned by association of the symbol with other things. In this way a symbol gradually develops an ability to influence us in its own right and to evoke common reactions.

Meaning is an attachment

Through a process that psychologists call 'discrimination learning' a symbol or a brand acquires meaning. An odd thing about this is that once we have learned via this process we become relatively unconscious of it. It is like our ability to drive to work without ever being conscious of braking or the process of changing gears. It takes place without much conscious awareness.

For example, when you see the letter q you are hardly likely to say to yourself 'Hey, that's romantic'. Nor do you say to yourself: 'This is a symbol that I am meant to decode as representing the letter q.' Instead, you simply experience the letter q. You have become unconscious of the mental process whereby meaning is attached to the symbol. The meaning is experienced not as something that we attach to the symbol. It is not experienced as us attaching meaning to it. The meaning is just there—*in* the symbol.

Meaning is an attachment. It just appears as though the meaning is in the symbol. Another telling example is the word 'window'. Its meaning has completely changed over hundreds of years from 'a hole where the wind comes in' to 'a hole where the wind does not come in'.[5]

A lesson in the origin of a kiss

Look at these symbols:

> <

What do they mean? Certainly, there is nothing romantic about them. To us they mean 'greater than' and 'less than'. In primitive society, however, either one could be used to represent a bird's beak and, by extension, a mouth.[6]

If you bring these two symbols together what do you get? An 'X'. If the symbols are read as mouths, you also get two mouths together—a kiss. Hence the shorthand symbol for a kiss that we often use on greeting cards and letters is an X.

We all use this symbol and understand that it means a kiss. Yet most of us don't know why it does. (This is a vivid illustration of how the meaning of a word or symbol, once established, can become divorced from its origins and operate independently of any knowledge of them.)

Our ancestors, looking at this symbol, decoded it as signifying two beaks in contact and deduced that this was meant to convey a kiss. As time passed, however, the intermediate associations gradually disappeared and the symbol came to elicit its meaning more directly.

The origins of such symbols and their meaning are often buried under layers of antiquity. But once a symbol's meaning is learned, it is no longer necessary for us to know its origin or how our reactions to it came about. Even though we are no longer conscious of how it was learned, we all use it and we all react to it just the same.

So symbols are like adults. We usually react to them as they are. But in order to understand them more fully we need to know something about their childhood and how they developed into what they are today. This is important because once learned, we regard meaning as being in the symbol itself rather than an attachment process that takes place below the level of consciousness. Any sense of the mental process of attachment disappears.

To learn how brands are built into symbols we need to understand the way symbols acquire meaning and how we interpret that meaning. The real differences between brands such as Coke and Pepsi, or Kodak and Fuji, or Colgate and Close Up may be quite small, but when the focal beam of attention is played on these symbolic aspects of the brand the differences may be significant.

Discrimination learning

Let's illustrate how crucial small differences can be. What do the following symbols mean?

q p 6 b d 9

To us they mean 'the letter q', 'the letter p', 'the number six' and so on.

When one of the author's daughters was about six years old she was learning numbers. She counted up eight toys. She was then given another one and asked how many she had now. She was asked to write it down. She said 'nine' but wrote it like this:

p

This is not uncommon when kids are learning to write. They sometimes get the symbol correct but write it back to front.

What happened next should teach us all a first-hand lesson about discrimination learning. She was told she was correct but that the number nine was written this way:

9

She looked at it, puzzled. Then, drawing on childlike logic, she said, 'But, Daddy, that's a q.'

Father, after recovering his composure, explained to her: 'No, darling, this is a q,' and drew a tail on her symbol, while realizing how small a difference it really was—q.

How subtle our learning of symbols and labels is! We take it for granted that the same basic symbol is a 'nine' when its tail slopes to the left but becomes an entirely different symbol, when its tail is bent up to the right.

It is exactly this type of confusion that turns out to be the origin of the phrase 'mind your p's and q's'. Apprentice typesetters were urged to mind their p's and q's because of the similarity in the shape of the letters.[7] As adults we are so accomplished at making the distinction that we are too close to it. We are no longer conscious of how we come to recognize instantly

q p b d g

as five quite different symbols.

Making brands into symbols

Brands are like letters. They can be transformed into symbols. They can become shorthand ways of communicating. They can be made to summon up associations or stand in for them. In this way small differences can have big implications. They can become triggers for different mental associations.

The expression 'Just do it' cues us to think of Nike; the expression 'Where do you want to go today?' cues us to think of Microsoft. In the same way brand names themselves can cue us to think of people and images that are closely associated with them. Nike may cue us to think of Michael Jordan; Sprint may make us think of Candice Bergen; American Express of Jerry Seinfeld; Revlon of Cindy Crawford.

If we want to identify with that image and feel closer to it, we can express it to ourselves and others by drinking, wearing, driving the same brand (see, for example, the Jaguar ad in Figure 6.3). Just as drinking alcohol can be a powerful sign to teenagers that they are now no longer children, so the consumption of other products can make powerful statements about us. The importance of this as communication is as much to the user or wearer as it is to the outside world.

A brand can become a badge of identity in several different ways:

Figure 6.3
Jaguar ad: 'You've made
a statement... Here's the
exclamation point.'

- by being a symbol of the group (e.g. football team logo);
- by being seen to be valued by members of the group (e.g. Pepsi is valued by pop idols);
- by being seen as supportive of the group (e.g. sponsorship of a football team);
- by being seen as characteristically used or displayed by members of the group.

Summary

We react to symbols. Whether our reaction is external or internal it is a learned reaction. It is learned via association of the symbol with other things. In this way a symbol can influence us in its own right by evoking certain reactions. Symbols come to stand for other things in our mind and the act of consuming a brand can become a symbolic way for us to express our identification with the entities associated with it.

Our internal reaction to a symbol may be emotional or unemotional. Brands are initially unemotional marks; advertisers use advertising to try to transform these (trade) marks into symbols that summon up certain mental associations. When a symbol elicits a cognitive or emotional response in us, we in turn can use it to express that idea or emotion to others.

We can identify privately with another person or a group without needing to tell anybody else. But often we want to signal this feeling of identification to the world. We do this by displaying and consuming symbols (such as football team badges, old school ties, Levi's, Reeboks, Mercedes, etc) or using products that are symbolically associated with our favorite entities. Identification is the flip-side of conformity. It is not just the avoidance of seeming to be different. It is a positive desire to be like something, to be part of it, to find identification with it.

The difference between brands in the same product category may be quite small, but when the focal beam of attention is played on these symbolic aspects the difference can tip the balance. Consuming or displaying certain products can make powerful statements about us. The importance of the communication is as much to the user or wearer as it is to the outside world.

7

Vicarious experience
and virtual reality

The theater is a form of hypnosis. So are movies and TV. When you enter a movie theater you know that all you are going to see is twenty-four shadows per second flashed on a screen to give an illusion of moving people and objects. Yet despite this knowledge you laugh when the twenty-four shadows per second tell jokes, and cry when the shadows show actors faking death. You know that they are an illusion yet you enter the illusion and become a part of it and while the illusion is taking place you are not aware that it is an illusion. This is hypnosis. It is a trance.

Robert Pirsig[1]

Virtual reality computer technology is developed partly from video games, partly from cinema and partly from flight simulators. It is based on the concepts of illusion and immersion. It creates the illusion of being immersed in an artificial world.

Years ago Morton Heilig (the inventor of Sensorama), after he had seen Cinerama and 3D, said: 'When you watch TV or a movie in a theater, you are sitting in one reality, and at the same time you are looking at another reality through an imaginary transparent wall. However, when you enlarge that window enough you get a visceral sense of personal involvement. You feel the experience and don't just see it.'[2] Anyone who has been in an IMAX big-screen theater will relate to this. As Heilig put it: 'I felt as if I had stepped through that window and was riding the roller-coaster myself instead of watching somebody else. I felt vertigo.'

What has this got to do with advertising? Sometimes, studying the extremes of a phenomenon can provide insights into its milder forms that would not otherwise be intuitively obvious. Ads that are mini-dramas work by mildly immersing us in a story rather than talking to us as viewers sitting out in front of the TV set.

Just as there are technological ways (like 3D, Cinerama and virtual reality) to increase the feeling of immersion or involvement in movies and games, so too are there ways that advertising can be designed creatively and structurally to increase the immersion of the viewer in a commercial, and thereby enhance its effect.

Ads as mini-dramas

Ads that are mini-dramas are those that depict a story or vignette. Mini-drama ads usually invite viewers to mentally migrate from their lounge-room reality and step into the fantasy world of the ad.

Take, for example, the Land Rover commercial that starts with the little kid knocking on the door of the Land Rover to ask the woman who winds down the window if his friend Jason is there and can he come out and play? She says, 'I'll check.' After about 20 seconds of silence she winds down the window again and says: 'Still looking.' Using mini-drama the ad very effectively gets across the message of 'hugely spacious interior' without ever actually saying it.

Or consider the serialized ads starring Gillian for instant coffee (Taster's Choice in the USA (see Figure 7.1), Nestlé Gold Blend in the UK and the Nescafé brand in Australia). Such ads invite us to step into the role of the characters in the same way we would in a movie.

Part of the reason for the popularity of movies is that they offer us a kind of out-of-body experience—a chance for a little while to be someone else. TV offers a less complete

Figure 7.1
The characters from the US version of Taster's Choice coffee commercial

out-of-body experience, but an out-of-body experience nevertheless. A chance to experience life, if not as someone else, then at least to experience someone else's experiences.

In these mini-drama ads the product is often cast in the role of hero. Take, for example, the American Express ad with Jerry Seinfeld being thrown overboard from a luxury cruiser and all the antics to get him back to the boat in full tuxedo in time to do his stand-up number. We observe an unfolding mini-drama that casts American Express Card as a hero that can help save our day.

Figure 7.2
Seinfeld starred in mini-drama ads with American Express Card as the hero

Role-play

Children's games are full of role-playing. Kids pretend to be firefighters, truck drivers, doctors and nurses. They imagine themselves in the role of their favorite TV or movie characters: James Bond, Batman, Robin Hood, Cinderella.

Television allows us to role-play in the same way. When we watch TV, we have the opportunity to 'try on' other people's identities. We do this with TV serials and soaps, our favorite movies, and even advertisements. Ads that use this process to get a message across are sometimes called 'slice-of-life' ads. They often portray stereotypical situations in which an individual experiences a problem and finds a solution. The solution is linked to the advertised product. In this way, we indirectly experience the self-relevant consequences associated with using or consuming the brand. We learn how the brand or product is (purported to be) instrumental in attaining the desired goal.

Identifying with a character

Our feeling of immersion in a TV program or an ad seems to be greatly enhanced if we find ourselves identifying with one or more of the on-screen characters. This increases not only the feeling of involvement but also the likelihood that we will adopt the trappings of that character. These trappings may be the character's:

- brand solution (American Express Card);
- behavior style (e.g. using Nestlé/Taster's Choice/Nescafé instant coffee);
- badges of identity (e.g. Coke, Nike, Harley Davidson, Pepsi, Levi's, Mercedes).

Because identification with a character in an ad is much more fleeting than with a movie character, it tends to be less conscious. It takes place quickly and evaporates. But it is fleetingly resurrected at the next exposure of the ad and, in this way, permanent associations or links can develop between the feeling of identification and the brand itself.

> During identification with an ad character, empathizing consumers begin to feel as if they are participating in the character's experiences. That is, consumers imaginatively experience the story's events from the perspective of the character with whom they identify: consumers begin to perceive similarities between aspects of their own self-identity and that depicted by the character.[3]

Immersion and empathy

Identification with a character is not the only way immersion can take place, although it is probably the most powerful way. So what else might make these ads work? If you can't have identification, empathy is probably the next best thing. Some ads invite us to observe the character and take in what the character is experiencing without any expectation that we will necessarily identify with, or want to 'be like', that character.

Empathy means that we understand at a deep level what the character is experiencing and feeling. It means that we have the impression we are experiencing some of the same feelings as the character. But we don't necessarily *identify* with the character. Identification goes one final step further in the process. It is a more complete projection. Viewers who identify with a character desire to be like that character or feel that they *are* like that character.

Immersion and image

The Nestlé Taster's Choice serial ads were entertaining. They were not necessarily addressing us as the audience 'out there', but rather inviting conscious identification with the characters. Some of us may not actually have identified with the characters but were simply entertained by observing the interactions between them. Our 'vantage point' seemed to be not out front as audience but inside the character, or somewhere in between. From this vantage point we were nevertheless able to immerse ourselves in the experiences of the characters and soak up the associations with the brand of coffee playing the comfortable, facilitating context role.

In this case no direct claims were made. In product categories like beverages it is often very difficult for advertisers to claim specific differences between brands and hence much advertising is vague on claims. Take soft drink as another example (e.g. 'the real thing', 'the taste of a new generation', 'time for a change'). The focal beam of attention is not on a claim as such but on the character's experiencing the brand and its attributes.

Emotions

Just as we experience life by observing the neighborhood out of our window so too can we vicariously experience life through our television window. Advertisements frequently show characters experiencing life and emotions. In the midst of these situations the advertised brand is cast either in a feature role or as a central prop.

Such ads utilize qualitatively different channels of communicating, which may be visual, musical or associational. They tap into our existing associations with such things as:

- personal desires (for fun, social recognition, achievement, dominance, power);
- belonging (acceptance);
- caring, human values (feeling good about and valuing others).

In other words, emotions and desires that we already experience.

A study that analyzed the content of American TV commercials found that 'happiness' or 'having fun' was the value most commonly depicted— in 57 per cent of all TV ads and in more than 80 per cent of ads for soft drinks, children's toys and restaurants. Social recognition was the second most frequently depicted value (in 26 per cent of commercials). These values were depicted as being achieved through a viewer or character becoming 'capable' (27 per cent of all commercials), 'helpful' (26 per cent) or 'smart' (24 per cent).[4]

Just as advertising can associate a piece of information with a brand (e.g. safety and Volvos) so too can it associate an emotion with a brand (excitement and Mazda Miata MX5). If we are concerned about safety then Volvo is a symbol of it. If we are interested in fun and good times Mazda Miata MX5 has a better symbolic fit.

The connection of a brand with an emotion by means of characters experiencing life and that emotion increases the brand's relevance for us. It connects the brand with an emotion that is already there inside us. It may be something that was previously inactive in our mind, or active but unassociated with the brand. The brand takes on these associations, and the more it does so the more it can function as a symbol—a symbol that expresses or stands in for that emotion and a symbol that tends to elicit that emotional response. Instead of being connected with a piece of information, a brand may thus be connected in our minds with emotion. The emotion may be:

- generalized positive emotion (e.g. 'You can't beat the feeling'—Coke; 'Oh, what a feeling'—Toyota; 'Bud Light...Bring out your best'; 'Come to Marlboro country');
- a specific emotion such as:
  - *caring* ('Reach out and touch someone...AT&T');
  - *fun* ('It's a good time for the great taste of McDonald's');
  - *achievement* ('Benson and Hedges—when only the best will do'; 'Inter-Continental Hotels—the place to stay when you know that you've arrived');
  - *power* ('Feel the power'...Drakkar Noir; 'The power to be your best'... Apple Computer);
  - *self-reward* ('You deserve a break today...McDonald's').

The viewer's vantage point

Ads can work without generating identification or even much empathy with the characters, but when they do they usually rely on registering in our minds the claims or associations conveyed about the product. The more entertaining commercials invite us to immerse ourselves in the mini-drama and experience events from the vantage point of a participant or bystander in the commercial.

These commercials vary in the degree to which they invite the viewer into a participant or bystander role. The role in which we are cast influences the way we are likely to process the ad mentally and what details of it we recall.

This suggests that the role or 'vantage point' we as viewers are invited to take in a commercial will influence how we mentally process the commercial and what specific details of it we are likely to recall. The implication of this is that in analyzing any commercial we should ask: What role are viewers being cast in? What character are they expected to identify with? Or empathize with? Are there structural aspects of the ad that enhance or inhibit identification? (Voice-over, for example, can be an inhibitor. Many narrative ads use voice-over to tell us what the character is thinking or feeling. This tends to interfere with the development of empathy by distancing us from the characters, in much the same way as using the third person in a story rather than the first person.)

Immersion as attentional inertia

Observational studies of children watching TV indicate that for much of the time they do not actually watch the screen. In one study 54 per cent of all looks at the screen were for less than three seconds.[5] However, if a look lasts longer than about 15 seconds, a child is very likely to become progressively 'locked in' to the program. After about ten seconds, the researchers often noted that the child's body relaxed, the head tended to slouch forward and the mouth to drop open.

This phenomenon is called *attentional inertia*, but at least one writer has related it directly to the 'hypnotic or trance-like quality of television watching'.[6] This 'attentional inertia' is not confined to children. It has been documented in samples of college-aged adults as well.[7]

TV, hypnosis and reality

The extract from Robert Pirsig at the beginning of this chapter likens TV watching to a mild form of hypnosis. TV and hypnosis do have some striking similarities.

A popular belief about hypnosis is that people have no knowledge of what they are doing while hypnotized; that they are compelled to do what is suggested to them; and that afterwards they can remember nothing of the experience. The truth is very different.

First, people do remember what happens to them under hypnosis and they feel completely conscious of it at the time. Only if the hypnotist gives them a post-hypnotic suggestion to forget everything will they be unable to remember.

If they know what is going on, why, you may ask, do they follow the hypnotist's suggestion? This is an intriguing question. Most people who have been hypnotized will tell you that they felt as though they could have ignored the hypnotist's instructions at any time, but went along with them anyway. In other words, they did not feel compelled to act as suggested.

However, this begs the question: Why do they go along? Most subjects say they just felt like it—that they could have acted differently if they had wanted to, but they didn't want to. This is not unlike our own response when we ask ourselves why we have just spent several hours in front of the TV set. It is because we wanted to. We could have turned the set off and returned to reality at any time. We watched because we wanted to, because we felt like it—just like the person under hypnosis.

The more an ad can immerse viewers (i.e. make the mediated experience momentarily more interesting, more involving, more immersing than what is going on around them), the more successful it will be. The best advertising does not remind viewers that they *are* viewers.

Tactics for increasing immersion

Immersion and identification are a matter of degree. The difference between reading a story written in the first person and reading a story written in the third person is that the former is like listening to somebody tell you directly about their own experiences, while the latter is like listening to somebody tell you about someone else's experiences. The action is more easily experienced in the first person because we project ourselves into the identity. The difference is in the degree to which we are reminded of our own identity or the external reality.

This is related to virtual reality. By decreasing the awareness of stimuli other than those coming from the cinema screen, TV or book, we increase the 'reality' of the mediated experience and lessen the sense of it as mediated. It is like the difference between listening to music on your stereo through headphones and through loudspeakers. With headphones we feel more immersed in the musical experience. The new technology of virtual reality is headphones for the eyes.

The more complete the experience of virtual reality becomes, the more we can let go temporarily of one reality and become immersed in another. This represents the ultimate in 'switching off'. So anything that lessens the salience of our own current 'reality' and helps to immerse us, the viewers, in the world of the ad makes the ad that much more powerful.

Summary

When we watch TV or sit in a cinema we are sitting in one reality and, at the same time, looking at another reality through an imaginary transparent wall. Just as we experience life by observing our neighborhood out of our window so too can we vicariously experience life through our television or cinema screen window. Advertisements frequently show characters in 'real-life' and emotional situations. In these situations the advertised brand is cast either in a feature role or as a central prop.

Ads that are mini-dramas work by mildly immersing us in a story rather than addressing us as viewers sitting in front of the TV set. We have the opportunity to 'try on' other people's identities. Identification with an ad character can build permanent associations or links between the experience and the brand itself. Some ads invite us to observe the character and take in what he/she is experiencing without any expectation that we will necessarily identify with, or want to 'be like', that character. Fantasy may not be true but we can learn from it, nevertheless, as *Sesame Street* showed.

Commercials vary in the degree to which the viewer is invited into a participant or a bystander role. The role in which we are 'cast' influences the way we are likely to mentally process the ad and what details of it we recall. What we often recall is the association of a piece of information or an emotion with a brand. The more the ad immerses us, the more the mediated experience is momentarily more interesting, more involving, more absorbing than what is going on around us, the more we can feel the experience and not just *see* it.

Registering a claim or an association in our minds in this way does not imply that we will necessarily believe it. We will, however, recall differences being depicted between the brands and will recall the name of the brand that was cast as the best or safest or most exciting. These are 'feathers' that, when everything else is equal, may be enough to tip the balance of brand selection—even if only to prompt us to see whether the association or claim is true.

8

Messages, reminders and rewards: how ads speak to us

With this chapter we begin to enter the mystical realm of the creative department of the advertising agency, whose art has traditionally been intuitive rather than encoded in any set of well formulated principles. The way an ad speaks to us can influence not only how the ad works but also whether it works at all. The creative team's job is to design and make ads, and good creative teams are paid a lot of money for their intuitive sense of what will be effective advertising. Their task is to make ads that are not only interesting and attention-getting but will also influence our brand choice and leave us feeling warm towards the brand and not alienated by it.

Articulating what makes for creative success in advertising is an under-developed science. In the past, researchers and psychologists who intruded on the creative team's domain risked finding themselves under hostile attack. Now their role is more acceptable, leading as it does to a better under-standing of the principles of psychological processing that underpin better prediction of ad effectiveness. In this chapter we bring these psychological principles to bear on messages, reminders and rewards and then in the fol-lowing chapter we examine the individual elements of ads.

'News' advertising

As we saw in Chapter 7, we tend to process ads differently depending on whether we feel we are being talked to as prospective customers or see ourselves as merely bystanders looking on. A related way of conceptualizing this is by asking 'Am I being informed or entertained?' because we can process an ad as 'news' or as 'entertainment'.

Some brands are heavily into news commercials. Others are more entertainment focused. There is evidence that ads seem to work best when they have something new to say.[1] As one US ad man put it: 'Ads are essentially about creating or broadcasting news about a brand...and News is the oxygen that lets brands live and breathe and grow.'[2] (News advertising is closely related to, but not quite the same as, informational advertising. The latter term is used in advertising in a very specific way.[3]) News advertising provides news or information about the brand. It may be:

- a new formulation (new, improved Colgate);
- a new benefit about the brand (removes plaque, lemon-charged, sugar-free);
- a new variant (fat-free Pringles, anti-dandruff formula); or
- a price comparison (now half the price of the leading brand).

Our minds are invited to process news advertising in the same way that we process the evening news on television or the contents of the morning newspaper. Our processing is focused on what the news is telling us that we don't already know; what it is adding to our store of knowledge; how interesting the news is; how surprising it is; and how important it is to us or to people we know.

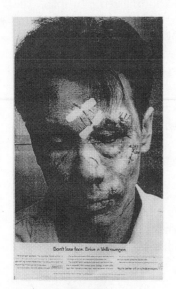

Figure 8.1
You don't necessarily have to like this ad for it to be effective

With news programs we don't necessarily have to enjoy what is being communicated. We watch news and current affairs programs for their information, not just for entertainment. Evidence is emerging that the same applies to news ads. It is not necessary for us to like the experience of it provided the ad is imparting valuable information to us (see Figure 8.1).

This explains why some ads that are disliked can still seem to work. Each country has its hated ad examples which, to the amazement of consumers, nevertheless seemed to work. The 'Ring around the collar...Wisk' commercials and the 'Mr Whipple...don't squeeze the Charmin' commercials irritated Americans for years, as did the Daz 'Doorstep Challenge' laundry detergent ads for UK viewers and the 'Mrs Marsh Colgate' ads in Australia.

When a news commercial reveals a solution to a current problem, then experience and enjoyability can take a back seat. For such ads to be effective it is not crucial that we like the ad if it gives us some news about the brand that is relevant to removing some irritation or problem we have with the product that we are currently using.

In our society, the history and culture of advertising has its roots in communicating news about products and brands. Today we see a lot of advertising messages delivered as though they are new when they are not. Unrequited expectations of being told something new tend to annoy us. News ads, by their very nature, are ads with messages formulated in such a way that they are almost guaranteed to irritate us if they are constantly repeated. Yesterday's news, like yesterday's leftovers, is stale. So a problem for advertisers is that pure news advertising can wear out more quickly than other types of advertising.

Advertisers know they have to keep their brand salient in our minds and keep reinforcing its key attribute(s). This inevitably leads to some degree of repetition because there is a scarcity of new things to say about a brand. Even brand managers and ad agencies can run out of new things to say about humdrum, old products. They may then look for ways to 'create' news rather than report it. Trivial and often irrelevant differences are sometimes created in order to have something to say (e.g. caffeine-free cornflakes). In the past there has been a certain reliance on 'beat-ups', as with that 'new and improved' (yet again) laundry detergent! These pieces of 'news' are mostly harmless creations that ultimately risk boring us.

Fortunately, for us as consumers, news is not the only way that advertising can prevent a brand from becoming tired and boring while keeping it salient in our minds. Instead of messages that give us new information about the brand, advertisers can wrap up an old message in fresh, entertaining ways. They can reposition them as entertaining reminders rather than new messages. The essential difference is not in *what* they say but *how* they say it.

Some ads speak to us in a way that irritates, and we detest their repetition. Others can be appreciated and enjoyed time and time again. The way in which we mentally process an ad is influenced by our individual interests, but it is also heavily influenced by *how* an ad speaks to us. And the way the elements of an ad are blended can help to determine which of our mental processes become engaged and which do not. In short, they can help to modify how our minds opt to process the ad.

Liking an ad

Liking an ad doesn't necessarily make it work but, other things being equal, advertisers would prefer us to like their ads. There are two reasons for this:

1. A brand's advertising is similar to its packaging in that it is part of the brand's personality wardrobe. Just as good clothes make a person look more attractive so a brand's advertising attire can add to its appeal. Ads that are dressed up to be cute and enjoyable are more acceptable than ads that speak to us in a way that grates and annoys.
2. Just as we feel more inclined to argue with someone we dislike than with someone we are fond of, so our minds tend to react similarly with advertising. We are less inclined to counter-argue when we find ourselves enjoying an ad.

Entertainment

When brands have nothing new to say they do not have to irritate the audience by simply repeating yesterday's news. Advertisers have become very adept at wrapping up old messages in fresh, entertaining ways. In product categories where brands are well established and there is little new to say, advertisers rely increasingly on reinforcement of the old message and on the entertaining quality of their ads. These ads are not news and our minds do not process them as news. But when news is removed and the ad relies on entertainment and reinforcement, it becomes more important that we, the consumers, like the brand's advertising.[4]

When the differences between brands are marginal or non-existent, and the brands on the beam-balance of choice weigh equal, it takes only a feather to swing the balance. It is important to remember that the advertising for a brand is part of a brand's personality. If we like a particular aspect of someone's personality, the chances are greater that we will like the person. If we enjoy a brand's advertising, the chances are greater that we will like that brand, however marginal this difference may be. It may be marginal but, when everything else is equal, it can tip the scales.

When we watch entertainment programs like *Friends*, *Baywatch*, *Frasier* or feature movies, our interest is not in the information they may be communicating but in the entertainment they provide. It is important that we like the experience—otherwise, why would we continue to watch? News ads, like the news bulletins, clearly cast the viewer as the recipient of information. Entertainment commercials are different. We are not being addressed but simply experiencing. With entertainment commercials we react like an audience rather than a sales prospect.

Entertainment ads may be 'drama' (the serialised instant coffee ads for Nestlé/Taster's Choice/Nescafé) or 'musical variety' (the commercials launching Diet Coke) or 'animation' (Snap, Crackle and Pop, Budweiser's Louie the Lizard, or the Keebler elves). Or they may be artistic, clever pieces of print or radio communication. As consumers we often appreciate ads for their cleverness in wrapping up an old message in a fresh new way. While they may not communicate news about the brand in the sense of delivering a new message, they nevertheless create 'feathers'. They increase the salience of the brand and continue to reinforce the image or feeling that we have about the brand (or its users).

One of the crucial ways in which entertainment commercials vary is how integral the brand is to the execution, and what role it plays. Here are some examples of the brand playing quite different parts:

- the brand as a prop (e.g. Pepsi ad with Queen of England crowd surfing);
- the brand as a setting (e.g. various McDonald's and Pizza Hut drama ads);
- the brand as the hero (e.g. Federal Express…if it 'absolutely, positively, has to be there overnight').

Some ads relegate the brand to a bit part while in others it is the star. The more integral the brand is to the ad the more likely the ad is to be effective.

Wrapping an old message in a fresh, entertaining way

Once we have heard them, ad messages start to get boring. For example, most people already know that Asic makes running shoes. And they know that Asic makes running shoes for women as well as for men. How does a brand like Asic continue to remind people of its name and target its message to women?

Consider this print ad:

Visual: A picture of rural surroundings where women are jogging
Headline: *'We believe women should be running the country'*
Advertiser: Asic athletics shoes

To take an advertising message and communicate it in this way is to repackage the message creatively. Shakespeare used the same technique. He was master of the play-on-words and, of course, his plays are regarded as poetic, works of art. At times ads are likened to aesthetic phenomena—just as though they were works of art (Coca-Cola or Absolut vodka ads, for example).

Our conscious reactions to such ads are quite different from our reactions to straight ads. Typically, we react with at least mild appreciation of how 'cute' or 'clever' the ad is. And such ads do more than just entertain. Research indicates that, other things being equal, we recall these ads better, we have greater liking for them and we are less inclined to engage in counter-arguing against them. Most importantly, when the brand is well integrated and communicated, it can nudge our attitude towards the brand in the positive direction.[5]

Why is this? What is the process going on here? An important point to note about such ads is that they often seem to stop us momentarily. There is a very brief 'interrupt' in the flow of our normal mental processing. Mostly, we don't have to stop and think about an ad. Mostly, we understand the communication immediately—usually automatically and without effort.

Techniques such as play-on-words, ambiguity or incongruity are used as creative material to force such an interrupt. Here is another example:

Visual: A close-up of a sandwich with a bite out of it
Headline: *The next thing that gets eaten is your teeth*
Advertiser: Colgate

We are stopped fleetingly by the headline: '*The next thing that gets eaten is your teeth*' when it is juxtaposed with a picture of a sandwich with a bite taken out of it. Our momentary reaction is likely to be 'Huh? What was that again?' But in virtually no time at all, and almost without effort, we puzzle out its meaning. 'Oh…I get it…Colgate helps prevent the decay that begins to attack teeth immediately on eating…hey, clever!'

This ad, like many others, plays on the fact that words have multiple meanings and can represent more than one mental address in our mind. In this ad the word 'eat' is used to mean both 'ingestion of food' and 'something that decay does to your teeth'. One reason why there tends to be less counter-arguing with such ads is that we expend more effort on understanding the ad and, consequently, there is less cognitive capacity available to contest the ad's claims. This creates a very fine line—if the puzzle is too hard the ad can fail completely because we are not going to be bothered… we just give up and turn the page.

However, if we do successfully 'get it', such ads provide a brief mental diversion not unlike a crossword puzzle.[6] Making sense of something from limited clues is rewarding. We gain a mild satisfaction when we are able to make sense of what is initially puzzling. The difference with ads is that we are prepared to invest much less time in puzzling them out than we are with crossword clues. So while ads, and crossword puzzles, that are too hard are likely to frustrate us so that we escape from them, ads that puzzle us momentarily, holding us just long enough for us to make sense of them and reach closure on them, are accompanied by a mild positive sensation—a sense of fleeting reward.

Repeating yesterday's news

Creating new variants or new developments of a brand can provide the source for new messages about the brand. Consider, for example, the ad in Figure 8.2, used to launch the Pringles fat-free variant. But the news of a new variant, once announced, has done its job. Repeating it is like repeating yesterday's news. So, wrapping up the same messages in a fresh way offers another solution to the advertiser to avoid the brand and its advertising appearing stale.

Consider how Colgate did it with the sandwich ad discussed above. There is no real news but in the unwrapping of the message we are reminded of both the brand—Colgate—and its key attribute—'protects against decay'. The ad reinforces the strength of both. Furthermore, it does it in a mildly entertaining way. How much more boring and irritating the ad would be if it just

Figure 8.2
'New Fat Free Pringles taste just as good as Original because they are made with Olean. Tasting is believing.' © *The Procter & Gamble Company. Used by permission.*

repeated the old message we have heard so many times: 'Colgate provides protection against tooth decay.'

When exposed to an ad like this, we immediately recognize it as an ad for Colgate. Then we store any 'new' information about Colgate (i.e. it 'protects against decay') at that mental address. If we find we already know this fact—in other words, we find it already stored in our mental Colgate pigeon-hole—our focus shifts to the clever wrapping instead of reacting negatively by thinking 'Why are you telling me that?…I already know it'. We tend to appreciate the cleverness of such ads and that makes us somehow more tolerant of seeing them repeatedly. The essential difference lies in the way we process the information.

How we understand ads

We are exposed to hundreds of ads every day but we process only a fraction of them fully. Some jump out at us immediately, others we miss completely and still others we deliberately ignore. When an ad catches our attention our minds automatically *try* to make sense of it. In this we may succeed or fail. We may fail because we find the ad 'too hard' to understand, or there is not enough time, or we are distracted by something else. Just how our minds set about trying to understand an ad goes something like this:

1. First, we recognize that it is an ad.
2. Then we immediately try to identify what it is an ad for. To do this, we look for something familiar. We look for something that corresponds to a memory address—something that already exists in our memory. In Figure 8.2, for example, we may recognize the name Pringles. 'Aha… we know that name. This must be an ad for Pringles.'
3. Once we have located this familiar memory address our minds can store any new information gained from the ad. We can put 'fat-free chips' into the Pringles pigeonhole.

Brand reminders

The important thing about this process is that, before any new information (like 'fat-free' or 'protects against decay') can be stored in our minds, a familiar mental pigeonhole or address has first to be activated (in this case, Pringles or Colgate). The opening of the mental pigeonhole, the triggering of that mental address serves to remind us of the brand. This happens whether or not the information 'fat-free chips' is new or is already stored there, and whether or not 'fat-free chips' is important to us. In other words, the ad reinforces the salience of the brand in our mind and this effect is independent of any new information. So brand reinforcement is one effect.

Then, depending on how important the new information ('fat-free chips') is to us, the news itself may have an effect, over and above the brand reinforcement effect.[7]

Heralding

New information—a special promotion, a new deal, a new pack or whatever—can be announced by 'heralding' the new information. Some ads virtually scream the news at us (e.g. used car dealers shout 'Have I got a hot deal for you!'). The more heralding the ad, the more it focuses our attention on the information as new. The more 'in your face' the ad message, the quicker it may get the message across. But once we have seen it and understood it, we don't really want to see it again. The more it is repeated the less affinity we are likely to feel, either for the ad or the brand, and the more tired and boring it makes them start to look.

On the other hand, if an ad is pitched in a more low-key manner, especially if it is done in a clever way that we can appreciate, we tend to receive it more courteously and are more tolerant of its repetition. The way an ad talks to us influences our reaction. Just as in our everyday interaction with people, *how* we are spoken to can heavily influence how we react. We like people who are fun, who make us laugh and don't harangue us. We feel affronted by people that are strident. They put us in a less receptive state of mind for what they have to say, and we are more inclined to argue with them.

Non-heralding

As we have seen, when a strident message is used, heralded repeatedly, it quickly becomes stale. Once new information is exposed and registered it is not new any more and repetition of it violates our cultural expectation that advertising is supposed to communicate new information. That is why we encounter a lot of advertising that seems to persist in delivering old information as though it were new.

Ads that communicate in a lower key and try to get the information across more incidentally, or as reminders, tend to be longer lasting and less annoying in their effect. Once the new message has been communicated, and before the repetition of the 'heralding' begins to annoy us, most advertisers would like to substitute a more toned-down approach. But in order to reach the mass of people some degree of repetition of the heralding ad is almost inevitable.

An alternative for the advertiser is to use a lower-key form of communication in the first place. It does not get the message across as directly, or perhaps even as quickly sometimes, but it does minimize annoyance and gives the ad a much longer life.

Even advertisers that adopt this method would be hard pushed to articulate exactly what they do. Rather, they can instinctively sense when an ad is 'in the consumers' face' and when it is lower key and less likely to irritate. What is going on here is governed in large part by the amount of focal stress that is placed on the newness of the information. In the lower-key commercial there is not the same focus on the newness of the information, and much less heralding of this newness. The difference is in how it is said rather than what is said.

Assertions and non-assertions

Information can be communicated by way of bald assertion—heralding— or with varying degrees of subtlety. Consider, for example, the statement:

> Pringles are now Fat Free and taste just as good as Original

There is no subtlety about this. It is a pure assertion, putting the focus on the information that Fat Free Pringles are new as well as tasting as good as Original. Assertions like this wear out quickly and, when they are no longer news, continued repetition risks becoming boring and irritating.

But ads often use more oblique techniques such as descriptive words (adjectives) in place of assertion. These can slip the same information in more gently with less focal stress on the newness of the information.[8] For example, consider the statement:

> Fat Free Pringles. As good as the original taste.

Using 'Fat Free' as a descriptive term like this rather than using direct assertion (that Pringles *are* Fat Free) causes the focus of our processing to be directed to the other part of the communication—'as good as the original taste'. 'Fat Free' is seen more as an identifying description than as an assertion. Adjectives appear less like assertions of new information, operating more as matter-of-fact descriptions.

Granted, such differences are subtle and the smallness of the effect may risk a 'so what' reaction. However, these more oblique forms of expression, by toning down the communication, can soften the degree of assertion while communicating the same information.

The part of the ad we focus on

As we have seen, not everything within a communication attracts equal attention. Our minds tend to process information that we already know quite differently from things that are new. The content of any communication seems to be classified by our minds into two sorts:

1. things that are already 'known', called the 'given' information—we are being reminded;
2. things that are 'new'.

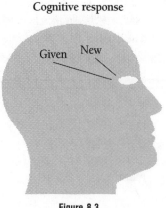

Cognitive response

Given   New

Figure 8.3
'Given' and 'new'

It is important to appreciate how our minds treat 'given' and 'new' quite differently. Think about your schooldays. Did you ever ask the other kids trick questions like: *How many of each species did Moses take with him on the ark?* Unsuspecting kids always gave the answer 'two'. You laughed derisively and pointed out to the other kids' embarrassment that it wasn't Moses who went in the ark. It was Noah!

This schoolyard trick worked because you positioned Moses in the question *not* as new information but as 'given'—that is already known. The kids assumed the given to be true and focused their processing elsewhere. It is easy for our minds to skip over something and take information as given when it is positioned in this way.

The trick worked even though we were unaware of the mechanism underlying it. Similarly, while there are ads that work to varying degrees because of this mechanism, very few advertisers would be able to articulate it or how it works. What we regard as 'given' simply registers in passing while we focus our attention on what we regard as 'new' in the communication. Our minds tend to regard given information merely as a reminder and assume the information to be true, leaving our processing capacity free to focus on verifying the truth of the new information.

Reminders

In various ways our minds pick up cues about what is 'new' and what is already known ('given') in the communication. In everyday conversation the term 'as you know' is frequently used. Consider the expression:

> 'As you know, Macintosh take less time than other computers to learn.
> Macintosh is the number 1 computer used worldwide in schools.'

The prefatory term 'as you know' has the effect of redirecting some of the focus of our processing away from evaluating the statement 'Macintosh take less time than other computers to learn'. If we are going to focus on evaluating anything, it is likely to be the statement '*Macintosh is the number 1 computer used worldwide in schools*' because this is the new information that is being asserted in the communication.

The expression 'as you know' operates as a signal to the listener that this is a reminder—the information is to be regarded as just a lead-in to something else. It pre-empts any premature annoyance that might get in the way of the communication and avoids the annoyed reaction 'I already know that! So why are you repeating it?'

More importantly, when something is signaled as a reminder instead of new information, we expect what is being said to be already stored in our memory. We expect it to be already known and therefore true.

Malleability of memory

When something is positioned as a reminder it has the effect of making us expect to find it in our memory. Just as we often see in people what we expect to see, so too we often find in our memory what we expect to find. Why is this important? To answer this, let us tell you about the classic experiments concerning eye-witness testimony. They reveal a lot about how human beings process information, when it is positioned as new, differently from how we process the same information when it is positioned as a reminder of something we already know.

In this famous series of experiments, psychologist Elizabeth Loftus showed subjects a videotape of a car accident and later asked them questions.[9] For example, 'How fast was the blue car going when it ran the stop sign?'

In fact, there was no stop sign in the videotape. But the form of the question led people to assume it was there. Subjects gave their speed estimates. When they were asked later if they saw a stop sign, more than half of them (53 per cent) claimed they had. The mental representation of the event had been 'altered' in their minds by the form of the earlier question.

Note that the information that there was a stop sign was positioned as 'given' information in the question. Using this technique Loftus found repeatedly that subjects were prepared to add buildings, see people that weren't there, make cars go faster or slower, and in general witness actions that were not originally there.

This is startling evidence of how we normally assume the given information in a communication to be true and concentrate on verifying what we see as the 'new' information. (As an aside, this factor is what lies at the heart of the controversy surrounding 'recovered memories'—of being sexually abused as a child, for example. The courts have to judge whether patients undergoing psychiatric therapy have been helped to 'recover' genuine memories or whether the memories have been accidentally created or altered in some way by the psychiatrist's questions.)

The general point is that expectations can be set up by the syntax or by other means that can significantly influence the focus of our processing.

Silent signals

Our minds receive signals from communications indicating to us what we should presume to be new and what we should take as given. When we listen to a radio ad, the amount of vocal stress in each part of the sentence helps signal to us what is new and what is given.

In written material and print advertising, it is the syntax and the graphics that provide the cues. For example, the position of an adjective can direct the focus of processing by signalling new information. Consider the statement 'Total clean Fab is gentler'. What is being signaled as new is that it is gentler than other washing powders.

Placing the adjective before the noun (Fab) signals 'given'. Consider the statement 'Gentler Fab gives total clean'. What is now being signaled as new is that Fab gives total clean. The attribute of 'gentler' is still being communicated but this time as given information.

In the last chapter we saw how our minds mentally process image ads and visual experiences quite differently from information ads. We can now see that information in ads can be processed by our minds in different ways depending on how directly or obliquely the information is asserted. What is involved here is a shift in our 'focus of processing' away from the information as new, to a focus on enjoyment, entertaining reminders or something else in the communication.

Oblique, less heralding ways have the effect of not inviting the same degree of annoyance when the information is repeated nor the same degree of counter-arguing. Wrapping up old information in fresh ways is just one form of rendering the information oblique and less heralding.

Summary

In at least five ways ads can minimize how likely we are to counter-argue with their messages, hence influencing how we react to the ad overall.

1. By not making assertions;
2. By toning down the assertions;

3. By positioning the information as something that is already known;
4. By packaging the information as entertainment;
5. By casting us, the audience, in a bystander role, 'overhearing' the information.

In Chapter 7 we saw how casting us as bystanders, rather than talking directly to us, can work for ads. In this chapter we focused on the other four methods—where, instead of heralding the new information, the ad is toned down or more subtly positions the information as a reminder.

Essentially, all communications work by triggering memories. Old images or concepts are triggered in our minds by something in the ad. We recognize various things as familiar. In the process, something new may be introduced and we are shown how to link this up with the old.

When something is positioned as 'new' the focus of our mental processing tends to be on evaluating (a) whether it is new and (b) whether it corresponds to our own experience, knowledge and beliefs.

The other parts of a communication, the 'given', we treat more casually. We assume we already know about it, so we tend not to spend as much time evaluating its validity. In other words, we take it as given.

Sentence construction, vocal stress and camera focus can be used to send signals as to what is given and what is new. While very subtle, these can also be very important. Don't let the subtlety distract you from their importance. Advertisers themselves are largely unaware of the mechanism involved.

9

What's this I'm watching? The elements that make up an ad

In the last chapter we saw that the way an ad speaks to us affects our processing of it—that news is processed differently to reminders. Ads vary enormously even though their basic elements are much the same: sound, voice, music and pictures. A brand like Coke will often have several different ads exposed in the same week. The message is usually the same but the ads may all be executed in different ways. As we have seen, the way the executional elements of an ad are blended can help determine which of the consumer's mental processes become engaged and which do not.

The art of the creative departments in ad agencies is traditionally intuitive rather than encoded in any set of well formulated principles. Articulating what makes for creative success in advertising is an underdeveloped science and even more especially when it comes to analyzing the individual elements of an ad. This chapter draws on advertising findings and the principles of psychological processing that are gradually coming to light to further our understanding of how the executional elements of an ad do, or don't, work.

Interaction of words and visuals[1]

It is important to note how the elements of an ad can interact—music with visuals, perhaps, or words with visuals. For example, consider the statement: 'The stripes expanded'. We can't process it effectively. What does 'the stripes expanded' mean? No mental address is activated in our mind that corresponds to the stripes. Unless we can locate one we can't make sense of it. If, however, there is a picture of a man blowing up a striped balloon on the same page, we can easily make sense of it.

In this way the visual element is used effectively to manipulate what is 'on stage' in our minds and help us locate the appropriate mental address for a word. Ordinarily this interactive process is extremely fast and automatic rather than conscious. So we rarely have any sense of expending effort to put these elements together. At other times it takes just a minuscule amount of effort to make meaning out of it.

Consider this example:

> Headline: *'This year, hit the beach topless'*—Pepsi
> Visual: The cap from a Pepsi bottle lies crumpled on the sand

Our minds are easily able to discover the underlying connection that makes this ad comprehensible. The process is rapid but goes something like this. Our mind locates two addresses. One in response to the headline—appearing partially nude. The second is a soft drink bottle-cap. How to make sense of the two? We must first search for and locate an alternative address for the expression 'topless'—ah, the Pepsi bottle with the cap removed is, of course, topless. Suddenly the image of opening a Pepsi has been triggered by something linking to nudity, rebelliousness and risk taking. The link is implicit and associative rather than explicitly asserted. And along with understanding it, go the fleeting satisfaction of having successfully puzzled it out (akin to solving a crossword puzzle clue) and appreciation of a cute or clever ad.

These interactions and the tiny effort we expend in the almost instant problem solving are partly what underlies our greater appreciation of such ads. But as consumers we are rarely motivated to expend much effort trying to puzzle out what a creative copywriter meant. Up to a point there is a certain reward that goes with puzzling out the right meaning, but this works only if the ad first gets our attention.

Attention-getting devices

Advertising has to get attention. It has to 'cut through' the clutter of other advertising and get noticed. The first principle of advertising is that it needs to stand out. To this end, advertising uses a variety of attention-getting devices, the best known of which are sex and humor. In addition there are other more subtle elements that almost involuntarily capture our attention.

101

What's this I'm watching? The elements that make up an ad

'People are social beings. Their attention often proves to be activated by other people, especially the portrayal of their faces and hands. Eyes in particular have an activating effect.'[2] Emotional characters, erotic stimuli, small children and animals are just some of the things that increase the probability of capturing attention. 'It is not for nothing they have frequently been used in advertising over the years—but not always functionally.'[3]

For example, advertisers who import sex into an ad and use it purely as an attention-getter when it has no intrinsic relationship with the product certainly gain attention. But, contrary to popular consumer belief, this device

Figure 9.1
Ad for Lever body wash

stands little chance of being effective if it is not directly relevant to an advertisement's primary selling point.[4]

Many readers will be surprised to learn that ads they are highly aware of may nevertheless be ineffective. This is because getting attention is just one component of making ads work. Eggs are necessary for making a cake but the cake will fail if you rely on eggs alone. Attention alone will not necessarily make an ad work.[5]

All too often in tracking the progress of an ad, we have seen that the very device that is used to direct audience attention to the ad also serves to distract the audience from the brand and its message. Devices such as humor, sexual arousal and emotion can give an illusory impression to the audience that an ad is highly visible and therefore must be a great ad, but is it in fact working?

An ad that compels our attention but fails to register the brand and its message is next to useless for any advertiser. Though such ads may stand

Figure 9.2
Victoria's Secret lingerie advertising

Figure 9.3
Ad for Jewelry.com. Sex is a natural
attention-getter

out, they frequently don't work unless advertisers make sure that compensatory emphasis is given to strengthening the brand and the message sufficiently to outweigh this distraction effect (see, for example, Chapter 15, 'The effectiveness of funny ads').

Sex is a natural attention-getter that is fairly widely used. Many products are bought partly because we want to feel more attractive, and they have a 'natural' association with our drive for sexual attraction. Products such as clothing, lingerie, jewelry, and fragrances often tie in to this 'natural' association—brands like Victoria's Secret (lingerie), Jewelry.com (jewelry) and numerous labels of fragrances for both men and women.

Controversial communicable ads

Some brands use attention-getting devices in a way that seems calculatingly designed to generate outrage. The effect is they become 'talked about' ads and are passed on by word of mouth. Resembling communicable diseases they are spread, virus-like, by people who say 'Did you see that ad for…?'

Three examples of ads that became 'communicable' by using sex in an explicit or controversial way were these:

- 'Nothing comes between me and my Calvins' (Calvin Klein jeans);
- 'Are you wearing any protection?' (Bolle sunglasses);
- Jaipur perfume ad showing a nude female from the back, 'handcuffed' by Jaipur. The 'bondage' overtones caused huge controversy.[6]

Humor

There are three main mechanisms by which humorous ads are supposed to work more effectively than straight ads:

1. Humorous ads are noticed more—that is, they gain greater attention.
2. There is less counter-arguing with humorous ads because viewers process them as entertainment rather than engage in true/false evaluation.

103

What's this I'm watching? The elements that make up an ad

3. They are liked more and there is evidence that ads that are liked have a higher probability of being effective.

These three points are dealt with in more depth in Chapter 15 ('The effectiveness of funny ads'). Suffice to say at this point that, while humor is another element that has the capacity to attract attention as well as entertain the audience and reduce counter-arguing, it does so at the possible risk of distracting us from attending to the brand and the message. Humor may hijack attention away from these other important elements. Consider, for example, this airline ad:

A man bursts naked into his living room with a rose between his teeth, only to find that his wife has flown her parents over on a cheap weekend fare.[7]

If you remember this ad, do you remember which airline was the advertiser? It was a very humorous commercial but, while the message is well integrated, the brand is not. Nothing in the execution ties in with the brand itself. It could be used as a commercial for just about any brand of airline. In fact it was—the same ad was used in different countries by *different* airlines. Where a brand is not inherently integrated into the execution, ads using humorous executions have to make doubly sure that the correct brand is successfully registered in people's minds. Otherwise, while highly entertaining, the commercial may be doing a job for airlines generally but not the advertiser specifically.

Sometimes, creative teams seem to feel a need to introduce humor almost gratuitously—for no functional reason other than that it appears clever—especially in sign-off lines at the end of commercials. Irrelevant throwaway lines (called 'klinkers') at the end of commercials do little to attract attention. Furthermore, they are likely to erase short-term memory and interfere with the main message of the ad.[8] They can be contrasted with sign-off lines that *reinforce* the message; for example:

'Volkswagen—it doesn't go in one year and out the other.'

Such reinforcements at the end of a commercial are called 'klitchniks'.[9]

Testimonials

Testimonials can be used to increase attention, particularly with radio and print.[10] Sometimes very effective as a form of advertising, they are not always done well.[11] The intention behind real-person endorsements is to depict a simulation of word-of-mouth advertising. They may show an 'expert' (e.g. the doctor-in-white-coat technique) but more often they present 'typical people' who appear to be just like us. This is the satisfied-customer technique. For example, in the USA, ads for Broadway musicals frequently show a lot of real people speaking glowingly about the show.

The process of empathy and identification indicates that the more like us the 'satisfied customers' appear to be, the more effective their testimonial. Consequently, in many countries testimonials are often used by companies marketing to specialist occupational groups like farmers, plumbers or builders.

Music

The inclusion in an ad of a tune that is already well known can help to get attention as well as set the appropriate mood and act as a memory jogger. Association of the brand with a popular piece of music increases the salience of the brand in our minds and makes it more likely that we will think of that brand whenever we hear the music. This principle is reflected in the saying: 'Sophistication is being able to hear the William Tell overture without thinking of the Lone Ranger.' Microsoft paid a reported $4 million for the rights to use the Rolling Stones' tune 'Start It Up'.[12] Can you hear that song today without thinking of Microsoft?

For years, Gershwin's 'Rhapsody In Blue' has serenaded us into seats for United Airlines. British Airways set the Lakme Duet behind their famous 'face' commercial. *The Partridge Family* provided lyrics for Levi's…'I think I love you'. Long-distance telecoms often urge us to 'mentally migrate' to music. Elton John's 'Rocket Man' provided a rhythm reminder of gadgets to let us stay in touch. And backing by a mobile phone gave us a Cindy Lauper license to enable working moms to be at the beach with their girls because… 'Girls Just Want To Have Fun'. Thousands of advertisers use hit tunes and other music to support their advertising. Music now appears in about half of all TV commercials.[13]

Words to music: the jingle

Many ads set their own words to established or specially written tunes. Coca-Cola, for example, was so successful in the 1970s with its jingle 'I'd Like To Buy The World A Coke' sung by an international youth choir that it was extended, recorded and released to become an international chart hit in 1971 called 'I'd Like To Teach The World To Sing'.

Consider these:

105

What's this I'm watching? The elements that make up an ad

- 'I'm stuck on Band-Aids 'cause Band-Aids stuck on me'
- 'You deserve a break today. McDonald's'
- 'Just for the taste of it...Diet Coke'
- 'Stayin' alive...Volvo'
- 'Heard it through the grapevine'...California Raisins
- 'Take good care of my baby'...Johnson & Johnson baby shampoo
- 'You can tell a Wella woman by the way she wears her hair'
- 'Come see the softer side of Sears'
- 'Be all that you can be' US Army
- 'Oh, what a feeling...Toyota!'

Such jingles can easily be dredged out of our past memories. A host of extraordinarily memorable campaigns owe much of their longevity in memory to the fact that the words were set to music. Music is a cutting edge that helps to etch a commercial into long-term memory. McDonald's set to music the incredible line: 'Two all-beef patties, special sauce, lettuce, cheese, pickles, onions on a sesame-seed bun.' A Canadian, Toronto-based pizza chain called Pizza Pizza set their telephone number to a jingle so successfully that, if you ask a Toronto resident what number to call for pizza, they will 'sing': 'nine-six-seven, eleven, eleven. Phone Pizza Pizza, hey, hey, hey!' On the strength of this, the company expanded to new locations across North America.

There is another effect that music seems to have. When the words of an ad are set to music they tend to wash over us rather than invite us to intellectualize. Why is it that, when the words of an ad are set to music, we do not have the same sense of somebody trying to convince us or sell us on something? Setting the words to music somehow takes the edge off what might otherwise be a strident message.

This is because we seem to process lyrics differently from spoken messages. As teenagers, particularly, we appear to learn to process lyrics and music in a different way from other communications. And we do this in terms of 'enjoy/don't enjoy' rather than in terms of truth or falsity. We learn to process the experience as an experience rather than as a proposition that is supposed to be a faithful representation of real-world reality. Much of the content of MTV (Music Television), for example, when it is processed in a rational way, is clearly unrepresentative of reality. It is designed to let fantasy and feelings in rather than shut them out.

Music is for appreciating and letting wash over us, not for arguing with. The mood that it sets can take the edge off potentially controversial topics. Words that might otherwise be processed in terms of truth/falsity are processed quite differently.

Musical commercials have become so much a part of our advertising environment that we almost forget they are there. We seem to respond to them as we respond to traffic lights: without thinking much about them. Putting words to music is a well established creative technique—the rhythm method of advertising. In putting words to music it lessens the chance of conception that anyone is trying to tell us or sell us something and it reduces our tendency to counter-argue with what is being said.

Who is talking to whom?

Analyzing the executional elements in an ad requires some rather subtle analysis. An invaluable starting-point to the process is to ask two questions:

1. Who is the ad talking to?
2. Who is doing the talking?

The way we experience a commercial depends on what role we, the viewers, are cast in by the ad. This in turn influences who is seen to be talking to whom.

Lecture-style ads

Consider ads like 'This week only at Merv's supermarkets, we have the following red-hot specials...' or 'I'm Joe Blow and have I got a deal for you!' Who is speaking to whom? These ads take a relatively traditional form in which it is clear that the advertiser (Merv's or Joe Blow) is talking to us, the viewer in front of the TV set.

We process these lecture-style ads in terms of the relevance of the information they convey. The advertiser hopes we will listen to what is said, find it of interest and see its relevance to us, then remember the information and act on it. For this to happen the ad has first to capture our attention and interest. In advertising jargon, it has to 'cut through the clutter'.

Look who's talking: face vs voice-over

Ads that reason with us often feature a presenter putting the case for why we should try or buy this widget rather than some other widget, or why the presenter's brand is superior to the leading brand.

One important way in which lecture-style ads vary is in whether or not

107

What's this I'm watching? The elements that make up an ad

we can see who is talking; whether we can see the face of the advertiser. In the typical supermarket ad announcing the week's specials, the advertiser is usually unseen. The focus is on the specials. The person doing the talking is merely a 'voice-over'. If there is any real sense of a human being in the commercial it is merely a disembodied voice informing us how much we will save. Car dealer ads, on the other hand, often have the dealer himself as the on-screen speaker. The words come out of the dealer's mouth. In advertising jargon, the ad has 'lip-sync'.

These ads are like lectures and the person doing the talking is like the lecturer. Some lecturers and some ads stick in our minds much more than others. Some lecturers like to work in a darkened room, hidden behind a lectern, with the audience's attention focused on a screen. Other lecturers are more lively. They work the audience from up-front, doing demonstrations or interacting with the audience and attempting to get participation from them.

So it is when we have a lip-synced, on-screen presenter like Paul Reiser as the spokesperson for AT&T, Candice Bergen for Sprint, Whoopee Goldberg for MCI or Dave Thomas for his own chain, Wendy's (see Figure 9.4). Such presenters engage us visually and verbally while they communicate.

Lecturers who stay in the background tend not to impress themselves, or their message, upon us and we feel less warm towards them. Similarly, advertisers who communicate with us only as disembodied voice-overs are usually less effective. Their commercials attract less attention.[14] In

Figure 9.4
Dave Thomas, owner and spokesperson for Wendy's

tracking lecture-style ads of this type over the last ten years, the ones with an on-screen human presenter and lip-sync emerge as the ones that almost invariably outperform those in which a disembodied voice-over is used.

This is no doubt related to why many people don't like talking on the telephone and prefer to talk to people face to face. Talking to someone on the phone is just not the same because you can't see the other person's face and expressions. This type of news or lecture-style communication where the advertiser is imparting information usually comes across as more meaningful and effective when there is a human face, a personality doing the talking, either on the screen or in your mind. Many car dealers are persuaded to appear in their own ads because we can see a face that talks to us and becomes a known face. It helps when the organization that is talking to us has a human face, whether it is Dave Thomas for Wendys, Lee Iacocca for Chrysler, Michael Eisner for Disney or August Busch IV for Annheiser Busch (Budweiser) beer.

Presenters

This raises the question of whose face? Some advertisers choose to use a human face but not their own. Just as governments use ambassadors to represent them overseas to be the human face of the government, some corporations prefer to use a presenter to represent the organization. So the presenter is not always the advertiser. He or she may be a model or actor with the 'right kind' of face (e.g. the 'fast talker' for the Federal Express ads, or the Maytag Repairman or the characters that Gallo wines created, Fred Bartles and Ed Jaymes, for the wine cooler brand, Bartles & James).

Or the presenter may be a famous person. Kramer (of Seinfeld) for Vodaphone; Yul Brynner for anti-smoking, Karl Malden and Seinfeld for American Express; John Cleese for Magnavox; Jim Palmer for Jockey; Cathy Lee Gifford for Carnival Cruises; Muhammad Ali for Rockport. Some advertisers use multiple faces: Madonna, Michael J. Fox, Michael Jackson and Cindy Crawford for Pepsi; Michael Jordan and Bo Jackson for Nike.

Cosmetic companies, especially, often use this strategy of someone else's face: Elizabeth Hurley for Estee Lauder, Cindy Crawford for Revlon, Melanie Griffith for Revlon.

The use of celebrity presenters is a global phenomenon. In Japan the majority of commercials feature a celebrity. In the UK, Rowan Atkinson (alias Mr Bean) was the face of Barclays Bank for many years. In Australia, where sport is almost a religion, Olympic medalists appear in ads for everything from breakfast cereals to cars.

Chances are you will recall one or more very old ad campaigns featuring the faces of those mentioned above—testimony to the durability of the memory trace that the use of such presenters can create. Celebrities and actors are surrogates for the advertiser. They can put a human face on the image of an organization.

As well as giving the advertiser a human face, the use of a presenter also acts a mnemonic device to increase the salience of the brand. Who can think of Karl Malden without thinking of American Express? In Australia Paul Hogan was ultimately prohibited from doing Winfield cigarette ads because of his huge popularity with kids and his mnemonic association with the name Winfield. The same happened with the animated face of Joe Camel in the USA. Whether it be the face of Marcus Welby (Robert Young), Joe

109

What's this I'm watching? The elements that make up an ad

Camel or Paul Hogan, every appearance of it in a movie, a variety show or a TV interview inevitably reminds us of the brand.

The use of a presenter instead of the advertiser to do the talking in an ad seems to lessen the sense of someone with a vested interest talking directly to us and doing a hard sell on us. We receive the message, from the company, but through a congenial and familiar figure (e.g. Candice Bergen for Sprint or June Allyson, the 1940s Hollywood star, for Depends adult diapers) who presents the advertiser and the product in a favorable light.

Voice-over

Whether the presenter is the advertiser in person or a hired face it is almost always more effective and more memorable than the use of anonymous, disembodied voice-overs. Why then do so many advertisers continue to use voice-over? The reason that so many ads continue to use voice-over in spite of the fact that they are almost always less effective is cost. They are cheaper to make and more flexible, especially if they need to be modified (e.g. to dub in another accent or language for use internationally).

Variations on voice-over

Advertisers sometimes have more success with voice-overs if they can vary them in some way. One way is the newer trend of using some of Hollywood's biggest stars as voice-over talent in major campaigns. When James Earl Jones, Richard Dreyfuss or Kathleen Turner lend their voices, we say 'I recognize that voice!' and we see the face in our mind rather than seeing the face directly in the ad.

Another variation is to set the voice-over to music. If we go out to an entertainment event like *Phantom of the Opera*, we clearly approach and assimilate the experience quite differently from a university lecture. When the voice-over of an ad is set to music it has a similar effect. Take, for example, the ads for Canon ('You can on a Canon'), or Gillette ('The best a man can get'). These ads are more entertaining and enjoyable than they would be if spoken as voice-over commercials. We process them differently—more as an experience—and their effects are thus more subtle. It seems to subtly change the way the ad is cognitively processed by the viewer. The way we process them is more akin to the way we mentally process musical drama.

A most unusual variation on voice-over is illustrated by the hugely popular Joe Isuzu ads. Isuzu cast Joe as the salesman presenter whose wild overclaiming for the product was corrected each time by supers-words that appeared on the screen coming from an invisible third person that we presume to be the advertiser. Joe is talking to us, the viewers, out front. But so too is the advertiser via the supers and, in contradicting or putting straight the wild claims that Joe makes for the car, the unseen advertiser earns our respect for honesty and credibility.

Who are the characters talking to?

What is important in an ad is not just who is talking or singing but who they are singing or talking *to*.

Take the 'fast talking' Federal Express presenter who is a business man, always talking very fast to employees, either on the phone or in person, communicating the need in business for documents overnight. Or the MCI 'Friends and Families' campaign where people talk to one another about the advantages of this MCI program. There is also the old but very famous spot for Chiffon margarine—'It's not nice to fool Mother Nature'. A woman talks to the narrator about how nice and creamy the butter is, and the narrator corrects her, pointing out that it's not butter; the woman gets angry, lightning flashes and thunder rolls, and she utters the famous 'not nice to fool Mother Nature' tag-line.

Ask yourself who the character on screen or in the voice-over is talking to. If we think carefully about this we will often find that the voice or character is not addressing us directly but some other character on the screen. At the same time we, on our side of the screen, are also experiencing the commercial and getting the message, but in the role of bystanders or passive observers.

The difference between being a bystander and being the obvious target of a communication was demonstrated in 1962 in an experiment by Walster and Festinger.[15] Subjects listened in on a conversation between two graduate students. Some subjects (Group A) believed the students knew they were listening. Others (Group B) believed that the students were unaware of their presence. Group A believed that what the students said could conceivably have been directed at influencing them, the listeners.

Group B was more influenced by the opinions expressed in the students' conversation. In other words, being in bystander mode seems to reduce the motivation for us to engage our defensive reactions and our tendency to be critical of what is being said.

As viewers we receive the message from these ads indirectly, much as we do when viewing a play or a soap opera or a movie. Our minds are not

111

What's this I'm watching? The elements that make up an ad

set to get a message but to be entertained. This contrasts with the traditional type of ad which addresses viewers directly—for example, the many retail ads for J.C. Penney or Woolworths in which the two main components are voice-over and illustrative visuals (usually of the products).

Such ads clearly and unambiguously talk to the viewer. Most early TV advertising was like this and we still tend to think of it as typical, probably because advertising's heritage lies in the print medium. Straight words with illustrative visuals is an approach very much in the style of, and a carryover from, print advertising. But if you watch today's TV ads closely you will see that this style has mutated considerably. Often the (off-screen) voice-over appears to be talking not so much to the viewer but to, or about, an on-screen character.

Voice-over talking to on-screen character

Having the voice-over in the ad appear to address an on-screen character is one of the primary ways in which a shift can be induced in our mental processing. It is one of several elements that invite us to take a bystander perspective. Oral B toothbrush did this with the voice over addressing Rob the dentist on screen and asking him to show us what brush he uses.

An Australian ad for Caro (a coffee substitute) illustrates the purer form of this technique. Throughout the whole commercial, the voice-over is not addressing the audience but a product-user on-screen character. In the ad, the man on the screen is told by the off-screen voice-over that there are many people just like him who now drink and enjoy the product. The viewer is a bystander and the viewer's 'focus of processing' is the bystander's perspective.

The difference between being a bystander and a target is the difference between overhearing a conversation and being told something directly. What is different in overhearing information in a conversation between two other people is that our attention and cognitive processing are focused differently (see Chapter 7).

When we are being told something directly we are more likely to engage our defensive, counter-arguing mechanism. We are more on the alert and ready for counter-arguing. The information gained from overhearing someone else's conversation may or may not be the same. However, the defensive processing applied to it is likely to be quite different.

Often this type of ad is very subtle and it is not immediately obvious that the primary role the audience is being cast in is bystander. Some well known commercials that have elements of this include 'This Bud's for you' and 'Where do you want to go today?' (Microsoft). Both address the people shown on the screen as much as, if not more than, those of us sitting out front.

The on-screen character as receiver

A seemingly strange but interesting question to ask of any musical commercial is 'Who is the voice singing to?' Who is the object of this communication? Sometimes the answer will be 'the on-screen character'. For example, in the famous Gillette (Best a man can get) commercials the voice sang to the on-screen character 'You're looking good'. In the Dr Pepper commercial the off-screen voice sings to the people on-screen 'Wouldn't you like to be a Pepper too?'

Think about ads like the US Army ad, 'Be all that you can be', or the Lowenbrau ad, 'Here's to good friends'. Setting the words of the voice-over to music can impart a sense that it is the on-screen character who is being sung to. This style further helps to disengage the viewer from acting the role of defensive customer. It engages the viewer more as a passive observer, a bystander enjoying the entertainment. The musical voice-over is not selling, talking or even singing to the viewer. Rather, it seems to be singing to the on-screen character.

To the extent that viewers identify with the on-screen character, they also receive the message indirectly and see it as relevant to themselves. In this type of ad, the pronoun 'you' occurs often (e.g. 'You oughta be congratulated' (Meadow Lea margarine), 'Aren't you glad you use Dial?', 'When you care enough to send the very best' (Hallmark cards).

This style engages us as passive observers and invites us to enjoy the ad while interpreting the 'you' as a reference to the on-screen character. However, if we identify with the on-screen character, we can simultaneously interpret the 'you' as referring to us.

Tuning in to the on-screen character's thoughts

In ads such as 'I'm stuck on Band-Aids because Band-Aids stuck on me' and 'I don't want to grow up, I'm a Toys-R-Us kid', it is as though the characters on screen are thinking the sentiments being expressed in song. Viewers have the impression of sharing what the characters are thinking or feeling. In these ads the words could be being sung by the characters, but they aren't. Instead the message seems to come from the characters' thoughts.

113

What's this I'm watching? The elements that make up an ad

If setting a message to music lessens the sense of being lectured to, this technique probably lessens that sense even more. We seem simply to be overhearing someone's thoughts. The on-screen characters in all these commercials are depicting other actions while simultaneously we are hearing what seems to be their thoughts, desires or remembrances coming through the audio track. The style is frequently characterised by use of the first-person pronoun 'I' or 'we'. To the extent that we find ourselves sharing the feelings of these characters and identifying with them, the pronoun 'I' or 'we' can be taken as referring to us as well. 'I Can't Believe It's Not Butter!'

Drama

Earlier we saw that people seem to process lyrics and music quite differently from spoken messages. Such processing, far from shutting fantasy and feeling out, deliberately lets it in.

'Drama' commercials are similar to music in this respect. Drama, like music, is supposed to be experienced and enjoyed. Experience and enjoyment are the focus of our mental processing. Our mental processing is not usually set to engage in analysis of the drama in terms of truth or falsity. Nor is it set to analyze what information goes into our heads in the process.

A classic drama commercial was Pepsi's 'archeological dig' which showed a bottle of Coke being found at an archeological dig in the next century and the 'professor' admitting that he doesn't know what it is. Classic long-running drama commercials include Impulse body deodorant ('If someone gives you flowers, it may be just Impulse'), AT&T's 'Reach out and touch someone' and the Nestlé Gold/Taster's Choice/Nescafé serialized ads. These ads appeal to us emotionally. We can relate to them and they entertain us at the same time as 'educating' us. They are like plays or dramas as distinct from lectures. They not only have people and faces but also characters and plots. All these elements help the ads to stick in people's minds.

There is a world of difference between listening to a lecture or debate and attending a concert or movie. Debates are an invitation to reason, movies an invitation to experience. With drama commercials, this is the difference. We record inadvertently the incidental information or message that happens to get conveyed while the focus of our attention is on being entertained. Sometimes by putting both music and drama together we get musical drama (e.g. Levi's 'Tainted Love' ad which used the 80s hit by Soft Cell featuring a Levi's-clad accident victim who 'comes to' in the operating room by singing the song to the beat of his heart monitor and is joined by the rest of the operating-room team).

Characters

When developing a commercial, ad agencies identify the target audience for the product (i.e. who buys it) so that they can make decisions about the characters. 'Young products' (e.g. jeans) usually feature young people and 'older products' (e.g. retirement plans) will feature older people. Similarity in age between characters and audience is usually a plus.

The ad maker attempts to weave roles and characters into the ad that we will welcome and that are consistent with the way we see ourselves or would like to see ourselves—roles and characters that we can easily identify with.

The closer we feel to a character, and the greater the similarity between that character and ourselves, the more effect a commercial is likely to have on us. This is why ads for Mattel toys usually star children, ads for Coca-Cola feature teenagers, and ads for All-Bran breakfast cereal show the whole family. The age, sex and lifestyle of the characters are chosen to maximise the probability that the target audience for the brand will identify with the character.

Multiple target audiences

Many ads have one specific target audience and the target character is designed accordingly. It is possible, however, for one commercial to address multiple target audiences and still achieve identification.

An example is the McDonald's ad that shows a working mom in a business suit showing her husband and kids everything in the refrigerator and freezer. She's going on a business trip and has color-coded the plastic wrap around all the foods—blue is for broccoli, red is for...—dad and the kids are just looking at her, not paying attention. Then you cut to dad pulling stuff out of the refrigerator for dinner, asking the kids, 'What do you want for dinner, blue or red?' They say, 'Let's go to McDonald's.' Lots of McDonald's spots work against multiple targets.

Another example is the typical long-distance telephone commercial used by carriers in various parts of the world that shows a young boy whose parents suggest he phone and talk to his grandfather. The warm emotion that ensues from the two parties to the call attaches itself to all the characters in the scene.

Such ads invite viewers to step into one or other of the roles by identifying with the actor's words, actions, feelings or thoughts. Successful identification should lead to suggestions for similar feelings in similar households.

115

What's this I'm watching? The elements that make up an ad

The point is that almost anyone can identify with one or other of the character targets. *Children* can identify with the young boy whose parents let him call his grandfather, prompting requests for permission to phone *their* grandparents. *Grandparents* can identify with the grandfather and hope their relatives will call them, or perhaps they will be motivated to make a call themselves. *Parents* can identify with the parent characters whose thoughtfulness in allowing the child to make the call lets them experience the joy of both the boy and his grandfather.

Another similar-style ad for long-distance carriers shows a son calling his mother to thank her for the sweater she has knitted for him—she receives the call while she is trying a similar sweater on her husband/his father. This is another example of multiple target audiences.

Two questions are therefore pertinent when we examine an ad and its characters. First, are we members of the target audience for the ad? Or is it aimed at people in some other age, sex or socioeconomic group? Tampon ads are not aimed at men, nor are women's fashion ads. Often, however, it is not that obvious. Assuming we are in the target audience for the ad, which character or characters seem to be most like us? Which character in the ad do we feel some identity or empathy with? If the ad is working on us it is most likely to be through that particular character.

The person playing the character

Michael Jordon is liked and admired by almost every adolescent, not to mention adults. People who are already admired generally have a head start in getting the audience to identify with, and project themselves into, the character. Almost every adolescent 'wants to be' a Michael Jordon and older guys would love to be Jerry Seinfeld, funny, rich, smart, handsome enough.

What if an unknown actor had been used in the Gatorade commercial or the American Express commercial? They would probably still have worked—but almost certainly not as well. Viewers would have taken longer to develop a feeling of familiarity with the character. This would have necessitated many more repetitions of the ad and possibly even the making of multiple ads. The identification process would not have been anywhere near as immediate or as intense. In other words, where the character has to be introduced and developed from scratch, the advertiser has to spend much more money for on-air time to elicit the same degree of identification effect. When advertisers develop identities and establish characters in their ads they regard them as an accumulating asset. They have an investment interest in the development of these characters. It is important for them to have in their ads attractive, recognizable characters that we, the audience, will want to identify with—whether they are known entities or (initially) unknown. This explains the advantage in ad campaigns of maintaining continuity in the star character. It is why we are beginning to see more sequels of successful ads. Advertisers are discovering that there are advantages to be gained in not changing the characters with every change of commercial (see Chapter 21, 'Sequels').

Animated characters

Fictitious characters in shows like *The Simpsons*, *Sesame Street*, *Home and Away* or *Neighbours* get fan mail all the time from people who empathize or identify with them. The fan mail is addressed to the character, not the actor. Why does this happen when everybody knows the characters are fictitious? It is because even though they are only characters they are real enough for us to identify with and empathize with.

We can even feel warm towards cartoon characters and puppets. A generation of people felt empathy, if not identity, with the Peanuts character Charlie Brown, the born loser. A different generation warmed to Big Bird and the Cookie Monster. And then came the Simpsons.

Animated characters have been used as both positive and negative role models. For example, in *The Simpsons*, Mr Burns (Homer's boss) and Barney (the drunk) provide clear negative role models. In *Sesame Street*, watching Oscar the Grouch is fun but acting like him is clearly absurd. Who wants to be perpetually grouchy? Oscar is the negative role model in *Sesame Street*; others, such as Big Bird and The Count, are positive role models.

Like 'drama' ads, ads with animated talent such as the M&M characters, Charlie the tuna and the Pillsbury doughboy seem to be most successful when the on-screen characters do the talking.

Animation can be used to change the whole feeling and tone of a commercial. In particular, it can be used to 'lighten up' what might otherwise be a serious, unpleasant message. Bug exterminators like Orkin and Terminex frequently employ the strategy of using animated or computer-enhanced bugs because they know that most of us are squeamish about seeing bugs on TV. AIDS campaigns around the world have used animated condoms to deliver a serious message. Similarly, many stomach cures use drawings of the stomach to deliver their message.

Advertising agency Doyle Dane Bernbach, in an ad for Kit 'N Caboodle cat food, needed to show a cat chasing a mouse. Although mice are the 'gold standard' in cat food they come in only one flavour, but Kit 'N Caboodle

117

What's this I'm watching? The elements that make up an ad

came in a variety of tastes. Instead of having cat owners watching their darling pussy on TV threatening the life of a real live grey mouse, the ad agency used animation. The agency wanted people to respond to the realism of the cat so they mixed live footage of a cat with an animated mouse.[16] The ad was a delightful example of animation's ability to lighten an otherwise unpleasant scenario.

One appeal that animated characters have for advertisers is that the makers of the ad are in total control of the characters' behavior. Their investment is protected. Advertisers using real people always have to hold their breath and hope. The character may get into trouble, developing a bad reputation that can cross over to the brand (advertisers are acutely aware today of disastrous examples like O.J. Simpson, Mike Tyson and Michael Jackson). With cartoon characters like Snoopy for MetLife or the M&M characters this can't happen. As one US film maker put it: 'Animated characters are…appealing because they don't age like regular characters and won't be caught in a crack house and then try to gang rape the arresting officers…They give advertisers control.'[17]

Figure 9.5
The animated M&M characters don't 'age' like regular characters.
Reproduced with the authority of the owner (Mars Confectionery of Australia)

Length of commercial

The 60-second commerical is becoming rarer today. Commercials are getting shorter rather than longer. But even a 60-second TV commercial is only about one-hundredth the length of a movie. This means that getting us to project ourselves into it and identify with a character is much, much harder to achieve than with a movie. In the time it takes to screen a movie you could watch about 100 60-second commercials or 200 30-second commercials, so any identification that does occur is much more fleeting with advertising. This is one reason that drama commercials seem to work better as longer, 60-second or 45-second commercials rather than at 30 or 15 seconds.

Time is both an enemy and a challenge for drama commercials. There is extremely limited time in which to develop the characters, depict the situation and get a message across (see Chapter 16, 'Learning to use 15-second commercials'). It takes time to build involvement and identification with characters. This is why sequels can work so well—because the characters have already been developed in an earlier ad.

Negative roles or characters

Some ads deliberately use a character designed to be a negative role model. For example, in an attempt to get people to save water, a water utility used a thoughtless, mindless, water-wasting character named 'Wally' in its ads, the theme being 'Don't be a Wally with water'. It urged us not to be like this character. This use of a negative character is one way of influencing the audience to avoid the same behavior.

Interestingly, some ads, in an attempt at humor, make the mistake of doing this inadvertently and depict the target identification character as something of a 'goat'. Yet the advertiser still hopes that we will react positively to the character and what he or she is saying. These ads often fail and can sometimes be seen to have marked negative effects.

For example, one ad showed a Fosters beer drinker who was so naive he failed to recognize the famous people he talked to in a bar (including the pro golfer, Bob Shearer). If the audience is made to squirm in embarrassment at a character's naivety, it is nigh on impossible for us to 'feel like' or want to 'be like' this character representing the brand user.

In another example, a one-time celebrity regarded as something of a 'has been' appeared in an ad for a gas hot water service. Referring to his own fall from fame, he proudly announced that with this hot water service the water 'will still be hot when you're not'.

When we were kids we identified with the goodies, not the baddies. We wanted the attractive roles, not the embarrassing ones. Who wants to identify with the baddies, the 'has beens', the losers or the naive?

Some advertisers, while not attempting to be humorous, can still fall into this trap and be amazingly incautious or unthinking in their choice of characters. They are obviously not thinking clearly about target identification. For example, in one country Toshiba inexplicably used a very obese individual to advertise its Toshiba Friend notebook computer. While obese people might have a special need for lightweight portability in computers, not too many people want to identify with that image. Ads that contain negative characters are very risky for advertisers when they are depicted as brand users.

A commercial is supposed to boost our positive image of ourselves, showing us as users of the product, our positive self-image mirrored in the users of the brand, people we want to identify with. If, on the other hand, the users are people we reject any identification with, these ads are very handicapped indeed.

So do negative ads like this work? We have yet to see one that did, unless it was strongly informational. A number of non-informational ads of this type that have been observed in market research tracking have, in fact,

119

What's this I'm watching? The elements that make up an ad

had negative effects, especially those that were not pretested before they were run. In one study of 147 commercials, 45 per cent were shown to have had a negative effect; even if commercials were pretested, 6 per cent were still shown to have a negative effect.[18]

Comparative ads

Duracell frequently names Energizer in its commercials—claiming that Duracell is the longer lasting battery. Today, from pain relievers to cars we see a growing number of comparative ads that ask the viewer out front to compare two brands. Particularly in mature markets, comparative ads are increasingly being used by small brands to attack the market leader head-on. For example in the USA, countless pain relievers have promoted themselves as 'More effective than Tylenol' or 'Longer lasting than Tylenol'.

Claims and counter-claims by the two brands may lead to such confusion that we as consumers give up trying to differentiate and simply buy the two brands interchangeably. We may be tempted to feel that this is another example of where advertising doesn't work on us, but wait. Note that this pays off in a big way for the small brand which thereby may become much bigger. So even though we feel we weren't persuaded by either brand's advertising, the smaller brand nevertheless achieves its objective of increasing its sales.

The focus is often on comparing the smaller brand's price with the long established market leader. It's all an attempt to say to consumers, 'Look, we're just like the leader, only cheaper.' It's not about building a brand personality, it's merely about setting a competitive framework and talking about one key attribute which is often price. For example, Equal is a relatively high-priced sugar substitute whose patent has now expired. So along comes NatraTaste and creates similar packaging. In its advertising it shows packs of Equal and NatraTaste side by side with the line 'Same Great Taste as Equal. Half the Price'. It makes for unexciting television, but its appeal is simple. 'Hey, same stuff, half the price. What's not to like?'

Summary

The art of advertising creative teams is traditionally intuitive but principles of psychological processing are gradually coming to light that further our understanding of individual elements and how these work. The blend of executional elements can help the ad capture our attention, as well as influence the way our minds process the advertisement.

Visuals interact with words to influence what is 'on stage' in our minds and to determine what interpretation we give to those words. Setting words to music influences the mental processes we use on words, in addition to making the ad more memorable.

Advertisers using sex, humor or other attention-getting devices have to be careful of the device stealing focus from other key elements of the ad and interfering with the registration of the correct brand and message. Nevertheless, elements that capture attention are important ingredients of ads. Sometimes they can be sufficiently novel, unique or outrageous that the ad becomes a topic of conversation in the community and becomes 'performance-enhanced' as it is passed along, virus like, by word of mouth.

The type of ad also affects the focus of our processing. It is very different when we see drama or 'entertainment' advertising compared to when we see 'news' advertising. When there is no news, established brands often turn to entertainment commercials. With entertainment commercials we tend to record any incidental information or message that happens to get conveyed while the focus of our attention is on being entertained.

One important question to ask of any ad is this: 'Who is doing the talking?' Straight news ads and lecture-style ads have more effect when we can see the person talking to us on the screen with lip-sync. Using a presenter character as a surrogate for the advertiser seems to lessen our sense of a hard sell. The presenter character also acts as an important mnemonic device. In drama commercials, the choice of character is crucial for the advertiser's hopes that we will want to identify with the character.

The second important question to ask of any ad is: 'Who is the ad talking to?' When it appears to be talking to an on-screen character, we tend to mentally process the ad as a bystander. The closer we feel to the character, the more effect the ad is likely to have on us. 'Overhearing' something can be more influential than being told it directly because we tend to apply less-defensive processing to it.

Liking for a brand's advertising can be a feather—especially when everything else is equal. While ads don't necessarily have to be liked if they are imparting valuable news about the brand, nevertheless a brand's advertising is an intrinsic part of the brand personality. If we like its ads we have a greater chance of liking the brand. So, the more that things weigh equal, the more important that liking of a brand's advertising is. Even as a feather, it can tip the balance of brand choice.

10

The limits of advertising

It should be clear from previous chapters that advertising's effectiveness has been much exaggerated. At the same time, this effectiveness is based on what seems to be powerful psychological mechanisms: learning without awareness, making brands into symbols, having people see a brand in different ways, the influence of conformity, and the use of brands to express identity. So why is advertising not more powerful than it is?

This chapter explores the many factors that severely constrain and often frustrate the power of individual advertisers to influence us. It shows how difficult it is for advertisers to make these psychological mechanisms work and how their unbridled use in any wholesale manipulation is virtually impossible. Just as democratic political systems have various checks and balances to constrain the power of elected governments to dictate to us, so too are 'checks and balances' inherent in the competitive environment in which advertisers operate. In addition, we consumers vote with our feet—the most powerful constraint of all. When the brand or the product does not live up to its promise, when it does not meet the expectations created by the advertising, then we simply don't buy it again. So, as we shall see, advertising's power is constrained as much by practical limitations as by absolute limitations.

Competitors' advertising

One of the most important limitations on any advertiser's power to influence us is the activity of its competitors. Competitors' advertising, more often than not, severely blunts an individual advertiser's efforts. If Pizza Hut was the only advertiser in the fast food restaurant category, its advertising power and market share would undoubtedly be much greater than they are.

For every advertiser there is at least one and usually several other advertisers in the same product category. These create a lot of advertising 'noise' and clutter. The 'noise' of competing claims often neutralizes or at least greatly dilutes the effect of any individual campaign. It also makes it much more expensive for any individual company to advertise at a level and frequency that can be heard above the competitive 'noise'. This imposes a limitation of its own.

For example, following the deregulation of telecommunications in several countries during the 1980s and 1990s, we saw long-distance telephone companies attempting to woo the consumer through heavy advertising. Inevitably, this triggered a reaction from competitors which escalated into an 'advertising war'. In America this took place between AT&T, MCI and Sprint who each spent significantly more than $US100 million talking about long-distance savings plans and cents per minute rates. Far from having the effect of manipulating the consumer, this served to create a high level of annoyance among customers who began to tune out the messages completely.

Money: limitations of budget

In the competitive environment it takes huge sums of money, sometimes over long periods, for such mechanisms to be really effective. Even the largest companies cannot afford the advertising that would be necessary to 'manipulate' us in the wholesale way that many opponents of advertising fear. This is especially true when the brand has no unique benefit or difference over other brands and the difference has to be created by advertising.

Even products that offer substantial real benefit over competitors must be prepared to spend very heavily to get that superiority message across. Zantac, for example, had to spend US$72.6 million on advertising in 1996 to make inroads into the US heartburn remedies market. And in the potato crisp category, Baked Lays ('lower fat and fewer calories, great taste') needed to spend in excess of US$46 million over the two-year period 1996/97 to make headway against the Procter & Gamble incumbent, Pringles, which spent US$67 million over the same period on its 'spend and defend' strategy.

L'Eggs pantyhose is an older but telling case in point. L'Eggs had a benefit, or difference—a super-stretch pantyhose that had no shape until pulled onto the leg when it moulded itself to the shape of the leg. It also differentiated itself with unique packaging. When it was launched in the United States,

L'Eggs had to be prepared to spend an amount on advertising for the first year that was double the total spent by all advertisers in the pantyhose category in the previous year.[1]

Even dominant brands like Coca-Cola rarely account for the majority of advertising in their product category. In countries like the USA, UK and Australia, for example, Coke accounts for less than a third of the total soft drink advertising. The proportion is even smaller if we take into account other beverages that are less direct competitors of Coke, such as fruit juice, milk, tea and coffee. So even the huge brands rarely have the advertising field to themselves.

'Creating' needs

People who are 'anti advertising' often feel that advertisers create needs and manipulate us into buying things we don't really need or want. To what extent can the psychological mechanisms of advertising be used to create needs or manipulate people into buying things they don't really need or want? Before answering this, we should look at two related questions. What do we really need, and what role does advertising play in bringing new products to our attention?

Advertising announces new products. It is generally quite effective in making us aware of new products and new brands (see Figures 10.1 and 10.2). This is a role of advertising that people rarely object to, unless the new product is trivial. They see it as a positive role—informing us of new events. In this sense it is like news, which is valued because it is informative.

Critics of advertising do not focus on the awareness role so much as the persuasive role of advertising—on its ability to make us buy things we don't need. In earlier chapters we have largely dismissed persuasion and pointed out that, of the many psychological mechanisms underlying most advertising, persuasion is often the least relevant. If it were truly relevant its record would be rather poor.

Figure 10.1
Ad introducing the Omron
ear thermometer

Figure 10.2
Ad for Palm Pilot, digital personal
assistant

Estimates vary but everybody agrees on this much—at least 40 per cent of all new consumer products fail, and estimates of an 80 to 90 per cent failure rate are not unusual.[2] There is a real interaction between what advertisers and marketers would like to sell and what we, as consumers, can relate to and, in the end, feel we want or need.

Advertising does not create these products. What it does do is help to accelerate their diffusion into the mass market. The more truly new and beneficial a product is, the more informational its advertising tends to be. We have a choice. Are we interested in this new benefit or not? Can we afford it? Are we prepared to pay the price?

Every household today needs a refrigerator, a TV and a telephone. Even the severest critic of advertising is likely to have one of each. What else do we really need? Heating and air conditioning are no longer regarded as luxuries. Video cameras and mobile phones are increasing rapidly in penetration and becoming mainstream. At the time of writing, the majority of homes have a VCR, a microwave and a dishwasher. Twenty-five years ago almost nobody did. The list goes on and on.

Yesterday's inventions and luxuries become tomorrow's necessities. Today 99 per cent of homes have a television set. More than 90 per cent have a telephone. Almost all have a refrigerator and a washing machine. More than one-third of homes now have a computer. Do we need them? Those who argue that we don't are technically right. We could live without them. But do we want to?

These are acquired needs, not biological needs such as hunger, thirst and sex. Were they created by advertising? No, they were created by inventors. Advertising's primary role is creating *awareness* of these inventions in the mass market. There is no doubt that, without such advertising, all these innovations (ranging from computers and microwave ovens to low-fat foods and combined shampoo/conditioner) would diffuse through a country's population very much more slowly.

How advertising accelerates mass markets

Communicating the existence of a new product (e.g. calculators, CD players, cellular phones, digital watches, personal computers, digital cameras) to the mass market, even without persuasion, expands the demand for that product because some proportion of us will always be interested in buying an innovation. These purchases then have the effect of increasing the size of the production run for the new product, which in turn reduces the unit cost of making the product. This creates economies of scale in production and translates into a lower price tag on the new product being offered for sale. When the product is advertised at a lower price, some of us who had previously decided against buying it because it was too expensive become interested. It has now become available to some of us who earlier could not afford it. This expands sales further, which increases production runs further, which reduces price further, which makes the product more available and affordable by even more people. Electronic calculators and digital watches are classic examples from the past. Home computers are an example in the present.

The whole effect is circular. Advertising, in communicating first the product and then the affordable price, accelerates the diffusion of the innovation into the mass market. Without advertising the process would probably still happen, but at an infinitely slower pace. Our mothers might still be using wringer washers. We would still be using manual typewriters, and computers would be something that only businesses could afford.

The critics of all this often seem to be nostalgic for the simplicities of the past. Nostalgia is an attempt to create an idealised past in the present.[3] It tends to gloss over the unpleasant aspects of the past and focus only on the pleasant aspects. However, there is no argument for staying where we are. Only the most naive romantics would argue that we were happier living in our caves as primitive humans. Who wants to go back to washing dishes by hand and stove-top heating of foods without a microwave? Only the most nostalgic conservatives would accept that our grandparents were happier doing the washing in a kerosene tin boiled over an open fire than we are now with our washing machine and dryer, and our many other creature comforts.

Ads for brands or ads for products?

The vast majority of advertising attempts to get us to buy one brand instead of another rather than new products per se. Earlier chapters focused on the low-involvement effects of advertising, which can tip the balance in the weighing up of brands when everything else is equal, or can influence which brands get weighed up. Only the rare category leader (like Kraft Philadelphia cheese or Campbell's soup) can afford to advertise just to grow the category. Hence, only a tiny proportion of advertising is aimed directly at affecting our decision about whether to purchase a product or not, as distinct from which of the various brands to buy. (The main exception seems to be the advertising of primary food products like milk, pork, beef, raisins, mangoes, cheese, rice, butter, bananas and avocados.)

Persuasion is not involved in the great majority of brand advertising that we are exposed to. To the extent that most brand advertising does influence our feelings of need for the product category itself, then this result is more a side effect than a primary focus of the advertiser. That is not to say that it is unimportant. Clearly, enough people think it is important to have banned cigarette advertising.

Research into the ability of brand advertising to create demand for the category as a whole is sparse and remains frustratingly inconclusive. Our own suspicion is that research will eventually show the spin-off effect to be substantial and that its mechanism is based primarily on agenda setting by creating an image of popularity and social acceptance for the product category—but only if enough advertising for enough brands is aired for long enough.

If this turns out to be true, it still implies very severe constraints on the power of advertisers to foist just anything onto us. Unless a new product finds reasonable acceptance quite quickly, it is likely to be discontinued before the agenda-setting process has time to take hold. There are limits to how long advertisers are able or willing to continue advertising a product that is not selling enough to pay for the cost of production, simply in the hope that it will eventually 'catch on'. This is why market research tries to determine beforehand what consumers would like to have, or at least what is likely to meet with ready acceptance rather than resistance.

Resistance to change

There is another limitation on advertising's ability to exercise unbridled influence and this is reflected in our resistance to change and in the natural working of our minds. We seem to have a strong inbuilt need for cognitive consistency, and tend to reject anything that is not consistent with what we currently know or have come to expect. To succeed, an innovation usually has to find the line of least resistance.

For example, for years after it was developed many people rejected instant coffee, which was advertised on the basis of ease of use. Research revealed that household food buyers (mostly women in the 1950s) saw the so-called convenience benefit as reflecting directly on their performance. Buying instant coffee (as distinct from coffee beans) was seen as the mark of 'a lazy house-wife who did not care for her family'. Remember, female role models in the 1950s were quite different from today's. This negative association slowed the rate of acceptance of many innovations pitched at convenience and time saving, including dishwashers, microwave ovens and automatic washing machines.

Another example was a noiseless food mixer, which was rejected for quite a different reason—because it seemed not to have much power. We tend to believe that powerful machines are noisy. A machine that is both powerful and quiet is inconsistent with our experience, so we find it difficult to accept.

Similarly, many packaged cake mix products have you add eggs to the mix. The eggs are not in any way necessary to the success of the cake but were added to the recipe after research discovered that women did not feel satisfied making a product they didn't have to put much effort into, especially something as indulgent and nurturing as a cake.

Perhaps the most telling example of this effect is dishwashing detergent. Before detergent was invented, when we washed dishes in soapy water in the sink, it was lack of suds on the top of the water that we used as a cue to tell us when to add more soap. Dishwashing detergent does not naturally foam, but manufacturers eventually had to add foam to the product to get it accepted. Without foam the detergent was not seen to be working. Unless new products fit with, or at least do not clash with, what is already in our minds, their advertisers are likely to encounter substantial resistance to the innovation. They are likely to face a long, hard and very costly battle over many years before the product eventually, if ever, achieves widespread acceptance.

Dishwashing detergent as a new product initially clashed with (was not consistent with) something that was well established in our minds—namely, that sudsing indicated when washing-up water was working and lack of suds indicated that it was not. For the product to gain widespread acceptance, it had to be made consistent with consumers' existing beliefs and expectations. This reflects a psychological principle known as *cognitive consistency*.

Cognitive consistency

Our minds seem to have a need for consistency, in our attitudes and beliefs, and between these attitudes and our behavior.[4] Let me illustrate the general mechanism that is at work here. If we believe that Volvos are very safe cars and we read in a consumer report that more people have fatal accidents in Volvos than in any other car, what happens? A motivation is automatically set up in us to try to resolve the apparent contradiction. Either our original belief is wrong or there is something wrong with the report. We are experiencing the need for cognitive consistency. We either have to change our mind about Volvo cars being safe or we have to find something wrong with the consumer report to discredit it.

When we receive information that is in conflict with, or is inconsistent with what we believe, we are likely to experience cognitive inconsistency. Our minds automatically try to resolve this. We try to keep our attitudes and beliefs consistent, as well as our attitudes and behavior. This is not a voluntary mechanism but more an unconscious one that goes into action automatically. It was first demonstrated by Leon Festinger in a classic series of experiments. During the Vietnam War, for example, Festinger gave experimental subjects who were opposed to the war an incentive to argue a position that was contrary to what they believed—that is, to argue *for* the war. He found that their attitude to the war tended to change in the direction they had been paid to argue—that is, in favor of the war.

This demonstrated how people's attitudes begin to change when they perform behavior that is inconsistent with their attitudes. Just as importantly, the same thing happens if we hold two attitudes or beliefs and then find out that they are not consistent. For example, what happens if you dislike mini-vans and your closest friend, whose judgment you respect, tells you he has just bought a mini-van? You have two attitudes, one positive and one negative. Your attitude towards your friend is positive. Your attitude towards mini-vans is negative. The two attitudes are inconsistent or out of balance. When this happens and we cannot avoid facing the inconsistency of the two positions, our minds automatically begin to change one or other of them to bring them into balance. The inconsistency weakens either our prejudice against mini-vans or the respect we have for our friend and her judgment.

Advertising is the weaker influence

Advertising is usually the weaker influence compared to what we already know or have in our minds. Any ad campaign is most likely to lead to advertising failure if the message is inconsistent with our existing beliefs. Advertisers have to strive to put a position that is credible, or at least is not inconsistent with what we as consumers already know and think.

For example, in several areas of the world light beer found greatest difficulty in gaining acceptance among young (18 to 24-year-old) male beer drinkers. It was found much more acceptable by older drinkers. The young tend to be searching for identity, and self-expression symbols play a role in this. Despite successful efforts by advertisers to get light beer accepted it has nevertheless been strongly resisted by younger people for a number of years. For them, the image of light beer as a product has been inconsistent with the strong male image that beer drinking has traditionally been identified with. Light beer will probably be accepted by this age group eventually but it will have been a long haul.

It is rare that advertisers can afford to engage in protracted efforts to change such entrenched attitudes by confronting them directly. Usually, they have to look for an approach that will be readily accepted because it fits neatly with existing beliefs. One example of this is the famous 'Avis— we try harder' campaign. This capitalized on the widespread belief that monopolies and big companies tend to become complacent. Companies that are still trying to get to the top will probably try harder. The ad is cognitively consistent with what is already known, so it is more likely to be accepted.

Our need for cognitive consistency means that advertisers who try to persuade us against our will, to get us to accept something that goes against our existing information or attitudes, are almost certain to fail (unless they have unlimited time and money to hang in for the long term). This big constraint on advertising's power is part of our psychological makeup. Like most of the other limitations, it is not an absolute constraint. Finding ways around it poses a real challenge to advertising agencies.

Positioning for cognitive consistency

Chapter 2 pointed out that humans have the ability to see the same thing (whether the same product or the same advertisement) in different ways depending on their frame of reference. The challenge for advertising agencies is to position the ad or the product in such a way that it is seen to be consistent with, rather than to clash with, our existing mindset. All too often this is unsuccessful, as evidenced by the fact that so many new products fail.

It is a creative task and it is difficult to give examples of this creativity at work without breaching client confidentiality but let us illustrate how it works with a couple of hypothetical examples.

Consider Oscar Mayer, the Kraft-owned US brand heavily identified with 'food your kids will eat'. Suppose Oscar Mayer wanted to market a hot dog—one that is 'good for you'. Almost everyone knows that hot dogs are made of leftovers—intestines and all the most undesirable parts of the animal. How can it be good for you? Even '100% beef hot dogs' translates in our minds as 100 per cent leftovers from cows. Because there is an active pre-disposition not to believe that these things are good for you, positioning the product in this way would be most unlikely to succeed. The brand would have much more chance sticking to its reliance on 'fun products/kids will love it' strategy, than attempting to confront existing attitudes head on with a 'good for you' positioning.

Consider another example of a similar type. This time a hypothetical brand of canned fish called Fine-C-Foods is long established globally as a high-quality brand and uses the slogan *'It's the fish that Fine-C rejects that makes Fine-C the best'*.[5] The quality image of the brand is paramount in its positioning. It decides to enter a new but related category. In certain parts of the world there is a product category known as 'fishpaste' which is a spread that comes in a jar. Fine-C wants to get into this market with a qual-ity fishpaste to compete with the existing brands, which are all of rather poor quality. Positioning it on the quality dimension *'Fine-C-Foods...superior quality fishpaste'* would make it consistent with the Fine-C quality image. It would fit with pre-existing beliefs and work in harmony with the pre-existing image of quality that the Fine-C brand has developed. So far so good. A real limitation however lurks below the surface. If there is a widespread belief among consumers (and indeed there is) that fishpaste is made of left-overs, (i.e. all the good parts of the fish have already been used for something else, similar to the general image of sausages) then *'Fine-C superior quality fishpaste'* is likely to translate unconsciously in consumers' minds into *'Fine-C superior quality leftovers'*. This is hardly the desired image. It would also be disastrous for the product. The cognitive inconsistency is likely to doom the product to failure from the start.

What can an advertising agency do in this type of situation? One way here would be to rename the product and market it as Fine-C Fish Paté. Paté is also a spread, but it has quite different associations that are consis-tent with the quality positioning of the Fine-C-Foods brand. This strategy is more likely to succeed than a strategy of directly confronting entrenched negative attitudes to fishpaste.

Much of the art of advertising, then, lies in finding ways to play the focal beam of attention on the attributes of the product that are consistent with what already exists in our minds. The existing set of our mind is a limitation or inhibitor on what advertising can do.

When everything else is not equal

Advertisers are beginning to find that advertising seems to work best when it communicates some positive benefit, or when the brand is at least equal to other brands on the market. Rarely can advertising succeed if a brand is inferior to the competition or if its qualities are cognitively inconsistent with the consumer's mindset. In other words, advertising is not magical. It is just one influence among many, and when there are real differences between brands the truth generally wins out eventually. Advertising may get us to try a product, but our experience with the product then overrides anything that advertising may tell us. If the product does not live up to the promise, we don't purchase it again.

Conversion/persuasion vs reinforcement

This highlights the fact that advertising's principal effect is to reinforce rather than persuade. That is, it reinforces us in the decision we made to purchase the brand and increases the chance of our buying it again. Using panels of consumers reporting on what they purchased each week, Professor Andrew Ehrenberg in the UK has studied the effects of advertising on purchasing probably more than any other person in the world. His conclusion is that 'advertising's main role is to reinforce feelings of satisfaction for brands already being used'.[6]

This is consistent with our observations. Advertising has frequently proved quite ineffective by itself at getting people to buy a brand for the first time. To achieve widespread trial of a new brand, advertising usually has to be heavily supplemented by promotions, in-store displays and free sampling. With supermarket brands this is very much influenced by simple locating behavior. The new brand has to stop us walking at more than 1 mile per hour (2 km/h), cut through the clutter and get itself noticed. There are limits to how much advertising alone can do here. (Advertising does seem to be more effective at getting people to buy a truly new product for the first time than at getting them to try yet another 'me-too' brand in an established product category. But, again, with supermarket products it often takes in-store displays and promotions to achieve widespread trial reasonably rapidly.)

Reinforcement is the reason why some campaigns, the ones conducted by the smart advertisers, talk to their own consumers. Users of a brand almost always react more positively to its advertising than non-users.[7] Toyota trucks used this to good effect in various parts of the world with the 'I love what you do to me' line. One US commercial for Toyota trucks featured vignettes of Toyota truck owners saying what they were doing when their truck clocked up 100 000 or 200 000 or 300 000 miles. It closed with an invitation to Toyota truck owners to phone a free number 'and tell us where you were and what you were doing' at these milestones. This ad undoubtedly reinforced the repeat buying of those who already owned a Toyota truck by reminding them of the durability of their truck and the number of miles it had endured. Just as importantly, however, it also got the message across indirectly to the 'bystanders', to those who had never bought a Toyota truck, that these must be very, very durable machines.

The long-running Dial deodorant soap campaign is another example of using a brand's own customers talking about their product in such a way that the viewer is cast as a bystander rather than the target of the message. 'Aren't you glad you use Dial—don't you wish everyone did?' Another example, this time from Australia, is the leading Australian margarine brand, Meadow Lea. Its ads sing to an on-screen buyer of Meadow Lea, 'You oughta be congratulated' (implicit is something like 'because of your good taste/ judgment').

Rather than placing the focus of attention on what might otherwise be perceived as an empty promise or claim, such ads address those of us already using the product, reminding us that we are happy with the brand. (Would we be buying it if we weren't? So who is going to argue?) Consider how much greater the invitation to rejection is if the ad were to say: 'If you switch to our brand, you will be glad' or 'If you switch to our brand you will be congratulated'.

So, instead of the typical promise style (i.e. 'Buy X brand and you will get Y result'), this type of advertising provides a verbal 'pat on the back' for its own customers. At the same time, it casts people not using the brand as bystanders who 'overhear' a communication between the advertiser and the buyers of the brand. Because they are bystanders, nothing in the ad is likely to motivate them to try to refute it. As we saw earlier, this technique can be even more effective than if it is addressed to that person directly.[8] Of course, should the bystander who overhears this be tempted to try the brand, he/she becomes a buyer and the commercial then becomes a verbal 'pat on the back'. The ad is a feather.

Deighton, in a brilliant new twist on this, pointed out that advertising tunes up our attention to a brand's key attribute(s) *at the time that we are consuming it*.[9] It is more likely that we will think of some aspect of the advertising at the time we use the brand, and consequently take greater notice of the advertised attribute. In the same way as we can direct your attention to the noises going on around you that you were previously not consciously aware of, so can advertising draw our attention to (or remind us to notice) the advertised attribute when we are consuming the brand. As a result of repetition of the advertising, when we consume the brand we may think to confirm that the brand does indeed have the advertised attribute. The advertising sensitizes us to experiencing those advertised attributes and confirming them. It therefore has the potential *to transform the consumption experience*. Without first experiencing the advertising we might simply consume the brand without noticing the differences between it and its competitors.

Confirming that a brand has the advertised attribute has two effects:

1. It reinforces the consumption experience and makes us more likely to buy the same brand again.
2. It makes us feel more positively towards the advertiser and the truthfulness of their advertising. (People use their experience with the brand to judge an ad's truthfulness and therefore its informativeness. Whether people regard an ad as 'informative' is greatly influenced by their satisfaction with the brand.[10])

Ads that work or ads that win awards?

Far from being omnipotent ogres who can manipulate us at will, companies that advertise often struggle desperately to produce an ad that works. They are frequently frustrated by the inability to devise a campaign that has a measurable impact on sales and market share. Creating something that is a clever piece of art is relatively easy, but they want to sell the product.

The people who are primarily responsible for making ads for them, the creative directors in advertising agencies, are artistic people. A number of them are making ads not because they choose to, but because they can't do what they most want to do—make feature films.

Denied the opportunity to make full-length films, it is natural that they will get at least some satisfaction from producing 30-second feature films instead. The result is that advertisers can end up with 30-second feature films disguised as TV ads, many of them winning awards. These 30-second feature films may look nice and they may be clever and entertaining but, if the brand is used merely as a prop with little regard given to the main purpose of the commercial, then the chance of it succeeding in its real purpose is very small. If it does work, it is likely to be more by accident than design.

Most advertising industry awards are not based on any measure of effectiveness but on subjective evaluation and artistic creativity. Objective measurement of effectiveness in selling the product has not been a consideration. As a result many advertisers in the past have not known whether these mini-films worked or didn't work. Until the last decade of new market research technology, most advertisers could not gauge effectiveness by their sales alone because there were too many other things (price promotion, what competitors do) that also affected sales—and, as we have seen, reinforcement rather than sales is often the primary effect. Advertisers have been able to do little more than grope towards effective advertising.

This is now beginning to change. With the advent of new market research technology and a more educated breed of product managers, marketing managers and marketing directors, companies are becoming less reliant on their advertising agency simply winning artistic awards to reassure them that their advertising is working. Awards (such as the 'Effies') based on objectively measured evidence of advertising effectiveness rather than artistic merit are now operative in most major western countries. More and more, the advertisers themselves are putting in place the market research mechanisms that will allow them to assess what is working and what is not.

Summary

Most advertising tries to get us to buy one brand instead of another and is not concerned with new products per se. It can tip the balance in the weighing up of brands when everything else is equal, and it can influence which brands get weighed up.

Advertising for new products announces more than it persuades. To the extent that persuasion is involved its record is extremely poor, because at least 40 per cent of all new consumer products fail. When advertising does influence our feelings of need for the product category, this is more a side effect than the primary focus of the advertising.

The effect of advertising is more often, therefore, not persuasion but reinforcement. That is, it reinforces us in the decision we made to purchase the brand and increases the chance of our buying it again.

Much of the art of advertising lies in finding a way to play the focal beam of attention onto the attributes of the brand that are consistent with our existing mindset. Positioning a product in this way is no easy task.

Advertising's power is constrained as much by practical limitations as by absolute limitations. These include:

- the fact that consumers vote with their feet;
- competitive advertising;

- money: limitations of budget;
- economic reality;
- resistance to change;
- the need for cognitive consistency;
- the fact that advertising is usually the weaker influence compared to what we already know or have in our minds.

None of these limitations is absolute but taken together they make advertising much less able to influence us than would be thought by the average consumer. This notion will probably not convince those who want to believe in the manipulative power of advertising, because advertising is one of those things that some people love to hate. The reality, however, is that the power and mystique of advertising and the people who make it have been much exaggerated.

PART B

What works, what doesn't, and why

Introduction

We saw in Part A that we can gain an important insight into advertising by asking the question, 'Who is the ad talking to?' The same applies to books like this one. Who is this book talking to? If it is aimed at the general reader it will have a different feel and style than if it is aimed at advertising practitioners or students of marketing or mass communication. Part A talked primarily to the general reader.

At this point in the book the general reader will sense a change of key. Many of the chapters that make up Part B had their origins in articles that were written for trade publications. The readers of these are advertisers and marketers who want to know more about how to make advertising work more effectively.

While this section talks primarily to these professionals, general readers should find it an interesting 'bystander' experience. In fact, they may like to imagine themselves as advertisers. By looking briefly through advertisers' eyes they will develop a greater understanding of advertising at work, and see the obstacles that advertisers strive to overcome in their attempt to influence us.

An understanding of only three technical terms is necessary for reading Part B. The first of these, 'ad execution', has already cropped up in Part A. A brand like Coke will often have several different ads on air in the same week. While the brand and the essential message are usually the same, the characters, dialogue or general scene may be different in each case. Each variation is referred to as an *ad execution*. Alternatively, you may see a 30-second ad, and a 15-second ad that is recognisable as part of the larger ad.

Advertising and the mind of the consumer

These are regarded as two different 'executions'. The creative execution, then, is the way that a particular ad is carried out or executed.

The second technical term is 'flighting'. Some advertisers schedule their brand's advertising to appear every week. This is known as a *continuous advertising schedule*. Others prefer to 'flight' their advertising, in other words to have a burst of several weeks of the same advertising followed by a few weeks off air, then go on air again with another few weeks of the same advertising and so on.

This is known as a *flighted ad schedule*. Each new burst of advertising is regarded as a separate *flight*.

The third technical term is TRP which is short for Target Rating Points. This is known by different names in different countries. In the UK the term used is TVR; in Australia, TARP. But the concept is the same. Loosely speaking, it is a measure of the exposure that an ad gets. Indirectly, it reflects the amount of audience exposure and the number of exposures that the advertiser pays for. The number of TRPs is a measure of how many people from the target market had an 'opportunity to see' because they were sitting in front of the TV set at the time the ad was shown.

Let us explain this with an example. Kleenex might define its primary target market for tissues as females 18 to 45 years old. If the ad for Kleenex tissues went to air on NBC at 8:50 pm last night and 20 per cent of this group were watching NBC at that time, the ad has 20 TRPs. If the ad is shown again several times in the same week, each time the percentage of the target market watching at the time is added to the accumulated TRP figure. So the ad might accumulate 210 TRPs for the week. Note that this is merely the gross total of people who had an 'opportunity to see'. Some of these will have seen the ad when it was shown earlier in the week but they are nevertheless counted again in the TRP figure. The total TRP figure can be calculated from the percentage of the target market that has had an 'opportunity to see' the ad at least once (called the *net reach*) and also the average number of times they saw it, which is known as the *average frequency*.[1] A total of 210 TRPs for the week could represent a variety of combinations of reach and frequency. The table below shows only a few of the possibilities.

Table B.1
Calculation of TRP figure

Net reach %	Average frequency	Total TRPs
100	2.1	210
50	4.2	210
35	6.0	210

For example, the whole target market may have seen the ad during the week and they may have seen it on average 2.1 times. Or perhaps only 50 per cent of the target audience saw the ad but they saw it on average 4.2 times. This still accumulates to 210 TRPs. In other words an ad can accumulate 210 TRPs through any combination of net reach (percentage of the target audience who saw it at least once) and average frequency (the average number of times those people saw it) that when multiplied together totals 210.[2]

The majority of ad campaigns run at 100–300 TRPs a week. Fifty TRPs would be a light weight while 400 TRPs would be a heavy weight of advertising in any one week.

11

Continuous tracking: are you being followed?

We estimate that among major packaged goods manufacturers, telcoms and financial services companies probably 25 per cent or more are now tracking their competitors' as well as their own activities with continuous customer surveys. Among durable goods manufacturers, utilities and pharmaceutical manufacturers the figure is lower but growing quite quickly. These are not once-a-year or once-a-quarter surveys. They are conducted every week, on small samples each week which accumulate over the year into a large database and provide a total, continuous picture.

Every week these organizations capture, in their computers, fresh information on a new sample of consumers. The information covers all players in the market. Ideally, it would cover the state of play for that week in regard to people's behavior, attitudes, brand awareness and brand image as well as direct communication effects such as advertising recall, advertising recognition and message take-out. This is then related to other information such as media data (indicating what advertisers were on air during that week, at what times and at what advertising weight) along with sales and market share data.

Continuous market research technology has rapidly become accepted as the best way of accurately assessing advertising effects in terms of what works and what doesn't.[1] Continuous monitoring of *purchase* information can reveal whether something worked or didn't. However, knowing whether it worked is one thing while finding out *why* or *why not*, is another. This diagnostic information also needs to be continuous and is obtained from continuous surveying known as *continuous tracking*.

From the 1950s through into the 1980s, market research was characterized by the large-scale, large-sample survey representing a single point in time. Known as 'ad hoc' surveys, these were conducted before an ad campaign and then again after it. Any differences in key measures between these two surveys (such as in the levels of people's brand awareness, ad awareness or the brand's market share) were supposed to indicate possible effects of the advertising. This 'pre-post' survey technique, as it was known, has slowly but inevitably been giving way to the new technology of continuous monitoring.

Conducting ad hoc surveys, or pre-post surveys, was the 'old' way of trying to understand what is happening in a market. It is like taking a couple of still frames from the beginning and end of a TV commercial and trying to get a sense of the whole commercial from just those two pictures. The difference between ad hoc surveys and continuous surveying resembles the difference between still photography and moving pictures. Without continuous moving pictures, the dynamics of what is happening can only be guessed at.

Take the dramatic case of a shampoo brand with around 2.5 per cent market share among females under 35. The brand launches a spectacular new commercial. The plot unfolds as follows: This new, different ad hits the tube. It is clearly an exciting and different commercial. The advertiser is putting quite heavy expenditure behind it. Quickly we see, to no one's surprise, that this ad successfully breaks through the clutter of shampoo advertising and delivers a message. We see this in the first two weeks of data (see Figures 11.1 and 11.2). So far so good, but will the ad sell product? If you are a competitor, do you react? Panic? Sit tight? You recall a previous ad for the same brand that broke through very well but, ho-hum, it didn't sell. Maybe this will be the same. Let's not worry too much yet! The key issue is, will consumer *behavior* change?

The continuous surveying that you are doing as a matter of course asks which brand the respondent last bought, and the answers come in each week in the sample data. You wait and watch agonisingly. Will brand purchase behavior move in response to the ad?

Figures 11.1 and 11.2 tell the story. Within a month of the ad going to air, you know the hair-raising truth (see Figure 11.2). By the third or fourth week of the new advertising, this brand's market share is clearly moving. By the fifth week it has doubled from 2.5 per cent to around 5 per cent. There is now no doubt this new ad is working. If this is a competitor, you

What works, what doesn't, and why

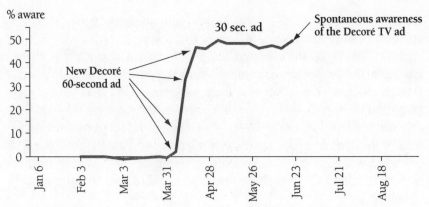

Note: Continuous tracking of people's spontaneous awareness of the Decoré advertisement

Figure 11.1
Shampoo advertisement awareness. *Source:* NFO MarketMind

had better move fast to try to find a way to counter it. Or start revising the annual market share projections for your brand *downwards*.

In fact, nine weeks after the launch of the new ad, the brand had successfully increased its market share in this target group to more than 10 per cent—a phenomenal achievement. If you are a competitor of this brand the news you are getting from your tracking is depressing. The upside of this, however, is that you know at the earliest possible moment. While it may be cold comfort, you do have more time to formulate a retaliation strategy.

We have also seen situations like this where the ad, while very visible and attention-getting, did not sell the product (sometimes because there was

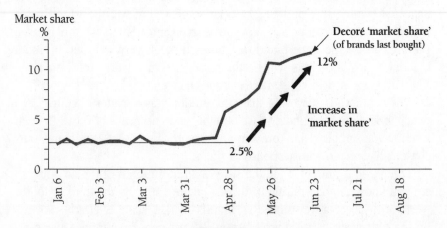

Figure 11.2
Shampoo market share. *Source:* NFO MarketMind

no relevant message or the ad failed to communicate the brand correctly or to link it with the message). In the absence of *weekly* information, there is sometimes an overwhelming temptation to react when there may be no need to. It is comforting to know at the earliest possible time whether you need to react to a competitor's move.

With the tracking results for this commercial, you have just received the clearest possible evidence that advertising can work in this market. Additional analysis over time allows you to draw conclusions as to the type of advertising that works and how it works in this market (because not all markets work the same way).

For example, in this market, did attitude change before behavior, or did behavior change before attitude? Did the advertising impact on image, then attitude, then behavior? What was the direction of the chain of events?

Product managers and marketing managers want to know what works in their market and what doesn't. If a competitor implements a new action, should they react? How do they judge what to react to?

While continuous surveying as a 'rear-vision mirror' has been around for a while, we can discern among advertisers a new trend in its use. They are not just using it to see where their brand has been and to evaluate the effectiveness of their moves, but to address the much larger question of how the market works. Increasingly, they are using continuous tracking before making important moves and to study their competitors' activities as well as their own. Their objective is to know what works and what doesn't before they make any important move in the market. The idea is to formulate the right move and ensure the maximum chance of success.

Not all are using it in this way but an increasing number are. They are not just tracking their own brand. They are also tracking and studying their competitors' actions and the effectiveness of those actions. By getting a handle on what is effective and what is not, they move towards closure on the question of what works and what doesn't in the particular market.

They address such questions as:

- Does advertising work in this market?
- What type of advertising works?
- How does it work?
- Does the advertising change attitudes and then behavior? Or behavior, then attitudes?
- Should we have advertising that primarily reinforces behavior ('Aren't you glad you use Dial?')? Or do we need advertising that will primarily generate trial ('Four good reasons to try brand X')?

In other words, What works? And what doesn't?

It is important to note that we are not just talking about advertising here. Product managers and advertising managers are also interested in promotions, changes in media flighting, different media weights, a switch to shorter-length ads, a free sampling campaign, a change in pricing, new positioning, a new presenter, or new creative advertising ideas. (The graph in Figure 11.1 shows what happened when this brand switched from 60-second to 30-second commercials. The flattening out of the growth in ad cut-through is very common after such a switch. It also happens after a switch from 30 seconds to 15 seconds.) Almost any action or event that takes place in a market can be plotted on the time line and subjected to this type of effectiveness analysis.

Snapshot, single-point-in-time surveys do not cope with this. Dynamics are needed. Snapshot pictures are too slow, and they don't capture unexpected events—such as the launch of this new ad campaign by a competitor. Pre-post or periodic snapshot surveys of the market every quarter or half year or so are yesterday's technology. The problem with them is that the time dimension is missing.

With dynamic measurement, market modeling and market knowledge accumulate over time and let a company know much more than its competition about how the market works, what works in it and what doesn't. The objective is to do more of what works and less of what doesn't.

It is no accident that Ronald Reagan was the most popular president than any before him—or that George Bush came from miles behind to take out the US presidency in 1989. The Republican Party discovered very early, the 'missing link' in research. This missing link was the time dimension: the use of continuous tracking. Bush was ultimately defeated in 1992 by Clinton which demonstrates the point made earlier—there are real limits to what advertising and promotion can do when the product does not perform or is looking old and tired. By the time re-election came around in 1996, Clinton and the Democratic Party had mastered the new technology of continuous tracking and were using it to great effect in evaluating and fine-tuning the effectiveness of their ads—especially in swing states.[2] Such expertise was then 'loaned out' overseas, in the form of former Clinton experts assisting in the election of Tony Blair as prime minister of the UK and Barak as prime minister of Israel.

By contrast with such overtly successful results, traditional, single-point-in-time market research has often failed to produce actionable information. It has been difficult to assess its value, precisely because the time dimension, reflecting the dynamic nature of markets, was either missing or very much mistreated. The time dimension has to be treated as a continuous variable and factored into marketing research methodology instead of being ignored or treated as a dichotomous variable.

With the time dimension included, the research becomes richer and its value much more easily demonstrable in terms of:

- Its role as an 'early-warning system';
- Its ability to reveal changing patterns in a market;
- Its ability to tease out inferences about causation and relate these to assessment of the effectiveness of advertising, promotions, etc;
- Its ability to capture unexpected events;
- Its asset value as a cumulative database resource.

Markets are dynamic. They are a moving picture and they need dynamic techniques to capture their richness. If you are not tracking your competition using continuous tracking, is your competition tracking you? In short, are you being followed?

12

New product launches: don't pull the plug too early

Why do so many new products fail?

In the last two decades in many parts of the world the NFO MarketMind™ system of tracking has been used to monitor hundreds of product categories. In many of these categories it has been possible to observe a range of new brands or products being launched. There is no single reason for the high rate of new product failure but there is one fairly common one. This has to do with the fact that the care and attention evident at the pre-launch stage is not carried through after the 'go' button is pushed.

Not enough companies closely and continuously monitor what is happening at the product launch and in the immediate post-launch period. The result is that many of the all-important fine-tuning adjustments necessary to marketing success fail to be made. And the product crashes.

Most companies these days put a lot of money and careful attention into development of a new product. They do the same with the development of the advertising and the promotional program to back it up. They pre-test the advertising and the acceptance of the product concept and try to put everything in place for the launch to succeed.

But then a funny thing happens. The launch button is pushed. And in this crucial immediate post-launch stage, the tendency is to do little more

---

™ NFO MarketMind is a worldwide proprietary system of continuous surveying and databasing, owned by NFO worldwide and located at www.NFOMarketMind.com.

New product launches: don't pull the plug too early

than take a deep breath, pray that everything has been done right, and wait anxiously for the judgment—the judgment of the market. Will the product be a success or a failure? If NASA launched space shuttles the way manufacturers launch new brands, there would be fewer astronauts!

The advertising resources necessary to fuel these new product launches are huge. (For example, in the USA one source estimates this at around 1400 to 2200 TRPs per year to launch a new packaged goods product—which equates to an estimated US$17–22 million.[1])

Durable products

Many new durable products fail because early sales do not come up to expectation. Pessimism then spreads within the company and often results in management 'pulling the plug' too early and abandoning the product.

Figure 12.1 shows a new brand of durable product that was launched with a continuous advertising schedule for seven weeks. At the end of that time the company took the advertising off air 'because sales were not up to expectation'. The whole mood of the company and its marketing team projected disappointment and an expectation of looming product failure. This is a real danger point in new product launches because the gloom is likely to be self-fulfilling.

Fortunately, in this case, for the first time in the company's history, not only sales but also the effect of the campaign on attitudes towards the brand

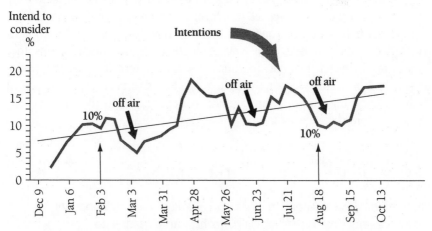

Note: Intention to buy new brand increases when on-air and decays when off-air, resulting in an overall upward trend.

Figure 12.1
Advertising influence on intentions. *Source:* NFO MarketMind

were being monitored continuously. On the basis of the continuous tracking data, the researchers were able to argue that the company should keep going; that just because sales had not yet responded was no reason to abort the advertising or to give up on the new product.

As a result the company went back on air with advertising for the product. The graph in Figure 12.1 clearly shows that since then, each time there was a burst of advertising, attitudes towards the brand improved (with one exception, when the launch of another new, competitive brand muddied the picture somewhat). Three months after the launch, the brand, far from being a failure, had a 15 per cent market share. The same brand is alive and well today, but if the abort decision had been made it might well have ended up in the annals of product history as just another new-product failure.

This case clearly illustrates the importance of continuous measurement. The market is a movie and its richness cannot be captured by a couple of snapshot surveys with a box Brownie. It needs continuous measurement.

Consider the situation in the first eight months of the product's life. If a snapshot-type survey had been conducted on 3 February, it would have shown that 10 per cent of people were prepared to seriously consider the brand next time they bought that type of product (i.e. were 'short-listers' for the brand). A good result. If another snapshot survey had been conducted on 18 August after six months of advertising, it would have shown no change as a result of all that advertising. Without continuous measurement, these snapshot-type surveys might well have given the false impression that further advertising bursts were having no further effect on people's attitudes.

However, as the trend line in the continuous data clearly indicates, there was a long-term positive effect of continuing with the advertising for this brand. Each time it went on air it was developing and strengthening attitudes towards the brand—it was strengthening the brand's consumer franchise. Between those on-air times, the mental territory that the advertising had previously captured would begin to erode because of the lack of advertising reinforcement but, overall, in the long haul, the product was gaining more than it was losing.

Repeat-purchase supermarket products

Continuous information on sales and market share is important for any product—not just new product launches. You need it to know whether what you are doing is successful in terms of behavior. Such top-level information, however, is not enough to enable you to *diagnose* why things are going right or wrong. It may tell you what worked and what didn't and as such it provides an important rear-view mirror picture. But to be able to decide on corrective or future actions, you have to focus on the diagnosis, the *why* of what is happening (see Chapters 24 and 25).

In new product launches, particularly, it is crucial to monitor other things—among them awareness (the proportion of people who are aware of the new product) and trial (the proportion who have tried it)—and do this continuously.

Why is this so important? It is because a 10 per cent market share in supermarket-type products can come about in either of two extreme ways.

1. Ten per cent of people have ever bought the new brand and they are buying it 100 per cent of the time. That is, they are completely loyal.
2. One hundred per cent of people have bought it, but they are only buying it 10 per cent of the time. That is, they are buying that brand only about once in every ten times they shop for the product category.

Depending on which situation the new brand finds itself in, the strategic implications are quite different. In the first case the company needs to get more people to try the brand if it wants to increase market share. In the second case, the company has managed to get people to try it but the only way it is going to increase market share is to increase their repeat buying.

So it is vitally important in the lift-off stage to measure not just market share but also how many people have ever bought or tried the new product. Incredible as it may seem, some companies fail to do this. And in the cases when it is done, a reading is generally only taken in a survey repeated every six or twelve months.

This is not enough. Companies need to know how the trial is progressing continuously. NASA monitors its space launches *continuously*. It doesn't press the button and then come back after lunch to see how things are going. It knows that anything may have happened in the meantime. Things occur that need correction, adjustment or fine-tuning! By the time some businesses come back and do a survey, one month, two months or six months after launch, it is too late. What they frequently find is that the product is out of control or has crashed—or sometimes, that it never even got off the ground.

A well known cookie manufacturer used to launch new cookie products this way. The company spent huge resources developing new varieties of cookies and then conducting in-home placement tests in which consumers were asked which one(s) they liked best and therefore which were the best candidates to put on the market.

This type of testing revealed which varieties people liked, how much they liked them, and how likely they were to repeat-buy those varieties.

The problem that this company failed to come to grips with was how to get people to buy and *try* the cookies in the first place. This company looked only at sales and market share information.

Typically, after launching one of the new cookie products, the company would look at sales. If sales were not up to expectation in the first three months or so, it would simply abandon the product. While it had some successes, it had many more 'failures'. The main reason for the failures continued to go unrecognized and the company continued to make the same mistake over and over.

The problem in most cases was not that the new variety was rejected by the market. It was to do with the inadequate level of marketing support behind the launch and the over-reliance on advertising alone without promotional activity to generate that key first trial. The company failed to monitor closely what was happening immediately after the 'go' button was pressed and the launch had begun. Because it didn't know exactly what happened between the launch and the crash, the crashes continued, largely as a result of the same problems. This is what happens when businesses rely only on sales and market share to indicate new product performance and then make critical decisions on the basis of these indicators alone. This is a common cause of new-product launch failures.

In one case in point a new cookie was launched but discontinued after about four months. When the decision to abort was made, this variety had about a 3 per cent market share in its segment, which was regarded as 'not enough'. Like so many of its previous new-product attempts, the company regarded this as a failure.

When the decision to abort was made the variety had only about 3 per cent share but this was primarily because only about 10 per cent of people had ever tried it. Its repeat buying rate was in fact quite good. The people who had tried it were buying it about one in every three times they bought cookies—which is not bad in the cookie market, where there are so many varieties to choose from.

The company had tested the product by in-home placement (i.e. 'forced' trial) and this had accurately predicted that people would accept and like the product once they had tasted it. The key words are 'once they had tasted it'.

Remember, only 10 per cent of people had tasted it when the launch was aborted. It was not the product that failed. It was the marketing activities designed to get it trialed that failed! Not enough resources were put into the launch to ensure successful communication of the product's qualities to enough people to prompt them to try it the first time.

The company aborted this variety and went off to develop a new one that it hoped would do better next time!

The point here is that initial trial is a key ingredient in new product launches for any low-cost product but particularly supermarket products. Even if the product was the greatest-tasting cookie ever and got a repeat buying level of 100 per cent, it could not have gone above 10 per cent share if only 10 per cent of people had ever tried it. On the other hand, with a 30 per cent repeat buying level, if the company had got another 60 per cent of people to try it, the product would have gained a potential share of 18 per cent (i.e. 30 per cent of 60 per cent).

Our cookie manufacturer wasted a lot of money trying to find outstanding product formulations that would guarantee success. But once you look at its activity in the light of the very low trial figures for its new products, the lesson is clear. The world will not beat a path to any company's door, whether it develops a better mousetrap or a better cookie. The product has to be effectively marketed. The company has to get people to try it.

Fine-tuning the marketing support

Instead of looking for ideal product formulations, the urgent need is more often to address the level and fine-tuning of marketing support for new products. To ensure that support is adequate and functioning as it should, companies need to monitor their launches closely, making appropriate adjustments, fine-tunings and corrections as required. Failure to do this is one of the most important causes of new product failure. Too often, marketers have too little information and pull the plug on the new product too early, before they have achieved the necessary awareness and trial.

Trial needs to be gained early, while the product has a newness and freshness about it. If it does not achieve good penetration in the first six months it is unlikely to succeed. This is particularly important for seasonal products such as new varieties of canned soup or chocolate cookies in winter or ice confections in summer. If trial is not achieved quickly and in the first season, the new product has to come back next season as an old product without the 'newness' factor that can be so important in getting interest and trial. Generally, it doesn't work (see Chapter 17, 'Seasonal advertising').

If the new product is going to succeed it has to achieve trial as quickly as possible before it loses its image of newness; that usually means, in the season in which it is launched. An obvious part of getting this first-season trial is making people aware of the new product and getting them interested in it. This is a communications task and, like everything else, needs monitoring.

Figure 12.2 shows response to a new product two months after launch. Only 26 per cent of target consumers have heard of the brand which means

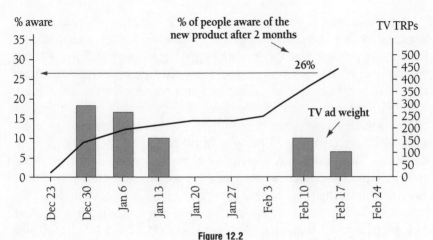

Figure 12.2
Awareness of a new food product. *Source:* NFO MarketMind

that advertising to this point has failed to communicate the existence of the new product to more than half of the potential market.

The implication is clear. It would be foolish to abort the product. What is needed is a change in the advertising or promotional strategy. Either the ad targeting and scheduling is ineffective, or the ad itself hasn't got the creative touch to break through clutter and get people to try the new product without more promotional support.

Launching new products should be like launching space shuttles—the successes should outnumber the failures. It is not an inevitable law of marketing that in the launching of products there needs to be more casualties than successes.

13

Planning campaign strategy around consumers' mental filing cabinets

Ads are like alcohol: the more you have the less you remember. After only two or three drinks your faculties start to become impaired. After exposure to only one or two competing ads, your memory for the first one starts to become impaired.[1] What is true of alcohol is surprisingly true of consumer memory for advertising—at least for competing brands in the same product category.

Over a period of a week, the more competing commercials that are aired for a product category, the less the average person will remember about any one of them. Most people think that forgetting is simply the fading of memory with the passage of time. However, it is now well established that forgetting is due not to the passage of time alone, but to interference from additional learning that takes place in that time.[2] When time passes but little or no further (competing) learning takes place there is very little forgetting.

On the other hand, where a lot of activity and new learning—especially competitive learning—fills the time interval, these 'interference effects' become very great indeed. These effects are one of the clearest of findings on the way human memory works.[3] They are also one of the most frequent findings to emerge from continuous tracking of advertising.

Memory, the ability to retrieve an event or message, can be severely impaired when a person is exposed to other similar events within a short time. While this is a well established finding in psychology, it is not widely recognized in marketing. Few people take account of it in planning advertising media schedules or when they are assessing why their ad campaign has 'failed'.

Models of memory and forgetting

At a crowded party, if you want to communicate you have to speak loudly. The more voices, the more competition and the louder the din gets. You have to shout to be heard above the clutter. On television you also have to shout for your ad to be heard. The greater the clutter the more you have to shout. In other words, the more competitors you have advertising against you, the more effort and money you will have to expend to get your message into people's heads.

Even when you shout, your communication may still not register successfully, especially if the target is distracted or tuned in to someone else's conversation, or musing on something else. How many conversations can you tune in to at one time? Two? Three? How many commercials for different brands in a product category can consumers hang on to in their mind? There is no single threshold. Rather, each subsequent input progressively diminishes the memory for any and all others.

The popular view of memory is that a trace of the remembered thing is either there or it is not. You can either remember it or you can't. This model of memory is demonstrably wrong. How many times have you been unable to remember someone's name even though you *know* that you know it? Forgetting has more to do with 'inability to retrieve' than with failure to store the memory. It is the inability to remember it when you want it.

It is sometimes helpful to think of memories as being stored in one of several mental filing cabinets. If you carefully file a new memory, a new ad, in a particular filing cabinet you should be able to retrieve it quickly and easily as needed. However, if you were distracted enough or unmotivated enough to stow the new memory away casually without paying attention to what you were doing or which filing cabinet you were stowing it in, the chances are that you will have great difficulty retrieving it. More to the point, you will be unable to retrieve it quickly. The only way to retrieve it will be to look painstakingly through every cabinet and every possible file.

With memory, the problem is usually not inability to retrieve, but inability to retrieve in any reasonable or functional time. So, for all intents and purposes, the information becomes 'functionally lost'.

Information can become functionally lost because it is a long time since you filed it. It can also become functionally lost as a result of interference effects—the competing exposures discussed earlier. You can think of interference effects as the outcome of trying to store several similar memories all in the one file. The more cluttered the file becomes, the longer it is going to take to look through it and retrieve a particular memory.[4]

When a consumer is exposed to competing commercials, this is what happens. There is interference from previously stored ads, exacerbated by the fact that the consumer is often fairly unmotivated or uninvolved when storing them. With these types of memory inputs the interference effect is all the greater when the viewer has low involvement.

Another way of thinking about it is that exposure to competing commercials is like laying down tracks on a two-track or three-track tape. After you have recorded the first one, two or three, the next one is laid down partly over previous recordings. And subsequent ones are laid down on top of that, setting up increasing interference and distortion in the memory playback.

Advertising application

It is for this reason that the 'effectiveness' or impact of a commercial is very much influenced by how much competitors spend advertising against it in a particular week. When trying to get the message into people's heads in the first place, it is rarely just a simple function of how much an advertised brand spends on advertising time (its media weight) in any week.

An advertiser cannot effectively plan or monitor a brand's ad strategy without information about competing on-air activity. This is why anyone who is serious about maximizing the effectiveness of their ad strategy needs to have access to weekly data (monthly or quarterly is not good enough) as to which advertisers were on air in that week and at what weight.[5]

It is always worth looking at the raw relationship between the amount spent on a brand's advertising and indicators of effectiveness such as sales, market share or advertising awareness. But don't be surprised or disappointed if you don't see any clear relationship. This does not mean that the advertising is not working. Try looking not at the total amount of advertising for the brand but at the brand's *share* of advertising in the product category, week by week. A strong relationship may then emerge. (This is more likely when you are first trying to get your message into consumers' heads than with reminder/reinforcement advertising.)

Figure 13.1 illustrates the point. The vertical bars indicate the weeks when this brand's advertising campaign was on TV. Their heights indicate the brand's *share* of the total TV advertising in its product category (share of media weight or share of voice).

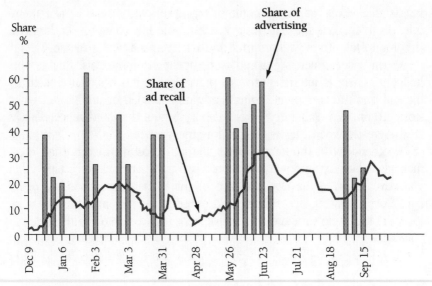

Note: For this brand a clear relationship is evident between its share of advertising and its share of advertisement recall.

Figure 13.1
Television share of mind and share of voice. *Source:* NFO MarketMind

The product is a consumer product and its share of voice is plotted against a measure of people's spontaneous awareness of the ad. This is a relative measure and is called the brand's TV ad *share-of-mind*. It is the brand's *share* of total ad awareness in the product category; in other words, memory for that ad relative to all other ads in the product category. It is indicated by the line graph.

A clear relationship is evident each time the brand comes on air with a flight of advertising. With each flight the brand's TV ad share-of-mind trends upward. (The graph also gives valuable indications of how quickly or how slowly memory of the ad decays between each advertising flight.) This performance graph can be compared with a similar graph for each competitor and inferences can then be drawn about whether the brand's advertising strategy is more or less effective than the ads for competing brands.

Components of clutter

This raises the question: What other ads does a particular brand compete with? In the broadest sense it competes with all other ads—even those not in the same product category. This is known as the general level of on-air clutter and any ad has to break through it. This general level of clutter is relatively constant, at least in the short term. However, it has tended to grow over the long term not only because of more time given to ads but also because of an increase in the use of shorter-length commercials.[6] Shorter-length commercials boost the total *number* of commercials on air and thus the number that people see in any given time period, and increases the general impression that there is more advertising overall.

As well as the general level of clutter there is, even more importantly, 'category clutter'. The ad in question competes with other ads in the same product category. This is called *category clutter*, and this *does* vary from week to week.

What may be surprising to many readers is that the ad also competes with any other ads for the same brand that may be aired in the same week. That is, multiple but similar advertising executions for the same brand frequently compete among themselves and can set up interference effects that impede their individual effectiveness (especially with low-involved audiences).[7]

Can a company compete with itself?

Is your ad being limited in its impact by competition from other ads run by your own company? If you are a multi-product, multi-brand company, the answer is almost certainly 'yes'. A Toyota Corolla commercial competes against ads for other vehicles manufactured by Ford, GM, Nissan, BMW or Volvo. It is not as obvious, but nevertheless real, that it also competes with all other ads screened by Toyota itself in the same week. These, too, are competing for consumers' mind and memory.

Commercials aimed at audiences with high involvement may be less subject to these effects than those aimed at audiences with low involvement.[8] This is because, in high-involvement situations, the consumer may consciously and deliberately process the message in such a way as to make it more resistant to forgetting. That is, it gets filed in a careful way that anticipates a future need to retrieve it. With high-involvement messages, the viewer anticipates a future need to use the information, unlike low-involvement messages.

The key point here is the level of involvement of the target audience. If vehicle ads are aimed at people intending to buy a new car in the next two or three months, then these people are likely to be highly involved. However, about one-third of all new-car purchases are made by people who did not intend to buy a new car but were overtaken by events. These include those whose old car suddenly gives them problems, and the growing number of people who separate from their spouse and find a need for another car. Such people are likely to be low-involved at the time of exposure to the advertising—at least up to the point when the 'need' is triggered by the unforeseen event.

So advertising for high-involvement products (such as cars) doesn't impact only on a high-involved audience. It also impacts on relatively uninvolved consumers. And this uninvolved audience will at some time in the future become an involved one harboring memories of past advertising.

In summary, successful advertising planning and evaluation demands detailed analysis of more than just one's own ad expenditure. It necessitates an understanding of consumer memory processes in regard to interference effects as well as memory decay. The on-air effectiveness of an ad is influenced by several things—not necessarily in this order:

- The execution. Is it a great ad?
- The dollar spend. How much 'weight' was put behind it that week?
- The reach. What percentage of the target audience had at least one opportunity to see it?
- The flighting. How is the ad being scheduled from week to week?
- The number of competitors who are on air in the same week and how much they spent.
- The number of different ad executions for the same brand that you have on air in any one week.
- The number of commercials for the same umbrella brand that you have on air in any one week.
- The level of involvement of the target audience and the complexity of the message that needs to be communicated.
- The ad objective. Is it a reminder of a message already established or is it communicating a new message?[9]

14

What happens when you stop advertising?

In tight economic times, the pressures are always on to cut advertising. Can a company do this? Can it get away with it? What will be the effect on the company a bit further down the track? These are the questions that are asked when the recessionary animal starts to bite.

If the company stops advertising and sales stay at the same level, the cessation of ad spending generates an immediate improvement in the bottom line. Hence the strong temptation to cut advertising in tough times and make the company's profit performance look good. What are the consequences? What do we know about ceasing to advertise?

What happens when advertising stops?

We do not know a lot about what happens when advertising stops but what we do know is enough to warrant caution. Most companies don't know what happens when advertising stops because they only look at the immediate sales figures. If sales don't go down, they breathe a sigh of relief. But it is critical to look at what is going on underneath, at the brand image and 'brand value' level. Here is where the early warning signs of erosion in brand value are likely to be seen first.

For example, in 1988, a major US food brand cut its advertising budget in half (from US$7 million to US$4 million). Before the cut, ratings of the product in taste-testing studies differed greatly depending on whether the brand name was on the pack when tasted. While the brand was supported by advertising at adequate levels, the brand name provided a lift of 24 per cent over blind taste tests (24 per cent higher than respondents who tasted exactly the same product, but without the brand name). Four years of greatly reduced advertising saw this differential erode so that it was only a 10 per cent lift over blind taste tests! The brand name lost more than half its power. Consumers were less impressed with it as a brand and it lost much of its ability to influence people's impressions of quality and taste.

Another example: Some years ago a leading brand in another food category, the only major advertiser in the category, decided to stop its previously consistent advertising. As might be expected, this premium brand's share eventually deteriorated along with perceptions of its value and quality. It not only eroded on these indicators but also in market share and in association with an image of 'good value for money' and 'high quality'. What was particularly revealing, however, was that ratings for other brands, the low-advertised, low-price, so-called 'value' brands began to *increase* over that time. In the absence of advertising reinforcement by leading brands, consumers are freer to raise their perceptions of alternative products and base their decision on what is visible on the shelf. It took a long time but this once leading 'premium' brand ultimately came back to the rest of the market and today is viewed as being at parity with the category bottom-feeder.

So stopping advertising could be a smart decision. But, then again, it could be a time bomb. A doctoral thesis on milk advertising in the United States some years ago revealed the delayed nature of the time bomb. It underlined the fact that maintenance of sales in the short or medium term after ceasing to advertise is no reason for complacency. In a prolonged series of test market experiments, it was found that nothing happened to sales when advertising of milk was stopped. Nothing, that is, for 12 months! After a year of no advertising, milk sales suddenly went into a sharp decline and continued to decline at a sickening rate.

Advertising restarted immediately, but it was too late. It took another 18 months to halt the decline and then begin to reverse it. So beware of the delayed time bomb. To regain a favourable position that is lost during belt tightening can cost more in the long run than to try to retain it by continuing to advertise at a maintenance level.[1]

For how long can a company afford to stop advertising?

Rather than ask the question 'Can we stop advertising?' it may be more meaningful to ask: Can we maintain our advertising support of the brand but at the same time reduce advertising costs overall? Capturing the mental territory for a brand requires much more effort and resources than holding it once gained. The cost of funding your occupation forces can be very much lower than initial capture. It implies cuts in frequency—that is, how many times people are exposed to the message within the week—rather than cuts to reach—how many people you reach with the message in the week.

However, in really tight recessionary times there may be no choice but to accede to a Corporate Board edict to pause the advertising. How long before you can expect the effect to show up?

Much depends on how much residual or carry-over effect current and past advertising has had. Some campaigns have amazingly strong residual memory effects. Other ads have almost none. They are forgotten almost as soon as they go off air. Continuous tracking of campaigns and advertising flights can reveal how much 'residual capital' has been built up and how quickly it is eroded once the advertising is stopped.

Some experiences

Figures 14.1, 14.2 and 14.3 demonstrate case experiences with cessation of advertising. Compare the first two graphs. They show what happened when two brands (from different product categories) stopped advertising.

Brand A and its advertising had a lot of residual recall even after the ads stopped. There is almost no memory decay of the brand or the advertising after three months. In the case of Brand B, on the other hand, the brand itself had good residual recall but the advertising didn't. When the advertising stopped, recall of the advertising declined rapidly while awareness of the brand held up well.

Brand A had been off air for four months. Brand B had been off air for seven months. Market share did not show any decline in either case. But that is where the complacency ends. When we look more closely, the indications are that other things are going on that could be very detrimental in the longer run.

Erosion of brand franchise

The third graph (Figure 14.3) shows total advertising exposures (TRPs) in one of these markets. Advertising stopped in this market three months previously. There had been no marked changes in sales or market shares for any of the brands in this market *at that point*.

What works, what doesn't, and why

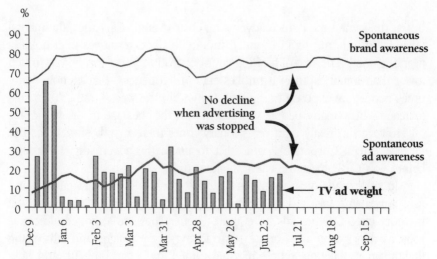

Note: When advertising was stopped for this product no significant decline was observed in spontaneous awareness of the brand or for spontaneous awareness of its advertising.

Figure 14.1
Spontaneous awareness: Brand A. *Source:* NFO MarketMind

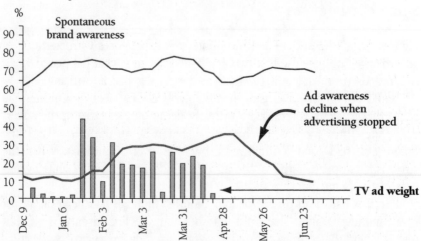

Note: When advertising was stopped for this product the spontaneous awareness of the brand did not decline significantly but a rapid decline in spontaneous advertising awareness took place.

Figure 14.2
Spontaneous awareness: Brand B. *Source:* NFO MarketMind

However, if we look further below the surface we find a worrying trend emerging. Brand loyalty is declining. People are still buying the brand but any feeling of 'commitment' they may have to the brand is eroding.

The market shown in the graph has two major segments—'brand loyals' and 'habitual buyers'. The brand loyals believe there are differences between

What happens when you stop advertising?

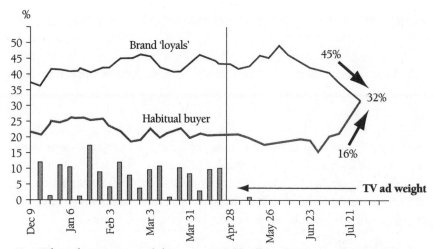

Note: When advertising stopped there was no visible effect whatever on sales. But after two months the 'commitment' of buyers eroded rapidly. The absence of reinforcement created habitual rather than loyal buyers, leaving the brand vulnerable to attack.

Figure 14.3
Share of market segments. *Source:* NFO MarketMind

brands and always buy the same brand. The habitual buyers also tend to buy the same brand each time but they believe there are *no real differences* between brands.

Habitual, repeat-buyers of a brand are not the same thing as brand loyals. Habitual buyers repeat-buy the brand for reasons of inertia rather than loyalty. With the cessation of advertising, the brand loyals diminish in the market and habitual buyers increase. While sales may not change immediately, the major brand(s) in the market become more vulnerable, more open to attack. They lose their brand franchise.

Even though sales and market share have not changed, if this trend is allowed to continue the market itself will be very different. Whereas the market in the past has been characterised by brands with strongly promoted brand franchises, it could well become more of a commodity market with little differences perceived between any of the brands. The market leader's sales could thus become wide open to a price attack from a new or existing competitor.[2]

Opportunity

'Rather than wait for business to return to normal, top executives should cash in on the opportunity that the rival companies (who are stopping their advertising) are creating for them. The company courageous enough to stay in and fight when everyone else is playing safe can bring about a dramatic change in market position.'[3]

Now we can see why. Figure 14.3 illustrates how a market can be made vulnerable even though sales and market shares do not appear to have changed in the short term. For a company that is a smaller competitor in the market, this is the time to go after the market leader. Like a pilot taking off in an aeroplane and picking out holes in the cloud-cover to climb through, the smaller advertiser can take advantage of these situations to steer its brand up to a higher level of market share and salience. At such times there is less advertising clutter and the smaller advertiser, even with a small ad budget, is more likely to be heard when the large advertisers are silent and mental commitment to their brands is beginning to erode.

Reinforcement effect of advertising

So the effects of advertising must not be looked at just in terms of increasing sales. To do so ignores the fact that advertising has a very important *reinforcement* effect.

One of the most important effects of advertising is consolidating and protecting what has already been built. It reinforces behavior. People are more convinced of the 'rightness' of their brand choice if they see the brand advertised. 'Good advertising provides people with the means to rationalize their brand preferences.'[4] And, all other things being equal, they are more likely to buy that brand again.

Some of the most avid readers of car ads are people who have just bought that brand of car. The ads provide reinforcement of their decision. This may not make a lot of rational sense, but that's the way we human beings are.

Belt-tightening strategies for tough times

In recession times, if the pressure is on, the key question should be how you can take surgery to the advertising rather than simply eliminate it. How can you improve the bottom line without jeopardizing the brand in the long run?

We have seen the dangers of ceasing to advertise altogether, so if you are not going to stop but are under budgetary pressure to economize, is there anything else you can do? Yes! You can consider some belt-tightening strategies for tough times. You need to make the ad budget that is available work more efficiently. Rather than stop the advertising, consider these ways of trimming the waistline and tightening the belt.

- A 'drip' media strategy—that is, rather than stop the advertising altogether, use reduced exposures (reduced weekly TRP weights) to try to hold the ground you have already captured.
- Look for ways to trade off frequency while maximizing reach on the target market.
- *If necessary,* examine the feasibility of having longer gaps in your advertising flighting pattern. How long can you afford to stay off air between flights without jeopardizing your brand franchise?
- If you are using several ad executions on air at the same time, cut back to just one ad and put all your media weight behind it. Be very single-minded. Most companies use too many executions, anyway, and have too few exposures (TRPs) behind each execution. In other words, avoid 'executional anorexia' (see Chapter 18, 'Underweight advertising').
- If you want to cut back, consider 15-second commercials—but use them not as attack forces but as occupation forces to hold the mental territory that has already been captured. Make sure you build ad awareness to a high level with longer commercials before you switch to 15-second ads. Don't just use 15s as substitutes for 30s (see Chapter 16, 'Learning to use 15-second commercials').

15

The effectiveness of funny ads: what a laugh!

- A young woman in a restroom strips in front of an apparently blind man, who is actually looking after his father's white stick and sunglasses. (Advertiser: Levi's)[1]
- An Argentine ad shows a pair of underpants on a washing line with a ragged hole burnt eloquently through the rear. (Advertiser: A brand of spicy tuna sauce)

Ten to 15 per cent of all TV commercials are estimated to contain humor.[2] It varies by country and culture so that, in the United Kingdom for example, estimates put the figure as high as 35 per cent.[3] In the last 15 years there have been many opportunities to track humorous ads. These are the ads that tickle us and make us laugh; they appear more often on television or radio but every now and again a print campaign comes along to be tracked that also makes people chuckle.

We are fortunate to have had the opportunity to track these funny ads because it is striking how little is actually written and known about humor in advertising and its effects. There is an amazingly small body of research on it, given how important humor is to us. And what little laboratory research there is frequently produces contradictory findings.

Part of the problem is that it is so easy to treat all humor as the same and generalize about it—when it isn't the same. Slapstick humor, for example, is very different from wit[4] (Figure 15.1). And what is funny to one individual can be uninteresting or even irritating to another. So you can't assume something is funny. British humor is very different from American humor, so it is not surprising that research that treats humor as generic often produces confusing and sometimes contradictory findings.

This chapter also generalizes about humor, but on the basis of what differs in the way people mentally process ads with humor in them. How is this different from straight ads? We will see why humor can have both positive and negative effects depending on how it is used.

Figure 15.1
Some humor relies on wit—
Suède-ish massage ad for Weatherproof
brand clothing

The history of humor

To have a sense of humor is a good thing. Everyone agrees, right? Not to have a sense of humor is a bad thing. Well, prepare yourself for a shock. This idea is only about 400 years old. You don't have to go too far back in history before finding that laughter and humor were viewed negatively, not positively. Indeed, they reflected the 'satanic spirit of man'.

Greek philosophy depicted humor as a cruel and brutal affair. Plato thought it was based on an unfortunate lack of self-knowledge and motivated by envy, which made it morally inferior and reprehensible. Aristotle described laughter as 'degrading to morals, art and religion, a form of behavior from which civilized man should shrink'. And Lord Chesterfield wrote 'there is nothing so illiberal and so ill-bred than audible laughter'.[5]

The historical origins of humor lie in the darker side of man—in derisive rather than friendly, enjoyable laughter. If you don't believe that, consider the expression 'pulling your leg'. It means having fun at your expense. It does today—but what's its origin?

Until the last century, public executions by hanging were a great source of entertainment. Often the victim's neck would not break and he was left to writhe and strangle slowly. His friends were allowed to pull down on his legs in order to put him out of his misery. This was an added source of amusement for the onlooker crowd.[6]

So much for the modern view that a sense of humor is something intrinsically good and has always been that way. Only 400 years ago laughter was 'seen as a socially disruptive force'.[7] Not exactly the stuff that ads are made of.

What has this got to do with commercials? Not much today perhaps— except that it should serve as a warning that humor is not as simple as it often seems. The more you study humor and the more you track the effects of humorous ads, the more it emerges as a Jeckyl and Hyde phenomenon that can have both negative and positive effects.

Anatomy of humorous ads

What makes ads humorous? Let us explore this with an actual ad. Readers may recall a classic ad that showed a lovebird pecking at what seemed like food but was really the keys of a touch-tone telephone. The beeps indicated that it was accidentally dialing someone. Of course, this had to be accidental. Everyone knows birds don't dial. And even if they did, who would they call? Ah, but in the next scene we see a courier arrive—he picks up the sleeping cat with delivery note attached and departs to the off-screen sound of the bird twittering—or maybe chuckling. We suddenly realize it wasn't just random food-pecking behavior—the bird phoned the courier company to dispose of its nemesis, the cat.

So what makes a commercial like this one humorous? What's in it that makes us laugh? The key is in the incongruity. The bizarre picture of the bird pecking is mixed up with what we identify as a peculiarly human trait—that is, intelligent, manipulative behavior. Seemingly random pecking by a bird at telephone keys turns out to be cunning, deliberate behavior that you just don't expect from a bird.

So writers create humor by surprising us—but in a particular way. They force us momentarily to fuse together two things that already exist in our minds but are otherwise unrelated and incompatible (in this case, food pecking and dialing). Incongruity is something of a general formula.

Our minds lead us up the garden path—a bird pecking at a phone is naturally interpreted in terms of buttons being mistaken for food. But only momentarily, before we are then forced to accept the alternative interpretation of the scene that the bird was dialing and not just pecking. This happens when we see the courier pick up the cat. This interpretation makes the two things consistent and while it is experienced as bizarre it is also enjoyable. And therein lies the key to humorous ads.

The interesting thing is that jokes as well as humorous ads are often built intuitively by writers.[8] They notice the ambiguity in something (e.g. a visual scene, a word or phrase or a concept) and then create an incongruity. Instead of adopting the most obvious interpretation that everyone will take, they develop instead an alternative one. An interpretation that 'fits' but which is highly unlikely or bizarre in the context (i.e. the bird is dialing someone).

The conceptual elements that go into humorous ads such as this, and induce a mental switch from information to humor and hence enjoyment of the ad, are these:[9]

- two concepts (e.g. dumb bird and human intelligence);
- incongruity/incompatibility between them (i.e. one violates the other);
- confidence that the stimulus elements occurring as depicted is impossible or highly unlikely;
- a way of fusing the two and making them momentarily 'compatible'.

The evidence suggests that the greater the degree of incongruity the funnier the humor is seen to be. The more impossible or incompatible the two things are that are fused together, the more enjoyment people seem to derive from it.

Humorists and scientists

Fusing incongruent ideas like this is part of the much broader process of creativity. Humor has a lot in common with scientific creativity, for example. Arthur Koestler pointed out that humor is 'the bringing about of a momentary fusion between two habitually incompatible frames of reference'.[10] The creativity involved in writing humorous commercials is not unlike the creativity of scientific discovery. One strives for the 'ha ha' reaction, while the other strives for the 'ah haa…' reaction. The difference is that scientific discovery is the *permanent* fusion of the ideas previously believed to be incompatible. Humor is only a temporary fusion.

Comedy writer, Herbie Baker, who wrote for comedian Danny Kaye had an intriguing way of looking at incongruity. He believed that ideas struggle against each other to fight their way up to our conscious mind from the unconscious. Under normal circumstances, certain ideas are incapable of combining with one another. Usually, their incongruity blocks these ideas from making it successfully into the conscious mind. Creative people like scientists can somehow circumvent this situation and bring incongruous ideas into their minds in spite of this otherwise natural blocking tendency. Marty Feldman, the great comedian, expressed this pithily when he said: 'Comedy, like sodomy, is an unnatural act.'

Humorous ads

Ask the members of your family what advertisements make them laugh. The chances are they will say spontaneously, 'Oh, lots of them!'—and then fall silent. If you persist, they will eventually dredge out of memory a commercial that made them laugh. You will probably note how difficult it is for them immediately to bring to mind a specific example and, when they do, it is even more striking how much difficulty they have remembering the brand name of the product advertised.

What emerges clearly, however, from this as well as from the tracking of numerous funny commercials of various types is the underlying Jeckyl and Hyde phenomenon. The ads are entertaining and a lot of fun but, when they come to mind, they do so often without the brand. The first step in being able to make humor work effectively is to recognize its two faces: it has the potential for positive effects but it can have negative effects as well. We will see that much depends on precisely how the humor is executed.

There are three main mechanisms by which humor is supposed to work in advertising:

1. Less counter-arguing. Because we process them as entertainment (rather than engage in true/false evaluation of the content), there is less counter-arguing with humorous ads.
2. Humorous ads are noticed more—that is, they draw greater attention.
3. Humorous ads are generally *liked* more. Ads that are liked have a higher probability of being effective—all other things being equal.

Counter-arguing

The first mechanism is that humorous ads seem to invite less counter-arguing. When we read a fiction book we mentally process it differently from non-fiction. With fiction we engage in escapist enjoyment rather than true/false evaluation of what we are reading. Humor is entertainment and tends to be mentally processed in a different way from informational commercials. We are less likely to process the ad in terms of true/false evaluation.

Freud observed that the world of humor is 'a place to which we temporarily and symbolically return to the playful and happy mood of childhood'. When we switch into our enjoyment/humor appreciation mode, we switch-off our attempt to process the ad in a normal, informational or logical way.

The incongruous elements in the ad tip us off that this is meant to be humor and triggers a reset switch in our minds. We stop normal processing and sit back—hopefully to enjoy the absurdity and a momentary return to the playful, happy mood of childhood. But Mr Hyde is lurking—a reduction in counter-arguing can often be at the expense of correct branding of the ad. The risk with humor is always that we may be so focused on processing it as entertainment that little if any processing registers for the brand and the message.

Attention and recall

The second mechanism is attention-getting. In helping the ad to gain attention and break through we see perhaps the most positive side of humor. But Mr Hyde is never far away and whether that extra attention has a positive or negative effect depends greatly upon *where* the attention gets focused.

People who are mugged at gunpoint often find it difficult to give the police much in the way of any description of the mugger. Why? Because if someone points a gun at us, it hijacks our attention. Understandably, we become so focused on the gun that we take little notice of anything else.[11]

Humor may provide big guns for advertisers to help them get noticed among the clutter, but humor can hijack attention so totally that people don't take in the message or even the brand that is shown in the ad—they are too preoccupied with the humor. Now we begin to see why it is not really surprising that a number of studies have researched humorous ads and found they were no more effective than straight ads, or worse—they even impacted negatively on results.[12]

If you conduct your own 'family poll', as suggested above, chances are you will confirm that humorous ads have an unusually high risk of suffering a message and branding problem. Just as the use of high-profile presenters can distract us from processing the important elements of the brand and the message, so too can humor. If not used properly it will hijack our attention from the brand and the message. That does not mean that we should stop using humorous ads. We don't stop using high-profile presenters because of this effect. But we do have to take deliberate actions to overcome it. We have to make sure that the brand-message communication in these commercials is *so much stronger* in order to compensate for the overshadowing effect of the humor.

Integration of brand and execution

How do we do this? Apart from making the brand *very* visible, the best answer is to try to heavily integrate the brand with the execution. How often do we see an ad that is an entertaining piece of film but with the brand message hardly integrated at all into the story? All too often the brand appears in the commercial almost as a 'tag', at the end of the ad.

Ideally, the brand should be made an integral part of the execution of the ad, especially in the case of humorous ads because of the 'attention-overshadowing' effect of the humor.

What do we mean by *integration*? To illustrate, consider the classic Budweiser frogs commercial in the USA. Three frogs are croaking in turn and at first it just sounds like nonsense croaking. But as the croaks speed up and run together, the camera pans so that a large Budweiser sign comes into view and it becomes clear that the sound the frogs are making is 'Bud', 'Weis', 'Er'. Here the brand is well integrated. It is not just a tag or packshot but woven into the storyline.

A good test of how integrated the branding is in any ad is to play a little game of 'imagine'. Imagine the ad with your competitor's brand substituted in it instead of your own. Does the ad still make sense? Does the substitution violate the ad? If the competitor's brand fits the execution as well as yours, you are at risk. It is likely to brand poorly (unless you are the market leader or take other steps to strengthen the branding in the commercial). The creator of the famous Volkswagen Beetle campaign went so far as to say that if you take the brand out of the ad it should no longer be funny.

Many ads have good integration of the product category with the execution but not with the brand. For example, recall the ad mentioned above, with the lovebird that successfully disposes of the cat by pecking at the telephone keys to dial a courier company that comes to pick up the cat as a package. This was a great ad that ran globally and that many people still remember. Which courier company was it for?

If you can't answer that question then you are among many who could not recall the brand even when the ad was on air. In fact, the ad was for DHL couriers. Note that you could easily substitute FedEx into the commercial in your mind and it would do no violation to the ad whatsoever. The brand is not integrated with the execution. However, the product category is. You couldn't as easily change the product category to something else. A courier company is fundamental to the story-line and a key ingredient in making the humor work.

Consider another example—the chimp and mouse ad (Figure 15.2) for Security First Network Bank. It has a great visual and a great message. Correct brand registration is its potential weak spot. There is no integration of the brand, and it could potentially be recalled as being for any Internet bank. Or recall the Land Rover ad—a little kid knocks on the door of a Land Rover and, when the woman winds down the window, he asks 'Is Jason there—can he come out to play?' She says, 'Hold on, I'll check.' This is another great ad but, again, one with the potential to 'slip' in memory to a competitor such as Land Cruiser or Jeep. Again, there are no integrative branding elements.

Poor branding is especially likely to happen in commercials where the humor is peripheral to the brand message rather than integrated with it. This is because the audience is overly occupied with processing the humorous, executional elements of the commercial—things that have little if anything to do with the brand message and which hijack attention from the brand.

Ideally, the brand name itself should tie in, as in the Budweiser commercial. This is not an easy thing to do. In fact, some would argue that when it does happen it

Figure 15.2
Security First Network Bank
'If you know how to handle a mouse you can earn 6% on a bank checking.'

is pure genius. By way of illustration, consider, for example, how the love-bird/courier ad would have worked much better with some kind of tie-in to the DHL company name. The ad would have worked wonderfully for Kruger Allstates Transport (we made that up) because it would have been much harder to confuse it with any other company (like FedEx), the cat being an essential part of the ad. The KAT courier brand could be easily integrated as an executional element in the ad as Budweiser was in the frogs ad. Like the chorused croaks in the Budweiser ad, the cat would form an integral element in the commercial and act as a retrieval cue for the company brand. While it is much harder to do, if integration can be achieved it works far better than simply tacking the brand on at the end.

So one of the guidelines is to try to integrate the execution with the brand, not just the product. Ads like DHL, where only the product is inherently integrated with the execution, are very common and have to rely on other factors to stamp in the correct brand association. Unless the brand is integrated into the execution, even great humorous executions must be extra careful to make sure they register the brand in memory and guard against doing a generic advertising job for the product category as a whole.

Liking

Liking for a brand's advertising is the third mechanism. Just as a brand's packaging is part of its brand attire, so too a brand's advertising reflects the characteristic way it communicates. Liking for the way it communicates can add to the liking for the brand. A brand's advertising is one dimension of its personality. Just as humorous public speakers are appreciated, so humorous ads are *liked* and this has the potential to wash over onto the brand itself.

As we saw earlier, liking for a brand's advertising is a feather that can tip the balance towards that brand. In low-involvement categories where all brands in the category are virtually identical and there is often nothing new to say about the brand, then the 'beam-balance' mechanism comes into play. If all brands are equal, it takes only one additional feather on one side of the beam-balance to tip the decision to that brand. Liking the brand's advertising can be that feather. It is of somewhat less importance in high-involvement categories.

Humor therefore tends to be more effective in low-involvement categories because it can be an effective feather. But there is another reason why it does not usually work as well in high-involvement categories. When people are already highly involved, humor can be somewhat superfluous in attracting their attention. If the advertiser has some important information to tell people about a product they are highly involved in, then they are likely to be all ears. It won't necessarily get any more of their attention if you include humor, and it may distract them from the key message elements. So for both these reasons humor is less relevant to high-involvement categories than to low-involvement categories.

Wear-out

Conventional wisdom says that humorous ads wear out quickly, and certainly wear out faster than other ads. But do they? It is nowhere near that clear-cut. Some studies find that they do wear out more quickly[13] while other studies find no difference between humorous and normal ads.[14]

In tracking we have seen situations where humorous TV ads worked very effectively for over a year without showing signs of wear-out. In one case, for example, the ad was on air for two years before showing any signs of wearing out. The advertiser and the ad agency would have pulled the ad off air 18 months earlier but for the clear evidence coming from the tracking data.

Why do such contradictory results exist? One clue is in the social dimension. Laughter and humor are contagious—that's why they put laughter tracks in comedy shows. When we watch a funny ad our reactions are likely to be different depending on whether we are viewing it alone or with others. Ads that are viewed by audiences that typically consist of just one person have less chance of being seen as funny. Studies are fairly consistent in showing that people laugh more if they are with other people, and the more people the more they laugh.[15]

Two leading researchers suggest that this is why we get contradictory findings on the wear-out of humor. As they put it:

> ...some [ads] seem to get better, as *anticipation* of what will be presented evokes an anticipatory humorous response. If, in fact, a listener or viewer laughs because others do or have,...wearout of humor may be postponed ...certain television commercials seem to become 'funnier' over time as their punch-lines enter the language of popular culture and are repeated by professional comedians, as well as the general public.[16]

This exposes the fact that humor not only helps an ad break through and get attention but it may also succeed in making the ad itself a point of discussion and attention of the social group. Quiz shows like *Millionaire* and *Wheel of Fortune* owe a considerable amount of their success to this. Unlike most other TV programs they stimulate participation and discussion between members of the living-room audience ('I got that one right.' 'Wow...how did you know that?' 'I know the answer to this one!' etc).

This is not just a case of gaining greater attention. It takes on a significance and a level of enjoyment that comes about by the ad emerging from the TV set to become the focus of a conversational interaction ('Oh, look...here comes that great ad again! Doesn't that just break you up? I love that ad').

Summary

Humor remains one of the least understood elements in advertising—indeed, one of the least understood sides of life. We have a lot to learn yet about how to maximise the chances of humorous commercials working effectively but we are getting there. The available research is thin and doesn't provide anything like a clear view. The glimpses of insight can be extremely valuable, however—like peeking through venetian blinds. The view is not perfect but as someone once said: *'If it were not for venetian blinds it would be curtains for all of us'*!

16

Learning to use 15-second TV commercials

In Japan 80 per cent of TV spots consist of 15-second ads, while in other countries it is more like a third. Other countries are not Japan, however. There are fundamental cultural differences as well as apparent differences in the way we process ad information. As one ad agency points out, in Japan to be tight-lipped is to be trustworthy. Product demonstrations and user testimonials are generally not well received. 'The harder you try to explain something, therefore, the pushier you will appear...Where our TV commercials tend to progress from beginning to end, the Japanese often dispense with chronology altogether.'[1] In a culture like Japan, the 15-second solo commercial may work. In the USA, Europe, parts of Asia and Australasia, it rarely does—especially with low-involved audiences.

Fifteen-second commercials were first introduced in the 1980s. They were attractive to advertisers who had not been able to afford television advertising before, with the result that money was redirected out of print into 15-second TV commercials. At the same time regular TV advertisers also began to experiment with changing from 30-second ads to 15-second commercials, hoping for better value for money.

When we were browsing through information about which advertisers were on air in the previous week, we noted that one advertiser went on air with a single ad but with a large media weight of 450 TRPs for the week. With such a lot of exposures you would expect it to be generating a reasonable return. However, we were amazed when we saw the advertiser's ad

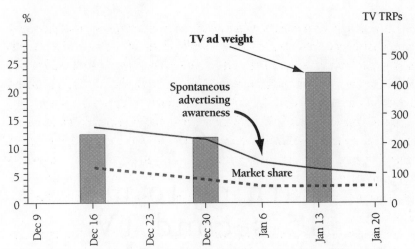

Note: The percentage of people spontaneously aware of this 15-second advertisement actually declined while it was on air as did the brand's market share.

Figure 16.1
15-second advertisement failure. *Source:* NFO MarketMind

awareness and market share information. Figure 16.1 shows that ad awareness and market share did not go up. They actually went down, despite all this weight of advertising! Crazy!

Intrigued by this, we played the ad. We wanted to see what ad could possibly be that bad. Fifteen seconds later we knew! It was a 15-second commercial, it had a fairly complex message, it was being aimed at a low-involved audience and it was being used as a solo.

Increasingly, in tracking 15-second commercials, we had observed that they rarely seemed to work when used on their own as a solo with low-involved audiences. Here was the starkest evidence yet. Even with 450 TRPs this ad seemed all but invisible. It did not break through, it was doing nothing for market share and nothing in the way of reinforcing people's feelings about the advertiser. It was a waste of money. The advertiser might as well have not been on air.

Conventional wisdom at the time was that a 15-second commercial is 'about two-thirds as effective as a 30-second commercial'. Driven by this erroneous belief, 15-second ads grew explosively in number throughout the late 1980s and early 1990s before levelling off as more and more people began to suspect that 'conventional wisdom' must be wrong. This point was made strongly in the first edition of this book, based on experiences like the one above.

Tracking numerous ad campaigns provided us with the opportunity, from time to time, to compare the performance of a 30-second ad aired in one region with the 15-second version of the same ad running simultaneously in another region. The results were generally clear-cut. Using 15-second ads as cut-down versions of 30-second ads rarely seemed to work, especially when they were used on their own as solos. *When* they work, 15-second commercials seem to work very differently from 30-second commercials.

United States researcher Lee Weinblatt has also questioned the merits of 15-second commercials, making the point that 'You can't communicate a believable message in so short a time, unless you started with 30-second commercials and built a case of communication, then brought in a 15-second commercial as a reminder'.[2] This is supported by the research findings of others.[3,4]

By the late 1990s there was less enthusiasm for 15-second commercials as the evidence continued to mount. The 'early call' in the first edition of this book was echoed in 1997 by researchers Von Gonten and Donius who concluded in 1997 from panel data:

> Wherever it has been possible to isolate the effect of 15's from 30's, the overwhelming majority of 15's have behaved as if off-air. Some few 15's perform strongly, but they are rare exceptions to the general finding.[5]

When our early warnings were first published, they aroused a big reaction. We were careful not to say that solo 15-second commercials cannot work. We did, however, emphasize that in our experience they almost never did. We had tracked a lot of commercials and it was the exception to come across a solo 15-second commercial that worked. They can work but the ones that do are the exceptions and not the rule. However, studying exceptions can be revealing.

One exception is shown in Figures 16.2 and 16.3. It had a lot of media weight behind it but it worked. Why? How did this campaign differ from the overwhelming number that we had seen fail? One difference was that it was extremely simple and single-minded, both visually and verbally. It did not try to do too much. The message was strongly communicated in both the visual and the verbal medium and it was an extremely simple message.

As a result of observing exceptions like these, we now have a greater understanding of how shorter commercials work and how they *can* be used to effect if advertisers learn how to use them, and also how *not* to use them. If you are going to use 15-second ads successfully they need to be designed differently and used in a different way.

What works, what doesn't, and why

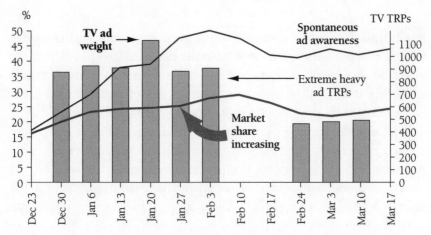

Note: This 15-second advertisement had an extremely simple and single-minded message along with extremely heavy advertising weight. It worked and market share increased— while it was on air!

Figure 16.2
A 15-second ad campaign that worked! *Source:* NFO MarketMind

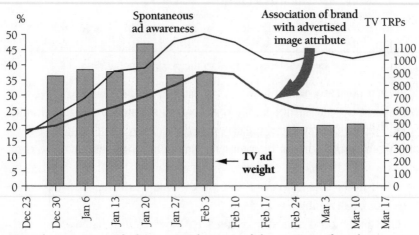

Note: The same 15-second advertisement also increased the percentage of people associating the brand with the advertised image attribute.

Figure 16.3
Percentage of people associating the brand with the advertised image.
Source: NFO MarketMind

Getting into people's heads versus staying there

A general principle in the psychology of learning is that it is harder to get into people's minds than it is to stay there. In other words, there are two processes: the process of learning and the process of priming and re-inforcement. One is original learning; the other maintains and reinforces the freshness of that learning. The process of reinforcement is not the same as the process of originally communicating something. It usually takes a longer commercial or more repetition to get an ad into people's minds in the first place than it does to keep an ad and its message there.

We know from psychology experiments that it takes much less time to recognize and process something that is familiar.[6] The more we prime (or activate) something, the more familiar it becomes. It is like priming a pump. The more it is primed the quicker it works.

A new commercial with new images and new messages takes longer for our minds to process than an established commercial. Fifteen seconds may be too short a time for our minds to process a new ad properly. Like fast-cut commercials they may just get lost. Even with words, the less frequently a word occurs in the language the longer it takes our minds to recognize and process it.

Familiarity and speed of processing

As Figure 16.4 shows, the time it takes us to recognize familiar words like 'chair' or 'book' when they are flashed on a screen is about one-tenth of a second compared with unfamiliar words (like 'bagpipes') which take *three times* longer.

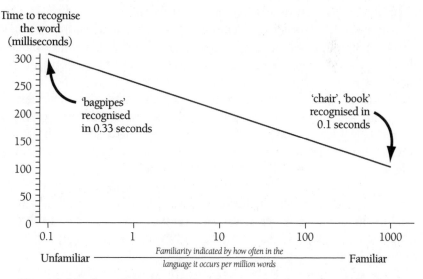

Note: It takes about three times longer for our minds to register and process relatively unfamiliar words like 'bagpipes' than it does to register common words like 'chair' or 'book'. (Adapted from *Journal of Experimental Psychology* 1951.)

Figure 16.4
We recognise the familiar more quickly

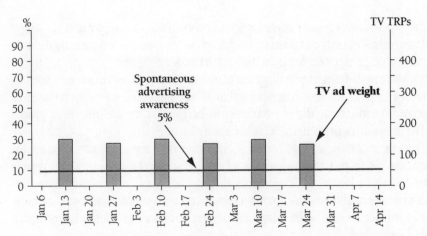

Note: The percentage of people who were spontaneously aware of this 15-second advertisement never rose above 5%.

Figure 16.5

Another 15-second ad failure. *Source:* NFO MarketMind

Our minds process words and ads much more quickly and easily when they are familiar. Hence, when we see shorter-length commercials or we fast-forward (zap) through ads on a prerecorded program, we are more likely to be able to pick up the communication if the ad is already familiar.

The general 'take-out' point here is that it is useful to advertisers to think about ads in terms of how much time our minds need to mentally process the elements of the ad and how many exposures it takes to develop a 'mental model' of it.

Shorter-length commercials are the occupying forces. They are best at occupying and holding the mental ground that has already been captured by the longer-length commercials. These longer-length ads are the attack forces. They are good for bringing about learning. They are good for getting a message into people's heads in the first place.

Our tracking research shows that 15-second commercials can be quite effective in holding mental ground *after* longer-length commercials have been used to capture it. However, when used on their own, as solos, 15-second commercials often prove disappointing and ineffective (see Figure 16.5, for example).

Lost in the clutter

Usually, the first thing you want an ad to do is to break through the clutter and get noticed. Fifteen-second commercials, when used as a solo with low-involved audiences, have great difficulty breaking through the clutter. Time and time again, we have found that 15-second commercials are generally disappointing at breaking through on their own except when the audience is highly involved with the product (Figure 16.5).

This is despite the fact that 15-second ads are usually screened at greater repetition levels than 30-second commercials. One of the seductive attractions of 15-second commercials is that advertisers can get more repeat exposure for the same ad budget than they can with a 30-second ad. But even at very high exposure levels, 15-second solo ads often fail to register at the level of conscious ad recall.

There have been amazingly few exceptions. And the exceptions are usually due to the great creative idea in the commercial or to the audience being highly involved with the product category. You need exceptionally creative ads or a highly involved audience or an extremely simple message, if you are going to use 15-second commercials as solos. Otherwise they just seem to disappear into the ether.

Message communication

Capturing mental ground means not only breaking through but also correctly delivering a message or an impression. We have found 15-second commercials when used on their own to be extremely weak in message communication with low-involved audiences. So when they do break through (which is rarely), they seem unable to communicate anything but the simplest of messages.

Table 16.1 shows the results of another 15-second ad campaign. Compared with a 45-second campaign for the same product category, run at a different time, its performance is abysmal.

This 15-second commercial campaign went for six weeks with a huge number of exposures (a total of 1850 TRPs, or over 300 TRPs per week). Despite this heavy media weight it achieved only 25 per cent prompted recognition and only 4 per cent correct message take-out.

Table 16.1 illustrates dramatically that a key weakness of 15s is in getting across a message. Their main function is one of reminder, that is, reinforcing an already learned brand or message. Fifteen-second commercials won't communicate unless the message is extremely simple, or the 15-second ad is a reminder ad following from a longer one (i.e. where the message is one the audience has been exposed to and internalised previously).

We stress that this is when used on their own, when the message is anything more than a visually supported, very single-minded statement, and

Table 16.1
Comparison of advertisement campaigns

	45 seconds	15 seconds
Length of campaign	2 weeks	6 weeks
Total TRPs	400	1850
Execution cued ad recognition	49%	25%
Share of voice	28%	19%
Correct message take-out	30%	4%

Source: NFO MarketMind

when the audience is not highly involved. When the message is a very simple one and one that has been established before by longer-length commercials, then 15-second ads can work cost-effectively. An example is the Trident chewing gum ads where the mother walks up to a group of kids and says: 'Who wants gum?' To which she gets the resounding response 'I do, I do!' An irritating yet simple use of 15s to help raise the brand's position on the mental agenda, with no reliance on anything but the simplest of messages to make them work.

Blame the creatives?

Some people take the view that the failure of so many 15-second commercials is the fault of the creative teams. This argument says that any commercial will work if the creatives and the media are right.

In light of the many solo 15s that we have seen fail, we think it is unjust and far too simplistic to blame this on the creative teams. To do so ignores what is now widely acknowledged—that there are inherent limitations to shorter ads. It ignores the fact that 15 seconds may be an impossibly short time in which to get across the great majority of messages—at least from a standing start.

Yes, part of the creative team's job is to package messages cleverly in such a way that they communicate easily, quickly and entertainingly. But 15 seconds is a very short time in which to communicate anything successfully. In those few instants the ad has to:

- tune viewers out of the previous commercial or program that they are watching;
- lock their attention onto the ad;
- communicate the brand name;

- get across an effective message;
- consolidate the memory trace before the next ad comes along (with the potential to interfere with the mental processing of what has just been said).

Tuning in takes time

We believe that the first and last of these are important reasons why so many solo 15-second ads turn out to be less effective than expected. It takes time for people to tune out of one communication and into another. This applies to conversations or any other abrupt changes in our stream of thought. And it also applies to ads.

It takes us time, even though it is brief, to switch from what we are currently thinking about or attending to and retune our thoughts to something else. All of us can relate to the experience of being interrupted while doing something and then having to ask the interrupter to repeat what they have just said. That's because we were tuned in to something else and it took time to switch over.

It is easy to be deceived by the fact that we are talking about only very small amounts of time for this mental switching to take place. It may only be a couple of seconds, but this is a couple of seconds out of our mental processing time. And it is sobering to realize that in a 15-second commercial a couple of seconds represents 13 per cent of the total exposure time that may be down-time for this reason alone.

A problem may exist in the final seconds of the commercial as well. The 'interruption' interference effect on mental processing may also apply to the last second or two of the ad content.[7] The memory trace for this has the potential to be interfered with by the next commercial. Psychological experiments show that interruption by, and switching to, the next event (the next ad) attenuates the mental processing and memory of what went on in the few seconds immediately before the interruption.[8]

So what this means is that, for up to a quarter of the time of the 15-second ad, the viewer's mental processing may be subject to interference effects of one kind or another (at the start and finish).

Fifteens as cost-efficient reminders

Many of the 15-second campaigns that critics say have worked turn out *not* to be solos or 'stand-alones'. Instead, they are often reminders reinforcing a previous campaign (such as the Trident 'Who wants gum?' campaign). This is not what we mean by 'solo' 15s. This is building on or retriggering what has gone before. It is advertising that ties closely back into, and reoccupies, the mental territory that has already been captured.

The point is that it takes more time and effort to get into people's heads in the first place than it does to stay there—or to retrigger memories that reside there and are well established. In such situations 15s can work well.

The general implication is clear. If we need to convey a message then the preferred strategy is to use longer-length commercials to get it across first, to firmly entrench it, before switching to 15-second (*reminder*) commercials. Fifteen-second commercials can definitely give us reinforcement and reminders at lower cost, but only if the main message has first been communicated with the longer commercial. (A lecturer can successfully shorten his delivery if the audience is already familiar with the topic.)

Ways 15s commercials have been used

- As a *reminder*: e.g. a 30-second ad followed, after initial bursts, by 15-second reminder ads. This works.
- As a *fast-follower*: e.g. a 30s and a 15s cut-down of the first one appearing in the same commercial break. The 30-second commercial is shown first up with the 15-second shortened version used last in the same break. More often than not, this works.
- As a '*sequel*': e.g. a 30-second commercial first up in the break with a 15-second commercial that extends the story appearing last in the break. More often than not, this also works.
- As a *mixture-ingredient*: e.g. 30s and 15s randomly scheduled in the same week. This seems to have little going for it.
- '*Back-to-back*': e.g. two 15s in a 30-second pod. Sometimes used in the United States. Unlikely to work unless the ads are for two *related* products (e.g. toothbrushes and toothpaste for the same brand—say, Colgate). These have the potential to appear as almost a 'seamless' 30 seconds of advertising for the brand's dental hygiene products.
- As a *solo*: 15s used entirely on their own. Usually don't work unless (1) highly creative, (2) simple message, (3) high involvement.

Audience motivation

How does the level of audience motivation change the situation for 15-second commercials? Are the principles different if we use 15s to advertise to a highly involved audience? People who are highly involved are more attentive and also have lower thresholds. To go back to our word recognition experiments, people who have not eaten for several hours recognize food words (like apple, bread, cake) faster than those who have just eaten. Hunger makes them process food words faster because their minds are more attuned to any stimuli that may be relevant to that immediate need.

Most of the tests we have done of 15-second commercials have been with low-involvement, fast-moving package goods. Funnily enough, until recently there seems to have been less inclination to try 15s in higher-involvement product categories such as cars or business products and services. Yet it is precisely here, with the more highly involved audiences, that 15-second ads should have a better chance of working—but the message still needs to be simple.

It is less demanding to get through to an interested, motivated audience. The communicator has to put in less work to get the message across because the audience is predisposed to put in more effort to understand and internalise the communication. Highly motivated students are likely to pay more concentrated attention to the lecturer and work harder at trying to understand and internalise what he has to say. There is less onus on the lecturer because the students are more naturally attentive.

We rarely find this level of involvement in advertising. However, when aimed at highly involved groups, a 15-second ad can work in its own right—if the message is simple. It may apply, for example, to a business ad with something new to say that is aimed at an involved audience watching a business program. Or a Toyota dealer advertising a red-hot price on Corollas to people actively shopping around for a Corolla. The key here is involvement, which affects not only attention but also the amount of work the recipient is prepared to do to take out the message.

Summary

What needs to improve is the ability of advertisers and ad agencies to realistically select the brands and strategies that lend themselves to 15-second commercials, and to use the ads in ways that maximise the chances for effectiveness. We can no longer afford to ignore the growing evidence on 15-second commercials.

- Solo, stand-alone 15-second commercials are all too often used inappropriately and rarely work, especially with low-involved audiences.

- If the audience is not highly involved and/or the message is not visually simple, don't use 15-second commercials as solos.
- Consider 15s as cost-efficient reminder ads after the mental territory has been captured with longer-length commercials.
- Or consider using a 15-second ad as a sequel, topping and tailing it with a longer length ad at the beginning and a 15-second ad at the end of the break.
- Remember that 15s have extreme difficulty breaking through the clutter. They also add to the clutter. (A three-minute ad break can consist of six 30-second ads or twelve 15-second ads.)

17

Seasonal advertising

All advertising is not created equal. And all product categories are not the same. It is clear to us from tracking numerous ad campaigns in various parts of the world that there are important seasonal influences on advertising.

Seasonal product categories

Products that are seasonal to a greater or lesser extent include:

- *Summer:* ice creams, suntan lotions, soft drinks, swimwear, beer and charcoal.
- *Winter:* canned soup, chocolate bars, chocolate cookies, cough and cold preparations.
- *Seasonal events:* electric razors (most of which are sold for Father's Day and Christmas); children's shoes and school supplies (start of school year); champagne (New Year) and greeting cards.
- *In addition:* some public-authority and utility advertising campaigns may be distinctly seasonal (e.g. save water (summer), prevent forest fires (summer), drink driving, speed kills (holiday seasons), etc).

Some of these things are pretty obvious, but all too often we realise this only in retrospect. It is easy to fail to be aware of them or to be distracted from them in the product management process.

Perceived popularity

We referred earlier to the 'perceived popularity' of a product and the role that advertising plays in it. Brand popularity can be self-fulfilling. If people see something as popular the chances are enhanced that, provided everything else is equal, they will follow suit and buy the brand. Perceived popularity can tip the balance.

Sometimes, products gather momentum through their advertising. The brand is seen as increasingly popular. And just when it is about to really catch on, the visibility and impetus suddenly stop. Why? Because 'the season' is over. This points to one key difference in marketing seasonal products, especially in the way we go about developing a new brand.

The need for accelerated trial

With product categories that are seasonal, advertisers have limited time to build momentum. They have to make the product 'catch on' in much less time than they would have for a non-seasonal product. They are always racing to beat the seasonal clock.

Even with non-seasonal products there is an unwritten rule of thumb that you need to aim for maximum trial for a new brand in the first three to six months. Otherwise, it loses that sense of newness. It risks acquiring an image of having been around for a while and not having taken off. If this sets in, it makes gaining further trial all the more difficult to achieve.

With a seasonal product the problem is acute. If the ad can't create a sense of the brand having taken off in the first season, chances are that by its return in the second season the brand will risk being perceived as 'old hat'. People will remember that it was around last season but 'didn't seem to catch on'. This can be the kiss of death.

Maximising the proportion of people who try the product is crucial to success. Remember, a 20 per cent market share can be achieved in two very different ways:

1. If only 20 per cent of people have tried the brand but they are buying it 100 per cent of the time.
2. If 100 per cent of people have tried the brand but are buying it only 20 per cent of the time (i.e. one in every five times they buy the product category).

To give a brand the maximum chance of success it is important to aim for maximum trial as early as possible. If the trial rate at the end of the first season has reached only 25 per cent it means the brand is relying on a very high repeat buying rate to achieve satisfactory market share and viability. More to the point, it will not be until next season that the brand will get a crack at the 75 per cent of consumers who have not yet tried the brand. By that time it may be too late.

The off-season pause

With seasonal products, the off-season period of inactivity is regarded by many advertisers as a temporary interruption. When it is over they simply expect to resume where they left off last season, in the same way as restarting a video after pausing in freeze frame.

But does it? It is dangerous to assume that activity will resume again next time, even if it has always done so. Memories fade, attitudes change, people change and competitors may try to influence the market during the off-season. If you have spent real effort and a lot of money during the season to capture the mental territory of consumers' minds, can you leave the opening round of next season's battle to chance?

It is worth considering occupation strategies during that off-season to attempt to hold onto the mental territory you captured.

Extending the season

In the USA Lipton very effectively expanded the tea 'season' into summer by promoting iced tea so that, today, about three-quarters of all tea in the USA is consumed cold. In Australia, the 'Speed kills' and 'Don't drink and drive' campaigns were traditionally seasonal. Now they run throughout the year, with demonstrable benefits. Kit Kat, formerly a winter product, extended its season from winter to embrace summer through its 'Cool Kat' campaign that urged us to keep our Kit Kats in the refrigerator and enjoy them cold.

The idea is to find ways during the off-season to maintain what has been built up in the season. This may be in people's minds or behavior or both.

An example

Figure 17.1 shows one example of a highly seasonal campaign. This was a 'save water' utility campaign which ran over two months each year. It was

What works, what doesn't and why

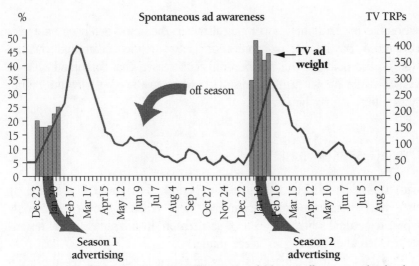

Note: A seasonal advertising campaign that is successful but its effect is very shortlived.
Figure 17.1
Seasonal advertising campaign. *Source:* NFO MarketMind

very successful. Note that it achieved about 48 per cent spontaneous advertising awareness in the first season.

The campaign was very successful...*while it was on air*. But it was on air for only two months of the year. This campaign built extremely good awareness but five weeks after the advertising stopped its effect had decayed and was virtually gone. Like the 'speed kills' campaign, it was aimed at influencing people's behavior. The need for this is more acute in the key period, but it is also present throughout the year albeit at a lower level.

A better strategy would be to have built the awareness in the key months (to 48 per cent) and then, instead of going off air completely until the next year, to implement a low-cost maintenance advertising campaign to run through the other ten months of the year. With a maintenance schedule of shorter length TV ads

- one week on air followed by
- one week off air followed by
- one week on air, etc

and at a low exposure (a maintenance weight of say 75 TRPs per week) and/or reminder ads in magazines and newspapers in that off-season, this organization would have spent the same amount of money but with much more continuous effect.

The point is that if you build public awareness to a high level and then let it come all the way down again by going off air completely, it takes just as much effort to build it from scratch next time. It is usually much more economical to build the awareness and then try to maintain it with lowered advertising weight or support media. The principle is that it takes more expenditure to get into people's minds in the first place than it does to stay there.

Get in early

If your product category is truly seasonal and you and your competitors always start advertising in a particular month, consider jumping the gun. Get in first. This recommendation is based on the principle that it is easiest to get into people's heads *when there is little or no competing advertising clutter.*

If you can capture the mental territory before your competitors come on air, your job is easier—a maintenance task, not a building task. You have already captured the mental territory and it is easier and less expensive in the face of clutter to hold the ground you have won. Getting in early can be an effective strategy. (But make sure you also send in the occupation forces in the form of a maintenance campaign when the competitors come on air.)

Who determines seasonality?

Is your product truly seasonal? For some products, seasonality is almost dictated by what the advertisers do—or don't do—in the off-season. With some products, all brands seem to observe a conventional promotional seasonal cycle. The dictum seems to be: We only advertise in the season.

As some of the previous examples show, it is sometimes the marketers as much as the consumers who determine whether something is seasonal. If marketers believe it is seasonal, this is likely to be a self-fulfilling prophecy. Products are rarely as inherently seasonal as we are inclined to believe.

Take the soft drink market, for example. Users consume primarily because they are thirsty. And it is true that people get thirstier more often in summer. Hence the soft drink product is seasonal. However, brands like Coca-Cola and Pepsi Cola have been deliberately given a social overlay—an image that makes the drink function as a 'social lubricant' for teenagers and not just as a simple thirst-quencher.

This adds functionality and at the same time reduces the seasonality of these two brands compared with ordinary soft drink. Like beer, they tend to be consumed more in summer but are also drunk in winter in substantial volume for social reasons.

The changeover-to-daylight-saving trap

Seasonal products have limited peak season time on TV. However, at certain times of the year, often the times when seasonal products need to advertise, there is a peculiar problem. In the summer holiday season, for example, there is significant doubt about how many people are going to be away on vacation and will therefore not be sitting in front of their TV sets being exposed to that advertising.

Another, not so well recognized, problem that is important in some countries with seasonal products is the changeover-to-daylight-saving trap. This is especially a trap for any brand that might think about relying heavily on advertising during the evening news. The changeover to daylight saving in summer means that a number of people this week, who last week at 6 pm were sitting in front of their TVs watching the news, may no longer be watching TV at that time. They may be out kicking a football or swinging a bat with their kids or doing something else in the new-found hour of daylight. With seasonal products, beware of this changeover-to-daylight-saving trap.

18

Underweight advertising: execution anorexia

How many exposures does an ad need to be effective? And in what period of time? No one knows for sure. Another way of putting it is: Is there a minimum threshold of media weight needed to make an ad campaign work? The answer seems to be 'yes'.[1]

A case example

We once saw a new campaign come very close to being cancelled by the client. A whole battery of effectiveness-tracking measures said the campaign was having a disappointing and marginal impact. The client was close to the point of concluding that 'the ads are hopeless'.

The media weight for this campaign was around 150 TRPs per week. This means that the people who were the target market for the product were supposed to be exposed to it on average about 1.5 times a week.[2] At least that was what was planned. But before labeling any campaign a failure, or concluding that 'these ads don't work', it is crucial to look at the actual TRP figures, the actual *delivered*, as distinct from the planned, media weight.

Sometimes ads do not go to air because of a mix-up. Sometimes the buying of air time is not as good as it should be. Sometimes (as in the changeover to daylight saving, holiday periods, etc) there are not as many people watching TV as there were the previous week. When these actual

TRP figures were obtained (some two months after the campaign had started), it emerged that only about 60 per cent of the planned weight was in fact achieved (i.e. about 90 TRPs per week).

Corrective action was taken and in the subsequent weeks the planned exposure rate, the full 150 TRPs per week, was achieved. With this weight the campaign went on to perform amazingly well in the test market and later nationally. The reason the campaign was not working originally had little to do with the creativeness of the commercials. It was like listening to a signal from deep space. The signal was too faint. The volume had to be turned up.

Here was a perfectly good creative campaign which could have gone down in the annals of 'great advertising failures'. The problem was not the ads themselves but a level of exposure that was too low.

Execution anorexia

Why was the difference between 150 TRPs (planned) and 90 TRPs (actual) so critical? Ninety TRPs was 40 per cent less than had been planned but, while it may be a light weight, many ad schedules have succeeded at only 100 TRPs per week. The difference between 150 and 90 TRPs a week may not seem much, but this campaign had three executions (three ads) being rotated on air in each week. This means that each ad was being exposed at the rate of only about 30 TRPs per week. This is a very low figure and evidently below a critical threshold for effectiveness—at least in that particular market.

There is a valuable lesson here. When planning a media schedule, the threshold TRP weights cannot be decided without taking account of the number of ad executions that will be used. The advertising weight must be set in terms of the number of TRPs per execution and not just in terms of an overall figure. Many advertisers use multiple executions (e.g. Coke, Ford, Microsoft) but recognition of this point is all too often the exception rather than the rule. The rule is that, in media planning, it is important to factor into the advertising schedule the number of TRPs per ad execution in addition to the overall campaign weight. Otherwise the campaign can end up, like this one, with execution anorexia and underweight advertising.

One execution or many?

This raises an important question. What is the optimum number of ad executions to air in any one week? One? Two? Three? Is it better to have one execution or many?

We wish we could tell you that the answer was straightforward and simple. It's not. One thing is for sure, however. Multiple executions have to be considered carefully in terms of tightness of integration, media weight, flighting of each execution and particularly the degree of involvement of the target audience. Especially with low-involvement products, the use of multiple executions can be counterproductive. We have seen as many as six ad executions used for the same brand in one week. Were they effective? No! If there is a general rule that emerges it is this: for low-involvement products don't use multiple executions or, if you do, be prepared to back each one with substantial TRP weight in its own right.[3]

There may be examples of tightly integrated campaigns where multiple executions have worked well but the general note should be one of caution. Being single-minded is usually best.

Low vs high involvement

How many TRPs you need to get effective response from advertising depends on the involvement of the audience as well as the number of ad executions you intend putting to air. Low- and high-involvement audiences process ads, and the information in them, quite differently.

Communicating to a target audience that is highly involved in what you have to say differs from communicating with people who don't care too much. How? Here is a summary.

- Highly involved target audiences are more motivated and actively looking for information.
- As a result the ad may require less repetition, and print media may often work very effectively.
- Advertising to highly involved audiences has been shown to be less subject to interference in memory when they see subsequent ads for competitive brands. The implication of this is that you should be able to get away with a lower share of voice (i.e. a lower share of the total ad spend in the product category) than would be the case for low-involvement products.
- Some evidence suggests that advertising to highly involved audiences is not as subject to minimum TRP thresholds as is advertising to low-involved audiences.
- Advertising to high-involvement audiences is therefore thought to be less sensitive to the number of ad executions on air—but only relatively.

Guidelines for the low-involvement audience

A crucial difference with low-involvement products is that the advertising has to capture the attention of the low-involved consumer. This is certainly the case with most packaged goods.[4] Advertising for low-involvement products puts a premium on highly creative and sometimes bizarre ad executions to make the advertising break through the clutter.

For low-involved audiences the overriding task is to break through the clutter of other ads and force people to notice the ad and its message. If you don't break through, the ad doesn't get noticed and the chances are that nothing happens. Consumers don't 'see' the ad and don't process the communication (see Chapter 24, '"Mental reach": they see your ad but does it get through?').

The ad and the message need to be very single-minded. Once you have forced attention, you have only limited time and tolerance to get your message across and have it processed effectively. The message has to be simple. The temptation to incorporate several messages in the same ad or in different ads needs to be cut off at the knees. An uninvolved audience just won't work hard enough to take in all the elements of your communication. If it requires anything other than easy processing, you have lost them.

Even when you get your message across with low-involved audiences, the way it has been processed makes it particularly subject to interference and memory degradation *through subsequent exposure to competitive commercials* for other brands. This is why, with low-involved audiences, repetition at that initial stage of getting the campaign into people's heads in the first place is so necessary. With highly involved audiences the desired effect may often be achieved and maintained with much less repetition because (a) the audience works harder on the message in the first place, and (b) this greater 'elaboration', as it is called, consolidates the information in memory, thereby rendering it less subject to subsequent interference and memory degradation from exposure to other competitive commercials.

With low-involved audiences you not only have to get the information in, you have to work to keep it there. This is where 15-second commercials come into their own, along with print media tie-ins with the TV commercial—that is, to provide repetition and reinforcement (see Chapter 16, 'Learning to use 15-second TV commercials').

For all these reasons, the number of executions on air and the TRP weight behind each execution are critical for low-involved audiences.

Underweight advertising: execution anorexia

Another case example

Research has revealed a number of occasions on which multiple executions have been a problem in effectively communicating a low-involvement product. Figure 18.1 illustrates one such case. This is a frequently purchased, low-cost and relatively low-involvement product.

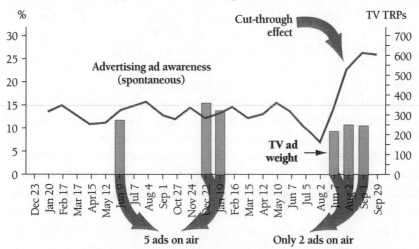

Note: This graph shows greater overall advertisement cut-through associated with fewer on-air executions for this brand. Executions reduced from five to two in any one week had a dramatic effect on advertisement awareness.

Figure 18.1
Number of advertising executions. *Source:* NFO MarketMind

   This brand was advertised with up to five different ad executions—that is, five ads on air for the same brand. The company then cut back on the number of different executions being rotated on air and this had a dramatic effect on advertisement awareness.

Mixed-involvement audiences

To make things even more complicated, some product categories have mixed audiences—a problem that some ad agencies do not seem to recognize explicitly in the ad planning process. For example, with most durable goods (cars, PCs, appliances, telephone systems, etc) you have at one time some people who are ready to buy and highly involved and some who may not buy for several months or years and who are relatively little involved.

   Audiences are rarely homogeneous. Some people will be highly involved and some will be less involved. In the planning process the advertiser needs to know the mix of the target audience.

To take one example, the audience for new car ads is often thought to be 100 per cent high-involvement because only people in the market for a new car are thought to be worth targeting. This is a mistaken view. A third of the people who will buy new cars in the next three months don't yet know they will do so. These people are unaware of what is just around the corner.

Some of them will find their present car starting to break down over the next three months; or, if not their car, their marriage. So some will separate from their spouse and find themselves in need of another car. Some will be relocated in their jobs; and still others will come in for an unexpected windfall such as an inheritance or a lottery win.

These are just some of the many things that put people into a market when they didn't expect to be there. Right now they may be low-involved but very soon they may well be much more highly involved. So, like it or not, in these categories an advertiser needs to communicate with both the uninvolved and the involved consumer. The ad strategy can ill afford to assume that the only people worth targeting and communicating with are the highly involved ones.

Summary

Not every ad campaign is going to succeed. But don't let your campaign die from underweight advertising. Here is a small checklist.

1. Check that your planned Reach, Frequency and TRP weights are in fact achieved.
2. Especially with low-involvement products, use a single execution unless there is a very good reason for doing otherwise.
3. If you are using multiple executions, make sure you check for the possibility of execution anorexia. Check the number of TRPs per execution per week. (Execution anorexia can be fatal to a campaign's health.)
4. As a rough rule of thumb, if you can't afford to put an absolute minimum of 50 TRPs per week behind each execution, don't risk using a multiple execution strategy. Stay with a single execution and do it well.
5. Check the involvement mix of your audience.

19

Why radio ads aren't recalled

Why is a lot of radio advertising so poorly remembered? It doesn't have pictures and it doesn't have the reach of television, but is there more to it than that? Even saturation campaigns don't seem to make it into the consumer's mental filing cabinet to the extent that one might expect. For example, one 'successful' saturation radio campaign that ran for a 16-week period in a specific target market was one of the highest-scoring campaigns we have seen in regard to radio ad awareness, yet it did not get more than 40 per cent of people to spontaneously recall the advertising.

Attention and pictures

Radio is not TV and it is not a substitute for TV. It could be used more effectively, but advertisers often seem to use it wrongly. The two main problems with radio seem to be listener attention levels and the fact that radio advertising doesn't have pictures. Advertisers can do something about both these factors by designing more effective radio ads and media schedules.

Radio competes with its environment for the listener's attention—much more so than TV, which usually has its own, relatively quiet exposure environment. When people watch TV they more often do so with fewer distractions. That is not to say that TV audiences are glued to the set. Brands in low-involvement product categories, particularly, have to rely on very creative ad executions to grab and hold their audience's attention.

Radio, however, competes with all sorts of things. At breakfast it competes with the clatter of cutlery, the sounds of breakfast preparation and breakfast conversation. Again, in the morning and drive-time slots, radio has to work exceptionally hard to break through a different kind of 'attentional clutter'. This 'clutter' is made up of the peak-hour traffic, the business of driving and passenger conversation, as well as the person's own thoughts.

So at certain times of the day, many listeners just aren't listeners in any full attentional sense. Radio's traditional listeners, who in its early days sat glued to programs like *Amos and Andy* or *The Goon Show* emanating from the bakelite mantle radio, have gone to television. Nowadays, peak-time radio listeners are a low-involved lot. They are schizophrenically pressured from minute to minute by the many stimuli that compete for their attention.

Whether it is radio, TV, or point-of-sale advertising, the ad has to break through. Then it has to deliver its communication. At the same time it has to succeed in registering the correct brand. So it is important with radio and low-involvement advertising generally not to look just for people's ability to recall the ad. Advertisers also need to look for behavior, attitude, image and salience effects before concluding simply from the lack of recall that the advertising is not working (see Chapter 26, 'The buy-ology of mind').

Lessons for using radio

The message we want to communicate here is certainly not that advertisers should use less radio—that would be throwing out the baby with the bath water. Rather, we think the need is to use radio more intelligently and more effectively. Here are a few pointers.

- **Don't rely solely on recall as a measure of effectiveness.**
Look also for other shifts, especially gradual image shifts, and any influence on stimulating product-category consumption (as distinct from brand selection).
- **Use more selective time periods.**
Clearly advertisers are likely to have more effect with radio (and TV) if they choose periods (or programs or stations) that offer less competition in the environment, less likelihood that the audience will be distracted. These may be the times when the listener base is at its lowest. So each spot may be more effective in itself, but among fewer people. This means using more spots but at a lower cost per spot.

- **Create better radio ads.**

Put money into making better ads—ads that demand attention and break through. Too many radio ads are awful. There is a logical reason for this. Radio is regarded as the low-budget medium. But keeping costs down at the expense of skimping on good writing and production seems to be the ultimate in false economy with radio.

- **Use radio for involved, dedicated listeners.**

Some segments (such as teenagers) seem to pay more attention to radio. They are more involved with and more dedicated to the medium because it, and its content, are an important part of their own peer-group subculture.

- **Use TV first to provide faces and visuals. Generate reminders and reinforcement through radio.**

Most people process something more easily and retain it better and longer when they associate pictures and faces with it. Pictures or 'visuals' act as memory hooks of the mind. This puts the focus on concrete messages and imagery. Use TV to give people the pictures and then use radio as a retrieval cue—that is, to *reinforce* the brand and the message that have already been associated with those pictures; for example, the sound track or jingle from the TV commercial. Fifteen-second TV commercials usually fail when used alone as attack forces. However, when used as occupation forces they can be remarkably effective. Radio can be used in the same way with low-involvement products.

- **Take advantage of the immediacy of radio.**

Exposure to advertising is attended to more (processed more deeply) and has more effect the closer the customer is to the purchasing occasion. Schedule radio tactically to hit the maximum number of consumers immediately before the purchase occasion (e.g. Thursday and Friday after 10 am is when a lot of supermarket shopping is done in some countries).

- **Take advantage of the flexibility and immediacy of radio to stimulate consumption.**

For example, Campbell's Soups in the United States sets aside $750 000 a year to run radio commercials on days when a storm threatens.[1] People are more likely to think of soup and eat soup when the weather turns bad.

- **Mention the brand name in the first eight seconds and a minimum of three times during the ad.**

This finding emerged from US studies of 30-second TV commercials. My guess is that it is probably even more important for radio than for TV.

Summary

The aim must be to break through the clutter and get attention in order to deliver the ad message, or the chances are that your communication won't have anywhere near the desired effect. The more attention an ad gets, the more effectively it is likely to communicate and the more it is likely to be recalled. If it gets only a low level of attention it is likely to be at best inefficient and at worst ineffective.

There is scope for using radio a lot more intelligently and to greater effect. Radio is a medium that is rarely well done!

20

Maximizing ad effectiveness: develop a unique and consistent style

Category conformity

Sameness, sameness everywhere! You can't see the forest for the trees. Too many product categories gravitate towards a single style of 'look-alike' advertising. The style becomes 'generic' to the category and we end up with entrenched category conformity.

For many years analgesics (aspirin, paracetamol) was one of these categories. Almost every brand's ad showed a glass with a tablet being dropped into it while the voice-over advised: 'If pain persists, see your doctor.' This is what we call the chameleon commercials syndrome. Instead of standing out from their environment, ads like this blend in with and virtually disappear into the background. The problem is that the ads are not distinctive enough to break through the clutter in the category and deliver the brand and the message.

In one dramatic case, before the commercial went to air we showed several still shots from it to respondents and asked if they had seen this ad recently. The ad was for a brand of pain-reliever. Forty-three per cent of the group claimed to have seen the ad on TV recently—before the ad went to air. Not surprisingly, most of these people said they had no idea who the advertiser was, or thought the ad was for some other advertiser.

How can people claim to have seen a commercial that has never been aired? What does this mean? It means that the visuals (and the audio) in the commercial were generic. They were similar to those used by other brands in the category. They could belong to anybody. If the brand were changed, it would do no harm to this commercial. One brand name could have fitted this ad just as well as any other. When it did go to air, it never achieved a recognition rate of more than 60 per cent. This was despite the advertising being scheduled to reach more than 90 per cent of the target audience—a very disappointing but nevertheless predictable result (see Chapter 24, '"Mental reach" they see your ad but does it get through?').

Beware of generic elements in commercials whether visual or verbal. A high level of false recognition before the ad goes to air is a good early warning indicator of this. It is telling you that the advertising is 'look-alike' advertising—that is, an ad that people already have a mental model of. If such advertising is allowed to go to air, many of those who see the ad will not remember who the advertiser was.

So here's a suggestion to improve your advertising. Conduct a small test. Take your ad. If it is a TV ad, turn down the sound track and, as you watch it, imagine a competitor's brand being substituted for your own brand. You can do the same thing with a print ad. Imagine a competitor's brand substituted for your own. Does it do harm to the ad execution? Or does the competitor's brand fit just as well as your own? If a competitor's brand would fit just as well, the chances are that your ad execution is lacking something and is suffering from 'category conformity'. The ad execution that works best is the execution that ties in uniquely to both brand and message.

Mistaken identity

One of our acquaintances wears a distinctive style of clothing. We can pick him out easily in a crowd. One day in a crowded airline lounge we caught sight of him, grabbed his arm and said 'Hi, Bob'. It turned out to be a case of mistaken identity. We realised that Bob had come to 'own' that style or position in our mind. Once somebody becomes inextricably associated with a particular style, it is natural to think of them whenever you see somebody dressed the same way.

Mistaken identity also occurs with commercials. If your brand is identified with a particular style, then anyone else who tries to use that style risks advertising for you.

'Owning' a style

As an example of a global style consider the De Beers silhouette-type advertising where the highly contrasting diamond earring is hung on a dark silhouette or, in another commercial, the diamond ring is slipped onto the finger of the silhouetted figure. (The music behind it is constant as well—at least in certain parts of the world.) Very distinctive. Very different. And very much owned by De Beers. The style is carried through into print advertisements (see Figure 20.1).

Figure 20.1
De Beers silhouette style

Or consider MetLife in the USA which has for many years had a distinctive style of advertising, always using one of the Peanuts characters to put a happy recognizable face on something that would otherwise be really boring (Figure 20.2). MetLife 'owns' this style and, if any other competitive company tried to use a Peanuts character or any other cartoon character in their advertising, they would risk doing an advertising job for MetLife.

This is exactly what happened in Australia when a soup manufacturer tried to use a similar style to that used for many years by the market leader, Heinz. Outside the USA the Heinz brand has a high profile as a canned

Figure 20.2
Consistency—MetLife advertising.
Reprinted with permission from Metropolitan Life Insurance Company 1999

soup manufacturer and for many years used high-profile presenters (English actors Robert Morley and then Penelope Keith). Along came competitor Continental soup which, for one year only, tried to use a similar high-profile presenter in the form of Dame Edna Everage (an alter ego of Australian entertainer Barry Humphries). What happened? The commercials broke through and people remembered the Dame Edna commercials. But almost as many remembered them as being for Heinz as for Continental. They were mistakenly recalled as being ads for Heinz because Heinz 'owned' that high-profile presenter style of advertising in the soup category. When a brand comes

to 'own' a unique and consistent style in its category, it prevents any attempt by its competitors to copy what it is doing without giving its brand free advertising.

Absolut vodka is another classic success story of a brand that has capitalized on a unique and consistent style of advertising. In the USA, particularly, Absolut has used this unique and consistent style based on the shape of its bottle and its name, and maintained this over two decades, while still finding imaginative ways within it to keep the same advertising style not only fresh but also involving.

Other examples include:

Figure 20.3
Consistency: Absolut Vodka

- Chanel No. 5, in its own unique style, consistently features multiple bottles on a yellow 'see-through' style background.
- Altoids consistently uses a pale green background. The very first ad was a strong man flexing his muscles, with the headline 'Nice Altoids'. It was followed by similar quirky representations of strength (such as the dominatrix, a girl with a whip) all alluding to the strong flavour of the mints.

Until a few years ago, car advertising almost always consisted of a cameo of visuals showing the car in motion accompanied by a male voice-over. The car was almost always red. A scene of it winding its way around a country road was obligatory. And then a few scenes would be cut in of it traveling in the city. Same. Same. Boring…sameness! Every now and again, however, an ad would manage to break out of the sameness, as Jeep did with its commercial that simply showed a mysterious object moving around underneath deep snow. This engaged the viewer's curiosity and when the mysterious 'thing' finally emerged from the snow it was revealed as a car—Jeep.

The award for boring sameness in ads, however, has to go to the retail industry and, in particular, supermarkets. This began to change a little in the 1990s but all too often we still see ads where there is nothing distinctive to differentiate one advertised store from any other. In department stores and apparel stores there has been much more individuality.

To escape the category conformity trap it is useful to understand some of the key dimensions of style (see Chapter 9), then apply this knowledge in your search for opportunities to differentiate your advertising and develop a unique style. A key dimension of style is constancy because of its importance in memory retrieval.

Style influences memory retrieval

Monet, Kandinski and Picasso are all artists who paint. But their styles are totally different. A style implies some sort of constancy. That is, the execution varies but a certain element remains the same. As a result, you don't have to be told that a painting is a Monet. You don't have to inspect its signature. You know it from the style.

There is a constancy in the style that acts as a memory trigger—a retrieval cue. It automatically retrieves from memory the identity (the brand) associated with it. Far too many advertisers have only one constant in their advertising from one campaign to the next and that is the brand or logo. The brand or logo is important: it is the equivalent of the advertiser's signature. However, the most successful advertisers and the most successful artists don't rely on signatures alone: they have a unique and consistent style!

So what types of constants are on the menu ? What should you be looking to include in your advertising? Here are some thought-starters on things that might potentially be constants you can use.

Slogans

A word, a phrase or a sentence can function as a constant. This usage is so common today that we even have a word for it—*slogan*. When we hear the expression *'Where do you want to go today?'* what do we think of? We don't need to be told who the advertiser is. We know the ad has to be for Microsoft.

Slogans are obvious ones. But there are other types of constants that we don't use as frequently. What makes it more difficult to discuss them is that we do not have any unique words, like 'slogan', to sum them up.

Symbols

Figure 20.4
The Nike 'Swoosh' symbol

Nike has come to own the Swoosh symbol it created so completely that it is synonomous with the brand Nike. You need only see the Swoosh on some article of clothing and it immediately registers Nike in your mind. This means that ad branding is not just dependent on the brand name. Indeed, this advertiser has flaunted its ability to advertise effectively without actually using the word 'Nike' just by using the Swoosh as a sign-off in some of their ads.

Figure 20.5
The Xerox digitized X symbol

In a similar but slightly lesser way Mercedes uses the three-point star symbol. At Grand Slam tennis competitions the symbol often appears embedded in the tennis net and immediately communicates Mercedes. Disney ads always have the Mickey Mouse ears and/or Cinderella's castle included as constant symbols. Xerox does the same thing with the digitised X (Figure 20.5). Symbols are one form of constant that act as a powerful branding device in the total style mix.

Visual devices

Used very rarely but sometimes very effectively is the action or gesture as a constant. For example, Nestea always had someone falling backwards into a swimming pool. Milk has people with milk moustaches. Revlon ColorStay lipstick has Cindy Crawford kissing everybody—proof that Revlon ColorStay doesn't come off.

When a brand uses a visual device like this as a constant, it comes to establish it as something that the brand 'owns'. We can't see it without thinking of that brand. In the USA, if you saw a foot on fire in an ad, you would

Figure 20.6
The Energizer bunny. *Used by permission
of Eveready Battery Company, Inc. Energiser
Bunny® is a registered trademark of Eveready
Battery Company, Inc.*

immediately think of Tinactin, the athletes foot remedy, even without seeing the branding in the ad or hearing the sign-off line: 'Tinactin…puts the fire out.' Similarly, in Australia, for several cough and cold seasons, ads showing people with sore throats could have been for any brand except that, as soon as the character started to 'breathe out fire', everyone knew it was for Anticol.

And in many parts of the world the Energizer bunny represents an icon constant that is associated with longer-lasting batteries ('Keeps on keeping on') established initially by a series of commercials showing the bunny keeping on while the others stopped one by one.

Sometimes, these highly visual and dramatic action devices are just used as part of the sign-off in the brand's ads. In the United States, for example, Sprint, the long-distance telephone company, consistently uses a pin dropping in slow motion, providing a visual for the telephone number to call, 1-800 PinDrop. The Toyota jump is a further example. The freeze-frame jump that often went along with the lyric 'Oh, what a feeling' was an action that became incorporated into the signature sign-off for Toyota in various parts of the world for many years.

Actions and gestures

Sometimes these visual devices take the form of simple actions or gestures. For example, the US insurance company Allstate held out the open uplifted palm in every commercial, accompanied by the line: 'We're the good hands people. . . You're in good hands with Allstate.' This and the Sure deodorant campaign, 'Raise your hand if you're Sure', are examples of tying your brand to an action that is commonly observed in everyday life. (Sure brand deodorant urged audiences to 'Raise your hand if you're Sure' and there were pictures of a variety of people raising their hands with, of course, no perspiration marks to be seen.) 'Raise your hands' has become a cue that almost involuntarily brings the brand to mind.

A simple action or gesture used as a constant can be very effective especially if it can be easily mimicked by the audience. Mimicry can be performance-enhancing and help to broadcast an ad and its brand by giving it free registrations beyond the advertising itself. For example, in the United States everyone was encouraged by the introductory ads for the new Dodge Neon to say 'Hi' to the Dodge Neon car with the result that you would see kids calling out 'Hi' as you drove your new Neon down the street. The technique is not new but it is effective. Back in the 1960s, the 'Hey, Charger' campaign for the Chrysler Charger in Australia did a similar thing. The ads showed people holding up two fingers in a V sign and saying 'Hey, Charger!' Anyone driving a Chrysler Charger could expect to be greeted by people making the 'Hey, Charger' gesture. Kids in particular love such mimicry which can range from V signs to hand raising to the flapping wings action of the 'Chicken Tonight' ad.

Presenters

Sometimes a presenter—often a celebrity—is used as the constant. The celebrity also helps the advertising break through. Michael Jordon for Gatorade, Kathie Lee for Carnival Cruises, Cindy Crawford for Revlon ColorStay. When Colonel Sanders had been dead for a few years, KFC managed to resurrect the continuity of this yesteryear icon by bringing him back as an *animated* character.

It is worth noting, however, that the person as constant does *not* have to be a ready-made celebrity. The alternative is the 'Do It Yourself' celebrity (or DIY celebrity for short). Examples include the Maytag man and Wendy the Snapple lady. We may not know their real names but they can become consistent visual properties for the advertisers. Some of the original DIY celebrities were cartoon characters: Tony the Tiger for Kellogg's Sugar Frosties (Frosted Flakes), Snap, Crackle and Pop for Rice Bubbles (Krispies). There are many candidates for constants and many possibilities. Some have been used extensively; others represent untapped opportunities.

Characters

The constant may be a character that always appears in the ad but who is not necessarily a presenter. Examples include:

- the Marlboro cowboy;
- the Intel guy in a hermetically sealed suit (Figure 20.7);
- the Michelin baby;
- Rob the dentist who uses Oral B toothbrushes;
- identical twins for Wrigley's Doublemint gum, acting as a mnemonic to reinforce the slogan *'Double your pleasure, double your fun, with Wrigley's doublemint gum'*.

Figure 20.7
Intel character in hermetically sealed suit.
Copyright 1998, Intel Corporation

Layout/Format

Some brands make effective use of a unique layout. By remaining constant it may come to identify instantly a particular brand. Absolut vodka has been very successful using its bottle shape in various guises as its branding constant that is also its layout. Similarly, Altoids uses its packs as the context for its constant layout.

For many years before the Compaq takeover, Digital Computers used a white-on-red, boxed print style as its communication device. When the company was taken over, its opposition seized the opportunity to turn that well known style back on Digital with ads reminding buyers that Digital had been sold and attempting to sow seeds of worry in buyers' minds.

Music

Music can function wonderfully well as a retrieval cue. Table 20.1 shows some of the songs used by brands in their advertising. While music is frequently used in commercials, it appears surprisingly rarely as a deliberate constant across campaigns.

Table 20.1
Examples of popular music used in commercials

'It's Not Unusual'	Heineken beer
'Danke Schön'	Amoco
'The Best Is Yet To Come'	Nestlé
'You Are My Sunshine'	Johnson & Johnson
'The More I See You'	Estee Lauder
'Rhapsody In Blue'	United Airlines
Cole Porter's 'Don't Fence Me In'	Embassy Suites
'Sing, Sing, Sing'	Nissan
Gershwin's 'Someone To Watch Over Me'	H&R Block
'I Want To Take You Higher'	AT&T
'Falling In Love Again' (sung by Marlene Dietrich)	Mercedes Benz
'Peter Gunn' theme	Apple computers

Sounds

Ameritech telephone services uses as a sign-off in its commercials the rising, tonal 'Bip, Bip, Bip' sound. Such sounds can become integral parts of the brand's advertising. Indeed, it is sometimes amazing what can act as a retrieval cue. We discovered this once while tracking for Nabisco. The sign-off for each Nabisco commercial was the brand. The brand name was sung, 'Na... bis...co...' followed by a little ping.

One could be forgiven for believing that the ping was irrelevant, incidental and hardly even noticeable. It was just a sound effect that punctuated the brand sign-off. However, when the ping was temporarily dropped to make room for a promotional tag to be included at the end of the ad, an amazing thing happened. The ads did not break through as much. More importantly, they lost a lot of their ability to link the execution in people's minds with the Nabisco brand. The principle was crystal clear. Even a simple sound like a little 'ping' can have far-reaching mnemonic effects.

Color

What about color? Can color function as a retrieval cue? No doubt it can, but we can't think of many good examples of where it has been used in TV commercials as a constant. Chanel No. 5 uses yellow. Kodak uses yellow. Pepto Bismol uses hot pink. And De Beers has used the black and white silhouette-style commercial to good effect. US retailer, Circuit City, uses a burgundy and white appliance plug that transforms into the burgundy and white Circuit City store, helping to build recognition of the store together with the commercials. But there seems to be surprisingly little use of constant color specifically related to commercials themselves. Although color is often carried across from the brand colors. For example, BP has used masses of green and gold to great effect in the design of its service stations. Shell similarly is identified by yellow and red. In soft drinks, Coke is red and Pepsi is blue (Pepsi changed some years ago from green).

Other constants

Various other things could serve as constants but have rarely, if ever, been used. For example, there is no reason why we could not make more use of things like:

- a place—always incorporating the same well known place in the executions for the brand (as Transamerica does for insurance: see Figure 20.9);
- a feeling;
- an emotion.

These are all potential memory cues that could enhance the ability of an ad to trigger automatic recognition of the brand identity. The general point is that the ad does not have to rely on the brand as the only constant.

When used consistently, such memory cues help to develop a style that is unique to the brand advertiser because they become part of the brand identity—just as the flashy style of dress became part of our friend Bob's identity or image. They are symbols as well as memory hooks.

Figure 20.8
Transamerica ads show the landmark Transamerica building

Voice-over ... and over and over and over

One of the key dimensions of style is the use of voice-over. As discussed in Chapter 9, voice-over seems to be ubiquitous in TV advertising. While it has the advantage of being cheaper and, in an increasingly global world, more flexible, using voice-over is almost always less effective than using on-camera presenters, whether direct or indirect.

Voice-over does not break through anywhere near as effectively as using on-screen speech and we have seen this many, many times in the course of tracking various campaigns. However, there is voice-over and voice-over. And just so we don't toss out the baby with the bath water, let us be clear that we are talking about traditional voice-over with on-screen demonstrations or illustrations.

The traditional style uses voice-over with on-screen illustration. In its loud form with fast cuts this is the classic retail advertising style (e.g. supermarket weekly specials). In its more subdued form, with slower cuts and more extended scene shots, it is used by car manufacturers, perfume manufacturers and so on. This traditional voice-over, when used for packaged goods, cars and the like, does not break through anywhere near as well as the voice of a person speaking on-screen.

Musical voice-over with visual illustration

This is typified by someone singing for the commercial but not appearing on screen—for example, Gillette—'the best a man can get'. This style engages the viewer as a passive observer, a bystander enjoying the entertainment. The musical voice-over is talking to the on-screen character. The viewer is expected to identify with the on-screen character and hence the message is received indirectly.

A subtle but important variation on this is where the on-screen characters are not speaking but the voice-over is meant to be what they are saying or thinking. The on-screen characters are 'sharing their thoughts' with the viewer. Because these thoughts are in the form of a sung voice-over, the viewer's sense of being spoken to directly is very much reduced and there is a particular feeling and style about this kind of ad.

The on-stage, all-musical singing commercial

There don't seem to be a lot of these around these days. The classic 'I'd like to buy the world a Coke' is one example. They were also used in the launch of Diet Coke. In recent years the big anthem-type ads have become much rarer, particularly as 60-second commercials have become less frequent.

The integral constant

The constant (character, gesture, sound or whatever) may become associated with the brand just through paired association. Ideally, however, it is better if you can find a constant that is, or can be made into, an integral part of your brand identity.

For example, the pink bunny in the battery ads is a constant character symbolizing longer-running batteries, but it's not integral to Energizer (except by simple paired association). It would be possible to take Energizer out of the commercial and substitute Duracell (because it is also a brand that is positioned as longer-lasting) without doing any real violation to the commercial. Constants like these that rely entirely on paired association are potentially subject to more competitive memory interference and forgetting. ('Is the bunny in those battery ads for Duracell or Energizer?'). Others (like the milk moustache) are unmistakably for milk because other aspects of it (such as color) are more integral to the brand.

Ad style—the brand's attire

A brand's advertising needs to be thought of as one of its most visible features. It is an attribute of the brand, no less real than the price, the package and what is inside it. A brand's advertising represents the brand's attire if you like. Imagine your mother walking in with her eyebrow pierced, sporting a tattoo and dressed like a 16-year-old. Just as it would be disorienting if our friends and family suddenly became wildly inconsistent in the way they dress, so too do we expect the brands we value to maintain a reasonable degree of consistency in their substance, image and dress. If the brand capriciously changes its style of attire every few months it would not only be disorienting, it would be difficult to get to know the brand. So we expect brands to remain true to themselves if we are going to get to know them and be attracted to them.

Advertisers have traditionally not been encouraged by agencies to get involved in advertising style. Some creatives fear that constants like those discussed above can all too easily become 'creative handcuffs' that restrict their freedom and make it harder to come up with great ideas. There is some truth in this. Just as a constant strategy limits the creative team to only those ideas that are on-strategy so too does a constant style constrain the team to ideas that can be executed on-style, that is, consistent with the brand's style.

A brand's advertising style is a component of its ad strategy because it is part of the way the brand's communications are identified in people's minds. Advertising is part of a brand's wardrobe attire. The brand's advertising constants and its advertising style are therefore valuable equities; with successful brands, they are woven into the fabric of the brand, constituting part of its heritage and thereby lending stronger identification and presence to it. Hence, it is legitimate to build in to the strategy brief a constraint in regards to ad style within which the creative process must work.

The winds of change are beginning to blow and an increasing number of advertisers and agencies recognize the benefits of maintaining a unique and consistent style. The style you choose can be a powerful form of non-verbal communication that identifies you and your ads.

Summary

Style is such a subtle characteristic of advertising that our language is hardly adequate for analyzing and discussing it. To maximize ad effectiveness, maintain a unique and consistent style. To do this, it is useful to understand how style varies. Style is like hair. It needs careful grooming, it is crucial to your identity, and how you look depends on how you cut it!

A consistent brand strategy supported by a strong symbol can produce an enormous cost advantage in implementing communication programs. It is much less costly to reinforce an established image than to create a new one.

David Aaker[1]

21

Sequels

Sequels are a particular form of advertising style where the character(s) are held constant and become associated with the brand. Sequels are something of a natural answer to the often overexaggerated problem of 'wear-out'.

Why is it that every new campaign for a brand has to be a total change? If your ad or campaign is worn out, it usually means people are bored with it or irritated by it. If you develop an entirely new ad that bears little if any relationship to the old one, then out goes another baby complete with the bath water!

Why change *everything* when your ad wears out? All too often, we seem driven to come up with an entirely new ad concept. The message may be the same but the new execution is a total departure from the old. We may have just spent a year and $20 million to break through the clutter—to build a strong awareness of the ad in people's minds. It has been a hard, competitive and expensive exercise but we have succeeded in taking the high ground. The ad now dominates the category in share of mind.

Then, suddenly, for some reason, someone decides to change the ad. The focus is now on unleashing another, entirely different ad execution. Why do so many advertisers make it hard for themselves by being intent on doing it all over again from scratch?

'Wear-in'

Think of a new ad as having to 'wear in'. Like a new shoe, it may take a little time. The better the quality of the shoe the less time it should take to wear in. Some ads 'wear in' very quickly. A great creative execution can capture the mental ground very quickly with a minimum of media weight. Other ads are of lesser creative quality and require more time and media weight to 'wear in'. Unfortunately, there are very few great creative executions. Most ads are more pedestrian and reliant on many media bursts over a period of time to build the assault and then hold the mental territory.

Residual recall barriers to mental entry

The more successful an old ad is in capturing and holding the mental ground, the longer it remains in people's minds even after the advertising is taken off air. (This is one reason why it is difficult for a new competitor to break through in the face of a long-advertised market leader.)

When a totally new ad for a brand is launched, it will be some time before the old one disappears from people's minds. In fact, the more successful and better performing the old ad, the longer it will dominate and the longer it will take for the new ad to 'wear in'.

A truly great ad execution does not take much time to 'wear in'. But if it comes hard on the heels of another good performer, it will generally take longer. This is because it takes some time for the new ad to displace all those well consolidated memories that surround the old ad and are linked to brand recall and recognition.

The consumer's mind is not a vacuum. It retains for some time the residual memories of the last ad for a brand. And this can act as an inhibitor or a 'barrier to entry' for the new ad.

The graph in Figure 21.1 illustrates this. An old ad dominated for seven or eight months after it came off air even while a new ad was being aired. The vertical bars represent the weekly media weight (TRPs). The horizontal lines represent advertising awareness for (top) the old ad and (below) a new ad for the same brand. There are a few points to note:

1. The first ad peaked in August/September (at 32 per cent recall rate).
2. With no further screenings, its recall rate declined.
3. Despite not being on air it was still in people's minds five months later (at 12 per cent).
4. In the meantime, an entirely new ad had been introduced and aired.

What works, what doesn't, and why

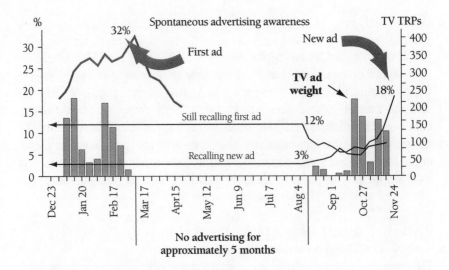

Figure 21.1

Note: Despite not being on air, the first ad was still in 12% of people's five months later. Not until about ten weeks after the new advertisement was introduced did it break through and dominate over the old one in people's minds.

Residual recall of old and new advertisements. *Source:* NFO MarketMind

5. Not until ten weeks later did the new ad break through and dominate over the old ad in people's minds; that is, the old ad held firm in people's minds for seven to eight months.

We might note that while this 'in-fighting' between ads is going on in people's minds, the sum total of ad recall for the brand (i.e. the old plus the new) is very low. It is not until the new ad breaks through and begins to dominate that net ad awareness for the brand starts to return to its previous levels.

The implication of this is that considerable time and media money could be saved if only the advertiser could somehow bypass or avoid this transition period when there is 'in fighting' in memory between ads. Is there a solution? Yes!

Greater use of sequels

Modern movie-makers such as Spielberg know that it is better to build on something you have already established than to start from scratch each time. In movie-making the 1980s and 1990s were the decades of sequels. There was a multitude of sequels, including *Rocky I, II, III, IV* and *V, Indiana Jones,*

Rambo, Mad Max, Die Hard, Superman, James Bond, Star Trek and Star Wars. They all testify to the success of the sequel strategy. It's the same with *Back to the Future, Lethal Weapon, Jaws, Home Alone, Gremlins* and *Terminator*. The list goes on and on.

This strategy consists of harnessing the interest and familiarity that has already been built by a previous movie success (the equivalent of a successful ad 'execution') and tying in the next movie (the next execution) to the consumer recall of the previous one. This is clearly a successful strategy—so why do advertisers so often launch a totally new campaign after the old one has had its day? Why not make more use of sequels, as has proved to be successful for movies?

A few great sequel ads

A sequel is one form of continuity of style (see Chapter 20) where the character(s) are held constant. For example, across the globe, the budding romance of the character, Gillian, with her next-door neighbor unfolded over convivial coffee and many sequels and the coffee just happened to be a Nestlé brand. This campaign started in the UK for Nescafé Gold and was used in the USA for Taster's Choice and in Australia for Nescafé. It portrayed an ongoing flirtation between two neighbors that began when one of them ran out of coffee and turned to the other to borrow some. Ultimately, the campaign shaded into the next generation of characters as the focus shifted to Gillian's daughter.

Over the years there have been some great sequel ads like this—built around holding the characters constant. Wendy, the Snapple lady, in the United States was created by the advertisers as a receptionist character for Snapple drinks who read the fan mail sent to the company by consumers. Wendy's quirky New York attitude and humor ran for years as the many sequels drove Snapple along in the non-carbonated soft drinks category.

What the character Wendy did for Snapple, Mr Bean did for 'BarclayCard' in Britain in a series of sequels that also ran for many years. And for Oral B toothbrushes, in a campaign that started in Australia and eventually went global for Oral B, the character always brushing his teeth with back to the camera was Rob the dentist ('This man is a dentist...we can't show you his face on camera'). Eventually, the ads showed Rob's young son alongside him, also back to the camera, using an Oral B toothbrush. Sequels in this way can offer a clever, smooth transition to the targeting of the next generation of buyers for the brand.

In the USA many sequels of white-haired Orville Redembacher, a maker

Figure 21.2
Frank Perdue appeared in all his ads talking about how his branded chickens were better. Today it is Jim Perdue (presumably his son)

of popcorn, smoothly transitioned to his grandson. Orville appeared in all his own ads for many years, proud as could be about his company and its popcorn, which had his image on the package. His grandson was introduced into the ads, appearing for a while with Orville in what was apparently a bridging campaign before Orville died soon after.

See also Frank Perdue in Figure 21.2. Frank Perdue appeared in all of his company's ads, taking a commodity product and making it into a significant brand image by talking about how his chickens were better than others and by using the slogan: 'It takes a tough man to make a tender chicken.' Today, his son Jim Perdue, who is now chairman of the company, is following in his father's advertising footsteps.

Resisting 'natural' forces

An anecdote often related in the ad industry tells of the head of a company complaining to his ad agency that there are 14 people working on the brand but he never sees any changes. To which the canny punch-line response is: 'We have 14 people working on your business precisely to see that nothing ever changes!'

Constancy in style in sequels such as this takes a lot of discipline on the part of the advertiser and the agency in order to keep them going. This is because the people involved tend to get bored with the characters and see them as 'creative handcuffs'. Also, brand managers tend to move on after a couple of years, and new brand managers naturally like to put their own creative stamp on the brand by introducing a totally new campaign rather than continuing to develop the old one. It takes discipline from top management for a company to resist these 'natural' forces and determine to keep things on track. (One brand we know that has paid the price has been around for only ten years but in that time has changed strategy four times and campaign style 15 times.)

With a sequel the ad doesn't have to wear in. Nor does it have to displace what is already there. It just hooks in immediately to existing memories. No waiting. No delay!

Continuity is the key

Like a good soap opera program, such examples hold constant the main character(s) and vary the situations. When new characters are created they are introduced through their relationship or relevance to the established characters. Each new ad is like a new episode. It provides continuity and the communications from the brand form a continuous unfolding story.

The important thing is that the new ad has a meaningful relationship with the one before; it is encoded or linked into the existing memory like pieces of a jigsaw puzzle that fit together. In this way people can file the two ads together in memory and retain both.

We have previously likened this to storing images in a mental filing cabinet (see Chapter 13). Many people defer office filing. It's a chore. People are even less motivated to file ads in their mental filing cabinets, let alone file them carefully or correctly. They have little motivation to remember a new ad at all, let alone with the correct brand name.

However, if something in the new ad immediately reminds consumers of something already stored in memory and then clearly presents a further development to it, the job is done almost automatically for them. Instead of storing everything that comes in as a separate file, we humans will store anything new that is related to an existing item in the most obvious existing file.

The more closely the contents of a particular file are related, the more it can act as a chunk—an integral whole in memory.

Human memory works best when new things that are introduced have an integral fit with, or can be related in some way to, old things that already exist in memory.[1]

Owning an ad style

Sequels are the epitome of maintaining a constant style. Absolut vodka has a unique style built entirely within the print medium and clearly illustrates how it is possible for a brand to own an advertising style.

The advantage in owning a style is that, when viewers see that kind of ad, the style instantly triggers an association with the brand. The brand comes to stand for the style and the style comes to stand for the brand. So if a competitor should try to use the same style, he/she risks communicating the wrong brand (your brand) and doing an advertising job for you. It would be difficult for any other spirit brand to use the Absolut style without advertising Absolut, just as it would be difficult for any other insurance company to use a cartoon character without advertising MetLife.

When you see an ad that shows a Peanuts character, which company do you think of? MetLife, of course, has been clearly associated with that style of mnemonic. It now owns that execution style. Not all ads are created equal. A sequel holds the character(s) constant and varies the situations so that the unfolding brand communications are identified with the character(s). Sequels have a lot going for them. Too many ads start anew every time.

Summary

- If your old ad has been successful but is now wearing out, consider a sequel rather than a totally new ad.
- If you do have to change horses and go for an entirely new ad, and if your past advertising has been very successful, then expect the new ad to take some time to 'wear in'.
- If you hit on a unique style that works, continue it in the next ad. Strive to 'own' that style in the consumer's mind.

22

Corporate tracking of image and issues

Look at Figure 22.1. We want you to think of the thing in the middle as our company. What do you see? You see the number 13, of course. Think of it as company 13. Note that it is surrounded by companies 17 and 21. Now read on; we will see the relevance of this when we come back to it later.

We saw in an earlier chapter that the same person, brand or company can be seen in different ways depending on the frame of reference we bring to it. Image is elusive. Your own image stares you in the face every morning, but do you have in your mind's eye the way you see yourself or the way others see you? Clothes, cosmetics, possessions and reputation can sometimes perform startling transformations of image and completely change the way others perceive us. Image is in the eye of the beholder!

The opponents of corporate image and corporate advertising argue that this is irrelevant for companies; that people buy products, they buy brands, but they don't buy companies. Even if it were true that corporate image has no effect on consumer behavior, how people perceive the company would

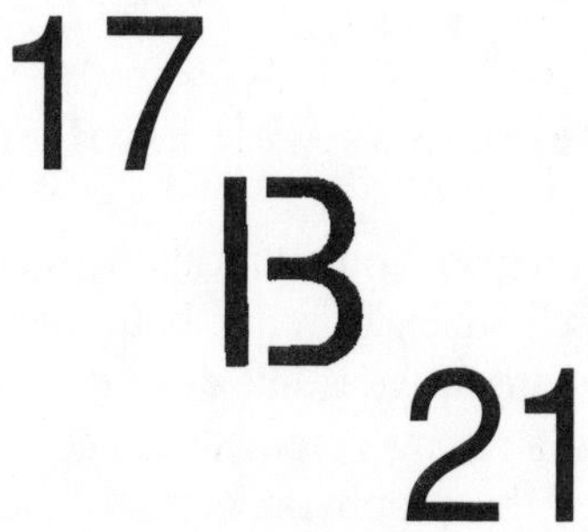

17

13

21

Figure 22.1
What do you see?

still be important because a well known and well respected company will always enjoy advantages in at least two non-consumer markets.

First, it will attract and retain better quality employees. A well known and well respected company is very different from a nonentity. When you are asked where you work, the importance of a corporate image is quickly apparent. If there is instant recognition of the name and what it stands for, the response is very different from: 'Who are they? What do they do? Never heard of them'.

Second, corporate image can and does affect the company's stock price. Even the people the company uses in its advertising can influence it. Stock prices often increase when companies sign up a famous celebrity to endorse their brand.[1] People do buy companies! At least they buy shares in companies and the price they are prepared to pay for the shares is influenced by the company's profile, image and perceived respectability.[2] This is so basic it is difficult to see how it could ever be far from the mind of top management.

A company's share price, like any other price, is a subjectively derived value—it is what people are prepared to pay. People pay more for brand-name products than for generics. A Gucci toothbrush is 'worth' more than a Woolworths house brand. The physical product may be the same but perceptions of its value can be significantly affected by image. So too can share prices. People perceive more value in, and expect the price to be higher for, something that has a substantial image. This has been very evident in the stock price of high-flier companies such as Virgin, Disney, Microsoft, News Limited, Apple, Amazon and ebay.

Companies increasingly recognize investors and the stock exchange as one of their key publics. For example, well known in Europe for its pharmaceutical and other products but relatively less known in the USA, global manufacturer Hoechst accompanied its listing on the New York Stock Exchange with a 'Great to be here!' ad campaign (see Figure 22.2).

Defense as well as offense

Corporate communication plans and corporate image development can be used strategically for both offense and defense. In a protective sense, corporate image is like a condom—both need to be used discreetly. By rolling on a strong corporate image and managing it effectively, management can get the prophylactic protection needed to keep out unwanted corporate invaders. A healthy corporate image, along with a strong share price, is what keeps the corporate immune system intact.

Figure 22.2
Hoechst's 'Great to be here!' campaign, introducing itself to Wall Street

Corporate raiders make a science out of hunting companies with under-valued or undermanaged assets. So top management's attention is forcibly turned to corporate defence as well as corporate survival. To survive cor-porately, the management of listed companies need to keep the share price up and be seen to be managing the company's assets effectively. If the com-pany is undervalued by the stock market, compared with the true value of its assets, this invites takeover attention.

Corporate raiders target undermanaged companies where changes in strategic direction can dramatically increase the value of the shares. Or they look for companies with high liquidation values relative to their current stock price. If the management of a company is seen to be weak, this can imply to the stock market that the company could be worth more under new management. This too could invite takeover attention. So it is impor-tant for the company not only to be well managed but also to *be seen to be* well managed. Perceived share value is not something traditionally thought of as a marketable entity. But there is no better means of avoiding a takeover than a healthy share price.

The most astute companies track the perceptions of their own share-holders—individual as well as institutional. They realize that it is important to know, week by week, month by month, how they and their manage-ment are perceived; what their strengths and weaknesses are. Is the company seen to communicate well with its shareholders? Is it vulnerable? What price would shareholders sell out at? What types of communications do they react to best?

Forewarned is forearmed. This type of tracking provides an early warning system of any weakness or vulnerability and forms the basis for managing the corporate image and the corporate communications plan.

The basis of image

Before you can change or create an image in people's minds you need to know what thoughts and associations are already there. The first step in image research is to find out

- which attributes are important in people's minds regarding the (product or industry) category;
- which attributes differentiate your company from companies generally.

A key aspect of this is to establish what things people know about, or associate with, your particular brand or company.

Research may reveal, for example, that people know you only as a manufacturer of one product and are relatively unaware of the much larger scope and size of your company, or its product range, or the fact that it competes in many other product categories. Hyundai, for example, in some parts of the world is known almost solely for cars. People have very little in the way of associations with the company other than as a car maker. The ad in Figure 22.3 shows Hyundai attempting to broaden that image by displaying its other products (such as aeroplanes and ships).

When researching people's knowledge and associations in regard to the company you may find that their associations are blurred, half-formed or even plain wrong—but they exist nevertheless. So the next step is to determine how you want your organization to be seen. Which image attributes does the organization *want* to dominate its perception? How does it want people to perceive it?

Wrong, blurred or half formed associations may also be an issue that critically impacts on the organization's success. The company needs to find out what consumers' current perceptions are in order to be able to 'engage the consumer in a dialogue' and put forward another way of seeing the issue. The timber and oil industries have for years engaged the environmental movement in a dialogue. More recently, companies involved in producing genetically engineered foods are also engaging the consumer in a dialogue—especially in Europe. The objective is to begin setting the agenda

Figure 22.3
Hyundai ad showing the diversity of its products

by giving people specific facts about the issue and playing the focal beam of attention on those facts.

The starting point is finding out how people currently perceive the company or the critical issue. Consider, for example, a company such as ADM. What do people associate with that name? In some parts of the globe, it is seen as simply a set of initials. In other parts the associations will be blurred—people having little more than a fuzzy sense that it is 'one of those big companies' that has 'something to do with food and agriculture'. A far cry from the reality that ADM (Archer Daniels Midland) is the largest agriculture company in the world.

ADM's sign-off line *'Supermarket to the world'* makes no secret of its bigness. However, while bigness and power are usually positives, they almost always have the potential to be seen negatively as well in terms of such things as monopoly, abuse of power, etc. The challenge is finding ways to communicate bigness while keeping the focus of attention on the positive aspect of that bigness. One way ADM does it is by focusing our attention on hunger and the human condition with the line: *'Feeding the world is the biggest challenge in the new century and ADM is leading the way.'*

Positive attributes like size, credibility, stability, national interest, human caring, responsibility as a corporate citizen, non-polluter, environment-conscious—

all these are possible attribute associations that a company might want to position on.

Being seen as a good corporate citizen is an increasingly common goal of many companies—especially, but not exclusively, those working in environmentally sensitive fields. Companies as diverse as BP ('call us at BP Solar'), Kyocera ('developing efficient, affordable, solar energy solutions') and GM ('the electric car') have tapped into the solar energy environment issue. 3M positions on society friendly innovation—for example, making the world's environment better with CFC-free inhalers—'so that we don't harm the world's ozone layer'.

Such positioning can be carried through into products as well. For example, Bosch advertises its headlights with the line 'Thanks to Bosch headlights, fewer things are going bump in the night' while the ad shows several animals (a raccoon, a tortoise, a squirrel, etc) spotlighted in a car's headlights.

In choosing an attribute to position on, organizations need to develop a unique and consistent positioning around that attribute dimension and resist the temptation to chase every other positive dimension to its burrow. Trying to position on more than one or two at a time is fraught with the danger of image diffusion—trying to do everything and accomplishing nothing.

When an organization decides on the image it wants to communicate, and confirms that it can deliver on that image, it should then track public perceptions and closely monitor the effectiveness of its corporate communications. The image dimension may be of the 'good corporate citizen' type or it may be focused on more pragmatic platforms that address different types of customer concerns. Often, it is a matter of keeping people focused on the positive side of what you offer corporately—keeping the perspective on the 'half-full' rather than the 'half-empty' perspective.

For example, Andersen Consulting may discover from research that people see it as a very big company—usually a positive. But at the same time, they would be aware that people sometimes think of big companies in terms of slow and cumbersome. Thus lurks a possible negative in the background. Can it be addressed by corporate

Figure 22.4
Andersen Consulting: 'Who says you can't be big and nimble?'

image advertising? Yes, as the 'nimble elephant' ad for Andersen Consulting illustrates (Figure 22.4).

Changing an image

There are three elements to an image, whether it's a brand or corporate image. That image is a function of:

1. the attributes associated with it;
2. the degree of those attributes it is perceived to have;
3. how important that attribute dimension is in people's minds when they make a decision.

What advertising or corporate communications are trying to do is:

- Move the organization along an attribute dimension—for example, honesty or corporate citizenship; or
- Add a new attribute dimension to the image—for example, environmentally responsible, financially secure; or
- Influence the perceived importance of an attribute dimension for the public in evaluating the organization—that is, change the importance that people place on a particular attribute.

By monitoring each of these three elements over time, an organization knows how well groomed it is all the time and this acts as an 'early warning system' for any changes. Image, like grooming, is something that needs continual attention, not a once-a-year inspection.

Tracking the agenda of concerns

In this era of environmental concern and corporate responsibility, the 'green' attack has had a real impact on corporate communication philosophy. Some organizations deliberately undertook to keep their heads down. Holed up in the trenches, they hoped that by keeping a low profile they would avoid being targeted by the environmentalists. Others, like the mining, timber and oil industries, took a more proactive approach and mounted specific ad campaigns that took their case to the people.

We would argue that, whatever approach is taken, there is usually a need to know what is going on outside the trenches—to know at least how many people are out there firing at you, and what they are most concerned about. To this end, a number of organizations (corporate, government and industry groups) track what might be called the *agenda of concerns* among the general public in regard to their particular organization or industry.

By asking people what concerns, if any, they have in regard to organization X (or industry Y) an agenda of concerns is generated. For example, see Table 22.1. This agenda is monitored continuously. It changes over time in response to the topicality of the environment, to strikes and to the organization's own news releases and radio and TV appearances.

Table 22.1
Agenda of concerns

	% spontaneously mentioning the concern
1. Too big and uncaring	24
2. Pollutes the environment	12
3. Poor handling of its labor relations	8

The important thing about this is that the information allows the organization to detect events that have had a positive or negative impact on people's perceptions and concerns. Furthermore, it allows the detection of these at the earliest possible moment. This is crucial if an organization is going to take a proactive approach to managing corporate communications and corporate image.

Image: you can't leave home without it

Image is not something that companies can choose to opt out of. Nature abhors a vacuum, and so does the human mind. If an organization doesn't effectively communicate the way it sees itself and its beliefs, and what it is associated with and what it stands for, then the public will do so for it. The environment will fill the vacuum and allow people to construct their own image of the organization, based on whatever evidence is around and what things the company seems to be associated with.

To illustrate this, take a look at Figure 22.5. What do you see?

If this is our organization then hopefully you now see us as we would like to be seen —as we see ourselves. We are company B.

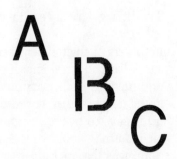

Figure 22.5
We now see the central item as a B. Its image changes when its associative context is letters rather than numbers.[3]

By making a few changes to the associative context within which we present ourselves this should help you to see us as we really are. We are company B —not to be mistaken for that unlucky organization 13.

Note that the two perceptions—letter B and the number 13—are as different as you can get. Yet it is the same physical stimulus that you were looking at in Figure 22.1. What has changed is your perception of it—influenced purely by its asssociations—the things that it is paired with. Changes to the way that real companies are seen are not as immediate and dramatic but over time they can end up being just as substantive. There is a lot to be said for a proactive, continuous tracking approach in the management of corporate communications and corporate image.

23

The Web: advertising in a new age

Home is where you hang your @

Anonymous

The Web is the medium of the new millennium. As this book goes to print, actual Web advertising accounts for about the same as outdoor advertising, barely more than 1 per cent of all advertising expenditure, but it is of course growing much more rapidly.

Also, any brand of any substance today has a Web site. The company Web site often starts out its life as just one more way to 'advertise' and provides a point of contact with potential and existing customers. But pretty soon it gets to be more than that. The focus builds on ways for visitors to *enjoy* the experience and the site is used to try to build closer relationships with them.

CLINIQUE HAPPY
chic,

Figure 23.1
Banner ad for Clinique

Having a Web address is an important part of a company's image these days. Companies that have Web addresses are seen as:

- more customer oriented and responsive;
- more informative;
- more sophisticated and hi-tech;
- more geared to a younger market.[1]

Web sites: a 'home' on the Web

A brand's Web address is becoming much more than just 'the company's home page'. When you invite someone to visit your home, that is traditional hospitality—a small but significant step towards building a closer relationship with them. Having people visit your home page and inviting them in to stay a while is also a significant step in hypertext hospitality. As we begin the 21st century the Web is becoming the company's 'virtual' home. Increasingly, for consumers, this is where they find a company so the Web becomes the company's real home as much as, if not more than, its physical address. For a growing number of companies, the Web is the primary point of contact—the place where people know where to find them. It is the place where the company holds open house and where consumers know the welcome mat is always out.

Prior to the Web, if consumers wanted to contact a manufacturer for service or for information on a product, or to complain or interact with the company, they would look up the physical address of the company. The company was then contacted at their physical location, by mail or by phone. Today, more and more consumers locate the companies they want, not by phone or by visiting their physical address but by visiting the company's virtual home on the Web. Indeed, for a growing number of companies, consumers have little idea of the company's geographic address, nor do they have any need to think about it. The company's primary home as far as the consumer is concerned is the Web. Amazon.com is a good example. Yahoo is another.

Types of products

If you want information on any product just click on the company's front door and you can enter, browse around and generally make yourself at home. Jim Beam lives here, at jimbeam.com. Jack lives over there, at jackdaniels.com. Can't see what you are looking for? Ask—interactively—or leave a message and someone will get back to you.

For Dell, Gateway, AOL, Amazon, Yahoo and the like it is clearly evident that the Web is increasingly the home of the company and its brands. For companies like these, what most Web advertising is about is getting people to visit the company's virtual home—that is, creating visitor traffic. The ad provides signposts and short cuts and directs people to the company. More than that, the ads draw the company to people's attention in the hope of making them recall that brand at the time they are interested in purchasing from that particular product category.

The Web is perhaps a more natural home for advertisers who sell directly through the Internet and for information-intensive products that require active consideration before purchase. 'By contrast, advertisers who sell more common household products have had more difficulty figuring out how to get consumers to request their ads.'[2] These companies have been the traditional heavy spenders on advertising in other media over the years and they seem to have the hardest time finding the right formula for a Web site that will continue to attract visitors. This is hardly surprising. Not everyone wants to have a relationship with every type of product. Some products are just too low on people's involvement scale for them to bother visiting the Web site of the brand—although if something goes wrong with the product, they may readily use the Web site as their means of contact.

Figure 23.2
An ebay cybernetic 'signpost'

One objective of a company's Web site is to set up a vehicle to enable a dialogue with the consumer. Another is to showcase the company. To attract traffic to the Web site and draw it to people's attention usually requires main media advertising of the Web site, or taking advertising space such as banner ads and sponsorship ads on other companies' Web sites. These are ways of erecting cybernetic signposts that point people towards the company's showcase site and offer a short cut (link) to it.

Ads on other companies' sites can do more than act as cybernetic signposts. Just as outdoor advertising can bring a brand to consumers' attention so too can these 'virtual billboards'. Virtual billboards can perform a communication role in their own right not only by displaying the company name but also a short brand message.

Banner ad effects

Outdoor billboards can deliver messages or reminders that are very short and compact and that communicate very rapidly (see Figure 23.3 for good

examples). Banner ads on the Web are similar. The messages to date have generally been short, sharp and very compact. Like the real, outdoor billboards these virtual miniature ones are capable of impacting brand salience, perceived presence, image and attitude.[3,4]

Figure 23.3
Outdoor ads for Federal Express and Lotto

As well as providing cybernetic signposts pointing the way to a company's site and inviting them to visit, Web advertising can:

- help build brand awareness and perceived advertising presence by displaying the brand name;
- convey extremely compact, very simple messages that help in brand building;
- reinforce/remind people with already known brand messages—if they are simple.

There appears to be little doubt that, like outdoor advertising, Web ads can make a brand stand out more and give it a greater degree of perceived

CLEANS THE AIR AS YOU DRIVE
INTRODUCING PREMAIR®
STANDARD ON THE VOLVO S80

VOLVO
for life

Figure 23.4
Banner ad for Volvo

presence. These awareness and image effects can range from marginal to sometimes quite substantial, meaning that it is important to know more than just how many people clicked on the ad. It is also important to have some measure of:

- *reach*—what percentage of the target audience had at least one opportunity to see your banner ad?
- *frequency*—how many opportunities to see it have they had?[5,6]

And it is important to know what effect the ad is having on awareness, image and attitudes to the company or brand. This means continuous tracking and monitoring of the ad day by day and week by week.

Continuous tracking

In essence, the concept of continuous tracking is the same on the Web as with telephone interviewing. However, in some ways, the Internet makes continuous tracking easier and quicker and can provide even better information.[7] Consider these benefits:

- Measuring recognition becomes more accurate and easier because visuals of the ads (or packs/displays, etc) can be shown so that people react to the actual stimulus instead of a verbal description.
- People exposed to banner ads are, by definition, on the Web and potentially accessible using that (cheaper) medium.
- The Internet enables rapid, cheap access to large samples via random sampling (e.g. of people visiting a Web site) or via panels of pre-recruited respondents.
- Pre-recruited Internet panels enable targeting of even low-incidence groups—such as Scotch whisky drinkers, expectant mothers, psoriasis sufferers, etc.[8]
- The low cost and super-fast turnaround of information means that it is capable of providing finer-grained information on a daily as well as a weekly basis.
- The use of control groups is all too often cost-prohibitive with telephone interviewing but the Internet makes these much more affordable and feasible.
- Continuous tracking of visitors to your site is possible. Who are they? Where do they come from? What pages do they visit? What are the most frequently visited places on your site?

Click-through

There are two essential ways of charging for advertising on a Web site. The advertiser can be charged on the basis of 'impressions' or, in other words, how many times the page with the ad displayed is exposed. The other way is to charge on the basis of the number of people who actually click on the ad. Some advertisers, most notable among them Procter and Gamble, insisted early on that they would only pay for 'click-throughs'.[9] As research provided evidence that Web ads can affect awareness, image and attitudes without click-through, the pressure grew for charging on the basis of 'impressions' and not just the number of people who click on the ad.

In this environment, advertisers understandably become worried when the incidence of click-through declines as they are still paying the same amount for the advertising. They are paying the same but fewer people, as a percentage of exposures, are clicking on the ad. In 1999 when the overall click-through rate plummeted to under 1 per cent there was much consternation.[10]

Let us put click-through into perspective. It has been likened by some people to a TV or print ad for a brand of car that prompts some percentage of the people who see it to visit the company's showroom. Others have likened it to a TV or print or radio ad prompting people to dial the advertiser's 800 telephone number. These examples are about prompting a behavioral follow-up response. However, such behavioral responses vary in the amount of effort involved. A visit to a showroom involves considerable inconvenience and travelling time. People are more likely to do something that takes less effort such as dialing an 800 number. Clicking on a banner ad on the Web is even lower on this effort scale. On a dimension of effort in making the response, click-through is more in company with things like opening a direct mail envelope or accepting a taste of a free sample in a supermarket.

This begs the question: since it is such a minimal effort response, why are click-through rates so low?

A key point is that the click-through rate will naturally vary with the makeup of the audience. People with lots of time, for example, who are in

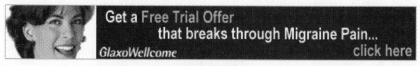

Figure 23.5
Banner ads often focus on a behavioral response—click-through

an entertainment frame of mind, are likely to be more exploratory in their behavior. Compared with those who are time-pressured and visiting purely to solve a specific problem, they may be more inclined to fill in their time by clicking through on ads or anything else. The same thing happens with those supermarket shoppers who have lots of discretionary time (e.g. they do not work full time). They spend more time in the supermarket and explore the items on the shelves much more than their time-pressured counterparts (e.g. people who work full time).[11]

As more and more people got connections to the Web, it surprised no one that the Web site audience composition changed somewhat. The types of sites that were becoming available on the Web were also changing. The click-through rate for ads on sites such as Yahoo (search engine), Ebay (online auctions), Amazon (world's greatest bookstore) and Microsoft will reflect to some degree the type of audience that generally frequents that site, and the frame of mind they are in.

So statistics on click-through rates are likely to be affected by the types of 'hot' sites that are proliferating fastest at that particular time.

The click-through rate will also depend quite crucially on the type of ad the person is presented with. If everybody doing a search on HotBot were presented with an ad for tampons, about half the people—by cause of their gender—would have no interest in it because the ad does not match the characteristics of perhaps 50 per cent of the audience. This is why more and more sites will display a different ad depending on what they have been able to glean about the user and what that person appears to be most interested in right then.

It is reasonable to expect that the more the displayed ad matches the person and the need state of that person at that time, the higher the likely click-through rate.

Context sensitive display

If, for example, you use the Excite search engine to explore the subject of computers and type in the search string 'computer', the page that downloads will show a banner ad for Gateway or something similar—along with your search results. If, instead, you are exploring the subject of 'entertainment' the results page will display a banner ad, not for Gateway but for Disney Store on Line, or the like.

This context sensitivity is a long way from perfect. For example, explore the subject of 'fast food' on Excite and, instead of showing you a KFC or McDonald's ad at the top of the page, your search results may display an

Figure 23.6
Context sensitive display: what you are likely to get at top of your Lycos results
page when researching the topic of 'baby'

ad for 'Peapod'—a place that will deliver groceries to your door. Not quite
a perfect match.

Clearly, the more this sort of thing happens the lower the click-through
rate is going to be. Ideally, the page will display an ad for one of the site's
advertisers that is closest to the need state that is inferred at the time from
the person's previous clicks and any information from previous visits.

So this context sensitivity enables the page that comes up to display not
just any old ad, and not the same ad that everybody else sees, but one that
is associated with what you are currently interested in—what is on your
mind at that particular moment. It is rather like being in the supermarket
and seeing a point-of-sale sign for a brand of the product category on display. It pushes that particular brand item to the forefront, making it salient
at a strategic time when you are in a need state related to that category.

What you type in as the search string (e.g. 'entertainment') functions
just like the product category retrieval cue that automatically elicits without
any effort from you one of the brand alternatives in that particular category
and pushes it forward. Of course, all this happens without your necessarily
being aware that you are being exposed to something different from anyone
else; or that you would have been exposed to a different ad had you typed
in a different search string.

Figure 23.7
Neutrogena Cosmetics: what you may get at the top of the page when you click
into the 'make-up' category on Yahoo or search for lipstick on Lycos

The Web—a very different medium

Unlike television where you can sit back and let it wash over you, the Web is a high-involvement, interactive medium. It does have some similarities to outdoor advertising but there are also fundamental differences. Most importantly, it is an environment that demands a continual stream of decisions from you. What is called the 'clickstream' is in reality a 'decision stream'. Each click is a decision. At every step you have to make a choice. 'Do I go here or will I click on this? Which of these will take me where I want to go? That link looks interesting but if I take it will I forget to come back? Will I click or won't I? Have I got time right now? Will it be worth it? I don't want to wait for half a minute and find it's not interesting.

The Web is therefore very different from other media. It is very active, very task-oriented and high-involvement in a very cognitive way. Its nature militates against the ability to lose oneself in the world of the medium, or what one writer has called 'telepresence'.[12] Increasing speed makes downloading of pages much more instant but this still does not alter the fundamental nature of the medium at this point—it is essentially decision making, not relaxation.

While things may change, people at the moment use the Web in a way that is heavily loaded with utilitarian rather than entertainment motives. It is dominated by search engines and portals, which are by far the most visited sites. Hence, people's state of mind when exposed to the Web and, thus, Web advertising is very different from other media, particularly television.

Functionality and aesthetics

One implication of this mostly task-oriented, active and focused frame of mind is that our values are generally more tuned to utilitarian than aesthetic considerations. We value stuff that is useful over stuff that looks attractive.

For example, an experimental study of attitudes to Web sites indicated that Web pages that are considered attractive tend also to be regarded as useless. The Web pages that were considered useful were thought to be most unattractive. This points to the value of having lots of relevant information even at the expense of attractiveness. Indeed sites that are rated as aesthetically pleasing seem to convey an image of being not very useful.[13] So the usual rules of design at this stage seem to be turned on their head.

Keeping track of the latest on Internet advertising

The area of Internet advertising is one of such dynamic change that any chapter written on this subject is bound to get dated before a book gets into print. Accordingly, in order that our readers may follow the latest developments in Internet advertising, we list the following recommended sites:

- **www.utexas.edu/coc/admedium** A helpful site at the University of Texas at Austin in the United States, where graduate students and faculty staff specialize in researching advertising on the Internet. The latest papers and presentations are available for download as well as links to other sites.
- **www.adage.com** This is the excellent site of the leading advertising trade magazine in the United States, *Advertising Age*.
- **www.arfsite.org** The Advertising Research Foundation undertakes research projects. Its mission is to improve the practise of advertising, marketing and media research.

24

'Mental reach': they see your ad but does it get through?

Whether communicating the corporate image or communicating the brand, an ad must generally break through in order to work. Many ads are mediocre at this. Others are compelling and involve us. Still others can be so boring that we skip over them mentally or tune them out and we can't recognize ever having seen them.

'Reach' is a media term that simply means the percentage of people who have had an 'opportunity to see' that ad. But even if they were in front of the television or exposed to a site page, to what extent does the ad reach them mentally and touch their minds as well as their eyes? Just what gets through? This chapter focuses on the difference between *media reach* (how many have an 'opportunity to see') and *mental reach*.

Let us look first at what people generally do when they see an ad. We focus on print ads for the moment and come back to TV later in the chapter. In an earlier chapter we saw that, in order to understand an ad, people seem to go through a process similar to the following:

1. First, they recognize that it is an ad.
2. They then immediately try to identify what it is an ad for. They look for something familiar that corresponds to a memory address that they recognize—something that already exists in their minds. Usually this is a brand or a product category.
3. When they have located a memory address their minds can then store any new information from the ad in that pigeonhole.

For example, consider the print ad in Figure 24.1. Leafing through a magazine and seeing this, people would recognize they were looking at an ad. They would then quickly recognize it as an ad for Colgate toothpaste, which is a known memory address for most people. Now, if toothpaste is not high on their agenda of interests or concerns, many at this point would flick over the page. They have identified it as an ad extolling the virtues of Colgate toothpaste, so any curiosity they had is quite satisfied by recognizing these two things.

This is a very low level of mental processing and, for many ads, not much more than this low level of

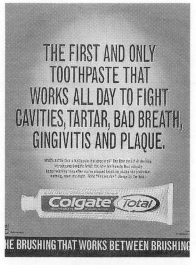

Figure 24.1
Print ad for Colgate

mental processing takes place. In this ad everything you need to know about the brand is included in the headline, so you might think that you don't have to work too hard to know what the ad is all about, even if you just skimmed it. The message is fairly instantly communicated provided that you read it. As Franzen reports: 'When something in our minds decides we have enough information, we move our attention on to the next advertisement, or to another constellation of stimuli.' That occurs after about seven eye fixations (about two seconds). *The average reader never gets round to reading an entire sentence (longer-than-average headline, for instance).*[1]

Recognition

Even with such minimal amounts of attention, an ad may nevertheless register enough at least to provide some brand reinforcement and help maintain the brand's salience in people's minds. The chances are reasonably high that they would recognize this ad again if they saw it. If, after being exposed to an ad, people can't even recognize having seen or heard it before, then chances are the ad is going to be a failure. This lack of recognition generally indicates the ad is not distinctive enough to 'cut through' the clutter and mentally reach its audience, even at this very minimal level.

So advertisers often show people an ad and ask if they recognize having seen it before. If they have been exposed to it, the chances are high that they will recognize it even though they may not have been able to *recall* it or describe anything specific about the ad. Recognition and recall are two somewhat different measures and we discuss this in more depth in Chapters 25 and 26. Suffice to say here, that advertisers can use ad recognition as an operational measure to validate that the ad is achieving at least some 'mental reach'.

In print advertising research, people are shown ads to see whether they recognize having seen them. With radio the ad spot may be played to them. For TV it is a little more difficult. It is impractical to carry around VCR facilities so an approximation is often used whereby people are shown a series of still shots taken from the ad. (The selection of exactly which shots are shown when measuring TV is critical, as we see later.)

'Mental reach' is defined as the percentage of the target audience that we can demonstrate had at least some level of *mental* contact with the ad. In other words, the ad has registered with them, enough for them at least to recognize having seen it. It quantifies how many of the scheduled 'opportunities to see' in the media schedule actually translate into mental contact, implicitly recognizing losses caused by bathroom visits, attentional distractions and simple, mental tuning out.

Reach versus mental reach levels

So what is important is not just the level of media reach ('opportunities to see') but the level of *mental* reach. A TV ad schedule that targets 90 per cent cumulative reach in a week will almost inevitably have a 'mental reach' that is somewhat lower. A reach of 90 per cent means that 90 per cent of the target audience have the 'opportunity to see' the commercial on at least one occasion. If this produces, say, 60 per cent *mental* reach it indicates that the ad has been exposed and registered with 60 per cent of the target audience…enough for them to recognize having seen it.

An advertising media schedule quantifies the size of the audience that an ad is supposed to reach. A reach of 28 per cent means that 28 per cent had an opportunity to see the ad—not that they actually saw it.

If the ad is shown several times over a period, the accumulated figure is known as 'cumulative reach'. 'The ad reached 48% of the target audience at least once over that period.' (See Figure 24.2.)

Such measures as these (along with TRPs, GRPs, TVRs and TARPs) can be misleading unless it is clearly understood what they mean. It is most important to realize that such figures do not represent *actual* exposures or mental reach. They are merely 'opportunities to see'.

'Mental reach': they see your ad but does it get through?

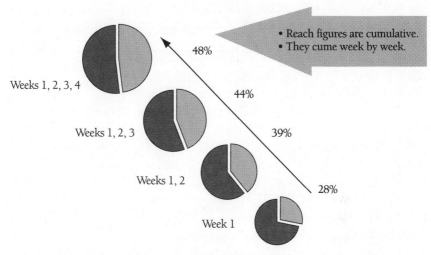

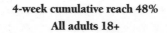

Figure 24.2
Cumulative reach of an ad

The reach figure measures the number of people who were in the room *around the time* the ad was aired. It does not mean they were in the room at exactly that time and in no way does it mean that the ad has mentally reached this number of people. For one thing, audiences do not necessarily remain intact during ad breaks. Some go to the bathroom. Others use the remote control to engage in zapping.[2] In general, when the set is switched on, there is no one in the room about 18 per cent of the time but during commercials this increases to about 40 per cent. Consequently, the size of audiences for ads should be assumed to be substantially less than for the actual program. In the United States, for example, audiences for TV ads are assumed to be at least 30 per cent less than for the actual programs.[3]

So it is very easy to overlook the fact that reach figures and cumulative reach figures are not mental reach figures. They are just the percentage of people who had an 'opportunity to see' the ad and it is for this reason that the concept of 'mental reach' is important. An ad's chances of achieving mental reach can be increased by a better understanding of the underlying psychology.

What is not widely understood by advertisers or consumers is that, for people to be able to recognize what they have seen or heard, they have to form a mental model of it. Comparison with this mental representation is what enables them to say whether they have been exposed to it before—

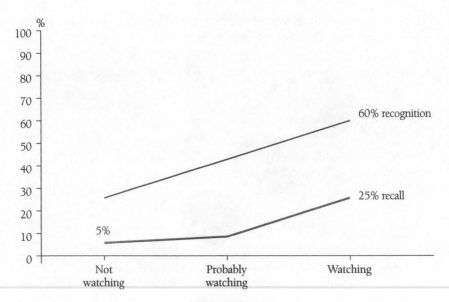

Figure 24.3
How 'eyes on screen' impacts on memory for TV ads.
Adapted from Thorsen and Zhao 1994

or if it is something new. The representation may be just bits and pieces that are stored but these provide a basis for reconstructing the past event, 'much as a paleontologist reconstructs a dinosaur from fragments of bone'.[4]

There are many print ads that people just flick over and ignore and would not be able to recognize again. Similarly, with TV ads, people's minds have the capacity to 'flick over' them mentally, as demonstrated by the work of researchers Thorson and Zhao. These researchers unobtrusively video-taped people as they were watching TV in a naturalistic setting where they were free to read, watch TV or chat.[5] Immediately after the program, the people were given a surprise test to check their awareness of the ads that had been shown during the 90-minute program. Figure 24.3 shows the relationship between viewers having their 'eyes on screen' while an ad was being aired (as evidenced by the videotaping) and subsequent recognition (and recall) of the ad immediately following the 90-minute program.

Remember that these were people who had their eyes on the screen when the ad was being shown. As the graph shows, only 60 per cent of these people were able to recognize having seen the ad. This is an average level across about 50 commercials. It *quantifies* what we knew intuitively— that even if people have their eyes on the screen and have resisted the urge to go to the bathroom or make a cup of coffee, an ad may nevertheless still fail to register mentally. (As expected, the percentage that were able to free-recall the ad without being prompted was substantially lower, at 20 per cent.) Clearly, there are a lot of other things going on in people's heads when they are exposed to ads—things that can neuter the effect of an ad.

Problem diagnosis

If, shortly after being exposed to an ad, an audience can't even recognize seeing or hearing it, they have either not noticed it or have been unable to take in enough to form a mental model of it. The main reasons for this are as follows.

- *Poor creative.* Boring ads that fail to attract attention are not distinctive enough. Or complex ads may make mental processing too difficult.
- *Insufficient processing time.* Many scene switches in TV commercials or very brief commercials limit the amount of processing time for under-standing. Time pressures and constrained reading time can do the same thing for print and website ads.
- *Distractions.* Even when people are in the room while a TV ad is on, they are often subject to distractions. Research shows that approximately half the time people are likely to be engaged in doing something else (e.g. talking, reading, using the phone, doing handicrafts, ironing, playing with kids or pets).[6] Naturally, when people are doing something else at the same time they don't have their eyes constantly on the screen. While they are reading or listening or watching, noises and distractions go on around them. The ad has to be compelling enough to 'break through' and engage people in the face of these distractions. Preoccupation with congested traffic and road conditions can have the same effect on radio commercials.
- *Lights on but no one home.* Even when they have their eyes on the screen, viewers may be thinking of something else, reflecting on the events of the day, perhaps, or listening in to another conversation. Even with eyes on the screen people don't necessarily mentally process the ad. Again it is the ad's job to 'break through', this time against internal distractions.

Overcoming the barriers

It is the creative execution, the creative elements of the ad, that are designed to 'break through' and capture attention. However, as estimated from the Thorsen and Zhao study, it appears that with perhaps 40 per cent of TV ads it doesn't happen. At least, attention isn't captured when there is only one 'opportunity to see' the ad. In the next scheduled 'opportunity to see' the ad, the minds of some of those 40 per cent who missed it on the first occasion may not be as preoccupied or distracted. This is a common justification for repetition of the ad—though usually a weak one.

Repetition and better media placement may go some way to improving the situation, but you wouldn't like to bet the farm on it. Good creative ads compel attention and there is a lot of evidence to suggest that repetition (in the form of more media exposures) will not make up for an ad if it is the commercial itself that fails to engage interest and attention on the first occasion.[7]

Relying on repetition alone to try to fix this problem is not only expensive but also risky. There is no guarantee that the ad will 'mentally reach' the 40 per cent on the next occasion or the next. So these single exposure results are a strong argument for the power of creativity and the need to design distinctive ads that do not have to rely on repetition to break through.

In this chapter we have focused on the difference between 'reach' (how many have an 'opportunity to see') and 'mental reach' (how many recognize having seen it). Measuring mental reach is best done through the ad recognition measure. But this is only one of a number of measures used in the diagnosis of where an ad is breaking down if it is not working. Ad recognition doesn't tell us whether the ad is working. But it does pinpoint whether the ad is being seen—whether it is getting at least the bare minimum of attention.

How then do we tell whether an ad is working? In the next chapter we show how to assess this through brand-focused measures (like brand purchasing, brand attitudes and brand awareness) rather than ad-focused measures (such as ad recognition and ad recall). In Chapter 25 we revisit ad recognition but this time in the context of the other ad measures (such as ad recall and message take-out) and show how they are used to pinpoint other critical areas where the ad may be breaking down.

25

Measurement of advertising effects in memory

Traditional measures of advertising effectiveness such as ad recognition, ad recall, message take-away,[1] brand awareness, brand image and purchase intention confuse many advertisers. The question often posed is: What do these all mean? Which one should I use? Do they really indicate how effective my advertising is? This chapter and the next focus on these mental measures. We look at what they mean, relate them to measures of purchase behavior and put them clearly into the modern perspective of how our memories work.

Diagnostic complementary measures

Mental measures are essentially diagnostic. They help with the problem of sorting out what is going on underneath the observed purchasing behavior. When there are changes in sales or market share they help us in sorting out what changes are due to what causes. How much is due to the advertising and how much to other things that happened at the same time (such as promotion, pricing, competitors' actions, etc)? Advertisers want to know more than just whether their ad worked or not. They need to know how and why it worked. If it didn't work, they want to know why, in order to avoid the same mistakes next time.

Let us make it as clear as possible that we firmly believe some form of purchase behavior measurement is crucial whether this be sales, market-share, scanner data or self-report.[2] Mental measures won't substitute for these measures of purchase behavior. But measuring purchase behavior by itself will not provide the necessary diagnostic ability to understand what is happening unless the behaviour measure(s) are combined with mental-response measures. In providing this diagnostic ability, mental-response measures don't substitute for behavior-change measures; they complement them. They help to sort out what is causing what. They provide understanding of how and why the ad works or doesn't work.

Indeed using purchase behavior alone can prove to be misleading and result in perfectly good ad campaigns being mistakenly jettisoned simply because they haven't led to increased sales or market share (yet). This is especially a problem for brands that already have large market shares. Increases in market share become harder to get the greater the existing brand share. Maintaining existing customer behavior is not necessarily a bad thing when you are a large, well established brand. An important role for advertising is to continually defend the established sales and market-share levels against the many would-be attackers. For established, larger brands, advertising's role must increasingly focus on defending or holding its established share. Judgment of advertising effectiveness *solely* in terms of increases in sales or market share is naive; among other things, it fails to come to grips with the role of advertising as an 'occupational force'.

To understand fully the way these other, mental measures work, to understand what they mean and how to use them, we need to discard the traditional, old-fashioned view of memory. There is often a gap of ten to 20 years between new developments in psychology and their dissemination and use in marketing. The past 35 years have seen significant developments in psychological research on memory, many of which have escaped marketing and advertising practitioners.

One reason for this is that some aspects of it are not all that easy to explain. It takes some effort to understand the full implications. The effort will be repaid, however, because an understanding of the modern view of memory is fundamental to understanding advertising's effects and to using mental measures diagnostically in the evaluation of an ad campaign.

Towards the modern view of memory

In 1959 a neurosurgeon by the name of Wilder Penfield inserted a microscopic electric probe into a patient's brain while the patient was conscious. This will make your eyes water, but Penfield used local anaesthetic and the patient was able to converse with him while this was happening. The patient reported various 'memories' being activated, like watching *Gone With The Wind* years earlier—complete with the smell of cheap perfume in the cinema and the beehive hairstyle of the person in front.[3]

When Penfield touched the brain at one spot the patient reported 're-experiencing' a piece of music. Penfield then shifted the probe slightly and into the patient's mind suddenly came the vivid 'memory' of an old childhood experience that the patient claimed had long been forgotten. Depending on the exact location in the brain that Penfield touched with the electric probe a different 'memory' might be reactivated. Whether these were true memories or not, they were often things the patient claimed not to have thought about in many years.[4]

Penfield's experiments eventually led cognitive psychologists towards what is called the 'spreading activation' theory of memory.[5] Cast in the framework of neural networks and distributed representation, this has become the best-accepted theory of how memory works today (notwithstanding that the strength of the original interpretation of the Penfield results appears to have been somewhat overstated).[6]

Association

Memory means retrieving a past experience.

> Retrieval of a past experience involves a process of pattern completion, in which a subset of the features comprising the particular past experience are reactivated, and activation spreads to the rest of the constituent features of that experience.[7]

To understand this notion we first have to understand association. When you hear 'MmmmmmMmmmmm', what do you think of? Chances are that it immediately brings to mind Campbell's soup. When someone says to you 'Where do you want to go today?' you probably immediately think 'Microsoft'. This is because our minds work by *association*.

Things remind us of other things. For example, we are often reminded, in the course of listening to someone else in a conversation, of something that we want to say.

This association process lets our minds 'fill out' more complete memories from fragments of information. We see the back of a head at a friend's party and before the person turns round we remember their face and, if we are lucky, their name. We catch a glimpse of Jerry Seinfeld in an ad on TV and think 'Oh, that American Express commercial again' even though we did not actually see or hear the words 'American Express'.

Our memory system can be cued with a fragment of a memory and, to the extent the connections and associative strengths are there, our minds tend to 'fill out' the rest through spreading activation that travels through the mental connections.[8] Neurophysiological laboratory studies now show us exactly what parts of the brain are active at any time (e.g. when we recall a person's face versus a person's name). This reveals the surprising fact that the various features or fragments of a memory are not stored together. The bits and pieces of a memory are distributed throughout different parts of the brain. What binds them together into a coherent memory is their connections and the associative strength of those connections.

If you really want to appreciate the pervasive and spontaneous nature of associative connections and spreading activation, try this exercise:

- Read out to a few people these words: *candy, sour, sugar, bitter, good, taste, tooth, nice, honey, soda, chocolate, heart, cake, eat, pie.*
- Ask them to write down as many of the words as they can remember.
- Finally, ask them if any of the words 'taste', 'point' or 'sweet' were on the list.

Chances are that about 90 per cent will say (incorrectly) that 'sweet' was on the list (up to 90 per cent of people do).[9] Why? The association is so strong that people mistakenly think they were actually exposed to the attribute 'sweet' instead of generating it themselves. 'Sweet' is an attribute that is strongly associated with a number of words on the list (candy, honey, sugar, etc) and it appears to activate the general category of 'sweet' in our mind.

Mental network

Recognizing something involves us in linking the fragments we have seen together—linking them by associative strengths into a coherent representation in our mind. We 'bind' the distributed features of the memory together. This representation of the memory is in the form of a mental network which may include not only things we actually saw or heard but also (as with the word 'sweet') things that are closely associated. This applies not just to memories but also to the meanings of things.

For example, when I say the word 'cars', what do you think of? You may have thought immediately of 'roads', or you may have thought of a brand of car such as Toyota, Ford or Volvo. What underlies these associations in our minds can be thought of as a gigantic neural network of interconnected associations.

Measurement of advertising effects in memory

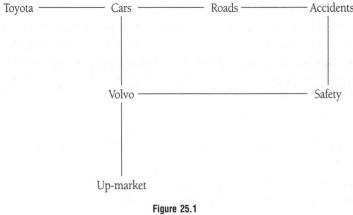

Figure 25.1
A memory network

These billions of neurons are all interconnected, some directly and others circuitously through other neurons. But the connections have different strengths. This is illustrated in Figure 25.1 which shows an over simplified version of what part of this network might look like.

Just as the touch of Penfield's electric probe might activate his patient's networks and cause the apparent recall of some memory, so may a picture that we see, or a word that we hear, activate a part of our mental network. The activation spreads through the distributed representation of that thing causing us to recall what it is and what is its meaning. For example, seeing a picture of a car or hearing the word 'car' activates their meaning. The activation is like an electric current spreading outwards and activating other close[10] things that are associated with 'car'. This is why an expression such as 'MmmmmmMmmmmmm' is likely to trigger not only its own meaning but also anything that is closely associated with it, like Campbell's soup.

Spreading activation

When we are exposed to words and pictures, each one activates a group of neurons that collectively represent that thing in the neural network. As we demonstrated with the word 'sweet' this does not have to be activated directly, however. It can be triggered by *spreading activation* from some close associate.

This is one of the main reasons why ad campaigns like 'Mmmmmm-Mmmmmm', 'Where do you want to go today?' and 'Don't leave home without it…' have been successful. They are frequently recurring expressions that crop up all the time in the normal course of our lives. So when we come across them in conversation it is the equivalent of inserting a probe into our minds and activating our mental memory network. 'Spreading activation' then triggers off any close associates, such as Campbell's or Microsoft or American Express, that may have become connected to the active representation. It gives the brand 'free registrations' and helps the brand stay 'top of mind'.

Meaning and brand image

The fact that our memories work through this process has far-reaching implications for advertising and marketing. It means much more than simply keeping something top of mind. In fact, it is the whole basis for the meanings things have for us, including the meanings of brands.

As Figure 25.1 implies, when 'Volvo' is activated it, in turn, activates any attributes that are closely associated with that brand, such as 'safety' and 'up-market'. These things that Volvo activates in our mind, the things that are closely associated with it, collectively represent the meaning of 'Volvo' for us. This meaning takes in the resonances of all the associations that are closely linked with Volvo and activated by it. This is the underlying essence of meaning as well as the underlying essence of brand image. It is why Volvo is seen as safe and Coke is seen as fun. It explains the ability of a brand name to activate (at least partially) these attributes in our minds. They are close associates of the brand.

Connections

Spreading activation extends through the mental network like an electric current. When there is low resistance between two points, the two items are said to have high associative strength and a high probability of the connection being made—the association being completed. On the other hand, when two items have low associative strength there is high resistance in the current flow. So things with low associative strength are less likely to be activated. The stronger the associative strength between an attribute like 'safety' and the brand Volvo, the more likely it is that activating 'Volvo' will spread activation to the attribute 'safety'. Conversely, the weaker the associative strength the less likely it is to be activated by that trigger.

Another way of thinking about this is in product-positioning terms. Simply put, it means Volvo 'owns' the safety position in people's minds. That is, Volvo is more closely connected to safety than any other brand (in its class).

The spreading activation view of memory thus gives advertisers a much richer way of thinking about product positioning as well.

Connections are like muscles. When they are exercised they get stronger. When they are not exercised they become weaker. We all have leg muscles, but if we want to use them for running long distances they need to be strengthened and exercised. Like leg muscles, connections that are not exercised may be too weak to perform.

When those of us who experienced the American Express campaign featuring Karl Malden encounter the brand American Express today, we rarely, if ever, think of Malden. This is not to say that we are unaware that he once advertised American Express. It is just that we don't think about it any more. The connection, in a sense, still exists but it has become so weakened by lack of use that it doesn't work of its own accord.

This all contrasts with the traditional view of memory that still dominates much of marketing practice. In this view, a memory trace is laid down. The memory is either there or it is not there. Either you remember it or you don't.

It is amazing that this model of memory has survived at all, because it is demonstrably wrong! How many times have you been unable to remember someone's name even though you know that you know it? Forgetting more often has to do with our inability to retrieve the memory (or some fragment of it) and we are unable to activate it again. Sometimes, we may have failed to store the memory in the first place but more likely we just 'forgot where we put it' or that part of it. In other words, our mind has lost the connections.

Retrieval cues

Our memories are triggered by retrieval cues. Retrieval cues enable us to remember other things. When we are trying to think of somebody's name, for example, and the name won't come to mind, we use retrieval cues. We may deliberately bring to mind the situation in which we last saw the person. That may help us remember the name. Why? Because we are hoping that the activation that spreads from the memory of that situation will activate the name of the person and allow us to recall it.

If that doesn't work, we may try other related cues to help us spread enough activation towards the person's name to trigger recall of it. What we are doing is looking for a retrieval cue that will help us to activate the name. Strong retrieval cues have strong connections with something and tend to remind us of it. They help pop that thing into our mind.

The relevance of this to advertising is that advertisers want their brand to be cued into people's minds when they think of making a purchase from that product category. If you are an advertiser, you would no doubt like to tie your brand strongly to a retrieval cue that is often in people's minds or in their environment—and ideally is also around at the time they buy the product category. This could be almost anything. It could be something visual (e.g. the pack or a dispenser label that we are likely to see at the point of sale). Or it could be something verbal (e.g. 'MmmmmmMmmmmm'). Or it could even be a piece of music (e.g. the 'Magnificent Seven'—the Marlboro music). So one test of the effect of an ad is to ask: Is it strengthening the association between a relevant retrieval cue (such as the product category) and the advertised brand?

Association measurement

As marketers, the retrieval cues we are interested in are brands, products, messages and image attributes. We have the ability to measure and track the changing strength of associations—to tell us how closely two or more things are connected in buyers' minds and how that strength increases with repetition.

Associative mental network

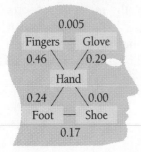

We are more likely to be reminded of 'hand' by the word 'fingers' than by 'glove'. Given the word 'fingers', 46% of people immediately think of 'hand' while very few (less than 1%) think of 'glove'. Fingers and hand have high associative strength. Fingers and glove have very low associative strength. Adapted from L. Postman and G. Keppel, *Norms of Word Association*, Academic Press, 1970

Figure 25.2
Association

The essential method was pioneered years ago by psychologists exploring relationships between words and asking large samples of people 'What is the first thing that comes to mind when I say...' The inserted word is the retrieval cue which might be, for example, the word 'fingers' or the word 'glove'. From the responses the researchers can derive a picture of that part of our associative mental network and the strengths in the associative mental network can be mapped (see Figure 25.2).

When advertisers use products and brands and image attributes as the retrieval cues the principles remain the same. The connection strength is measured by the percentage of people giving each response. Direction is important—for example, the likelihood of the expression 'credit card' triggering 'Visa' is not the same as 'Visa' triggering 'credit card'.

But how do you relate associative mental networks and strength of connections to advertising effectiveness? Exactly what associations should be tracked, and which of them indicate effectiveness?

An example

Let us illustrate using the print ad for Minute Maid fruit juice as an example (Figure 25.3). A young girl with plaited hair is holding up her juice glass and asking 'Mom, can I have some more calcium?'. The copy explains that Minute Maid is enriched with calcium—as much calcium as milk and that 'it's one delicious glass your kids will actually drink'. This implies images of Minute Maid being:

Figure 25.3
'Mom, can I have some more calcium?'
Ad for Minute Maid fruit juice enriched
with calcium. © 2000 The Coca-Cola
Company. 'Minute Maid' is a registered
trademark of The Coca-Cola Company

- 'healthier' (fruit juice); and
- a more delicious way for kids to get their calcium than drinking milk.

When this ad is run, the ultimate test of it is this: Are more buyers purchasing Minute Maid? If not, are they at least more disposed to purchasing Minute Maid?

The underlying logic of the process is this:

- if people, when they think of fruit juice, are more likely to think of Minute Maid (*brand awareness*);
- and when they think of it, they think of it as 'healthier/good for you' (*brand image*);
- then, if 'healthier/good for you' is important in fruit juice purchasing (*attribute importance*);
- we can expect a greater likelihood of people buying Minute Maid fruit juice will follow.

(Additionally, the ad very cleverly attempts to tie the brand to milk as retrieval cue and remind people of the fact that some kids don't enjoy the taste of milk and are reluctant to drink it. In other words, the hope is that when they think of milk, this will tend to trigger Minute Maid fruit juice as an association and as a possible substitute that parents might entertain as a way for their kids to get their calcium. This is a mechanism that could generate perhaps a bigger effect than the simple one of giving Minute Maid the image of a healthier fruit juice. So we should also ask: Is it strengthening the association between milk as a retrieval cue and Minute Maid fruit juice as one of the other alternative ways their kids can get their calcium? Because, this is another way the ad could be working and having its effect in addition to making the brand into a 'healthier' fruit juice. To keep things simple for the purposes of illustration here, we will ignore the 'milk substitute' mechanism in the explication of the measures that follow and focus only on testing for evidence of the healthier fruit juice mechanism. It should be noted however that the same type of analysis procedure can be very easily extended to test the associations involved in building up the milk substitute mechanism—in other words, positioning Minute Maid as a more acceptable way for kids to get their calcium, than milk.

Whether a greater likelihood of purchasing Minute Maid does result, is a question to be answered by sales, market share or other form of behavior data (such as self report.). Table 25.1 summarizes the primary measures that need to be available. Note that in addition to behavior (1), we need to look at attitudes (2). People may feel more predisposed to buy Minute Maid but, if they get to the supermarket shelf and find their regular brand of fruit juice on cut-price special, they may postpone their trial of Minute Maid until next time. That does not mean that the ad has failed.

Table 25.1
Primary measures of effectiveness

1. Are more buyers purchasing Minute Maid?	**Behavior**: Do sales, market share, scanner data, or survey self report show more people buying Minute Maid?
2. If not, are they more predisposed to purchasing it?	**Attitudes**: Has disposition or intentions towards buying Minute Maid improved?
3. At point of sale, what is the likelihood they think of or notice the brand?	**Awareness**: Has spontaneous brand awareness for Minute Maid increased?
4. When they do notice or think of the brand, what is the likelihood that the image information (from the ad) is activated?	**Image**: Is Minute Maid now more associated with 'healthier (because it has calcium)' than it was before?

Measure 3 (brand awareness) and measure 4 (image) are not meant to substitute for the behavior and attitudes measures, but they are diagnostic —they help us analyze whey the ad is or is not working and, if it is not they give us pointers as to what to do about it. Figure 25.4 depicts measures (3) and (4) as two diagnostic connections that need to be measured in the associative mental network.

Do people when they think of fruit juice, think of Minute Maid? The connection strength of measure (3) represents the likelihood that people will think of (or notice) Minute Maid when they get to the point of sale. Pack displays, special promotional material and all sorts of other things can influence this as well, but these things aside and other things being equal, the product category is one thing that is always present in the situation.[11]

The other connection is the brand image connection: when people think of Minute Maid do they think of it as healthier? There is nothing too complicated in measuring the strength of this brand-attribute association. It is simply a matter of asking something like 'What brand(s) of fruit juice do you most associate with 'healthier'? or 'What attributes do you associate with Minute Maid?'.

Note that none of these four measures asks questions about the ad. They are all focused on the brand itself. If the tracking shows that the both brand connections get stronger when the ad is being run, then all else being equal, we expect more people to be buying Minute Maid. Of course 'healthier because it contains calcium' would need to have been pre-researched and established as a potentially important attribute in fruit juice choice. If that has been done and these two connections are strengthening, then purchase behavior in the form of sales or market share (or at least attitudes) should also be moving in consequent response.

Under such circumstances where these four *brand*-focused measures are moving as expected, analysis of *ad*-focused measures such as ad recognition, ad recall and message take-out are rather irrelevant. The ad is working and even if such additional analysis showed the ad with poor recognition or poor message take-out (which is rather unlikely), nevertheless the *brand* connections that you want to influence are somehow strengthening and the key outcomes are happening. Something is working. Unless it can be accounted for

Mental connection

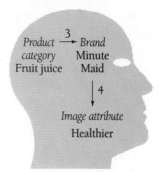

Product $\xrightarrow{3}$ Brand
category   Minute
Fruit juice   Maid

$\downarrow$ 4

Image attribute
Healthier

Figure 25.4
Brand associative mental network

by some other activity (such as brand-building promotion or PR), the ad must be working and, while this may be in a way that you don't fully understand, nevertheless it is working.

This is an important point because, while we know how a majority of ads work, we don't understand everything about the way that all ads work. In our experience, it is the exception for them not to work through conscious advertising recall, but sometimes it does happen. We should *never* throw out an effective ad that is working just because we don't understand exactly *how* it is working. Poor ad recall or poor message recall should never be allowed to override the stronger evidence of movement in the strength of the *brand* connections, (together with sales, market share and attitudes, of course).

But what if purchase behavior and attitudes to the brand have *not* changed? This is when the ad-focused measures like ad recall and message take-out, as well as ad liking, can become really important because they give further diagnostic aid in working out what is going wrong.

When an ad isn't working

It is when these key indicators (of sales, market share, brand attitudes and the two primary brand associations) reveal that an ad isn't working that the ad-focused questions become valuable diagnostics. This is when we need to delve deeper into the underlying related associations in an attempt to diagnose why the breakdown might be occurring.

We need to answer questions like 'Are they seeing the ad?' and 'Is it communicating the right message?' We know that an ad can work despite its apparent failure on one or both of these questions, but that is the rare exception not the rule. If an ad is clearly not working (as indicated by the behavior and attitude evidence discussed above) then ad-memory questions may help to identify whether the problem is one with mental reach (getting attention) or branding or message registration.

With a high degree of confidence, this will point to a key reason why the ad is not working and hopefully allow us to do something about it. We take this up again in the next chapter.

Summary

Mental connections are like muscles. When they are exercised they grow stronger and when they are not used they get weaker. The primary role of mental measures as an indicator of connection strength is essentially a diagnostic one. Measuring the strength of connections can help with the problem of sorting out what is going on underneath the observed purchasing behavior.

These are all brand-focused measures. They measure performance and associations with the brand. Measures that are focused on the ad itself (ad recognition, ad recall, message take-out, etc) are important when the ad is not working; they aid the diagnosis and supplement the brand-focused measures. As we see in the next chapter, they help to pinpoint exactly where an ad seems to be strong and where it seems to be weak and what actions we need to take to fix it. Understanding this can help advertisers do much more of what works and less of what doesn't.

26

The buy-ology of mind

The suffix '-ology' is used to mean either 'the study of' or 'the science of'. This chapter is about the science of consumption (or buying). In particular we address the role of the mind, how it influences buying and brand choice, and how to go about measuring it.

The last chapter peeked inside our 'necktop' computer to see how memory works. Memory consists of the firing or activating of an interconnected network of neurons. If our brain is touched internally at any point with a probe, a picture or a word, some part of our mental network is activated and we may recall a particular memory or meaning of that word or picture.

Like an electric current, the activation spreads out in all directions from the original point of activation, gathering up the meaning of the stimulus as it goes. The meaning of a thing is represented by the total pattern of the 'spreading activation' that the word or picture initiates. Knowledge is retrieved (or recalled) by activating the appropriate network in memory.

What we haven't discussed is the fact that there is more than just knowledge in these networks in our brain. Not all memory is knowledge. There is also memory for things that happen to us—of autobiographical events that are not knowledge per se. We remember episodes in our life—like driving to work this morning. Or perhaps we remember tasting a new brand of coffee yesterday. And we remember watching the Channel 5 movie last night and seeing that great Michael Jordon ad for Nike again.

These are autobiographical events or episodes that are retained in our memory, at least for some time. They form memory networks that can be activated later to be re-triggered in our mind. Psychologists label memories for episodes like this, 'episodic' memory, to be distinguished from remembering that is in the form of knowledge which they call 'semantic' memory.[1] The two are seen increasingly to be related.[2]

When we are exposed to an ad that gets our attention, such as the Minute Maid fruit juice ad (discussed in the previous chapter), there are usually four distinguishable components or fragments that can potentially be stored in autobiographical memory. Under normal ad-exposure circumstances it is all too rare that we remember all four of them. These fragments are:

1. the ad execution (girl with glass asking for more calcium);
2. the product category (fruit juice);
3. the brand (Minute Maid);
4. the message (healthy/good for you—kids ask for it).

The first component, the execution, is the creative vehicle that we hope will make the audience sit up and take notice; that will make the ad break through the clutter so that, having captured some attention, it can deliver its message. The ads shown in Figure 26.1 for Volkswagen (the 'Save Face' ad that we saw earlier) and for Dairy Soft spread are good examples. These executions almost compel us to stop and take a closer look at what they have to say. Once the execution has got our attention, it has a better chance of delivering its message and linking this to the brand.

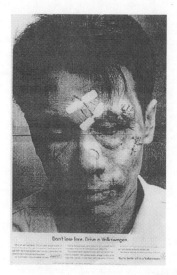

Figure 26.1
The ad executions for VW and Dairy Soft spread grab attention and, having done so, can then deliver a message

If the ad execution does its job of successfully breaking through the clutter, that is an important but just a first step. Getting attention is the first stage but the other elements are also important. Having broken through the clutter, what message does the execution register in memory? Is it what the advertiser intended? And if it is, did the consumer connect all of this in memory with the correct brand and the correct product category? If not, the advertiser could be doing a great job of advertising for some other brand or product.

These four elements of any ad experience that need to be represented in memory as fragments bound together by connections can be depicted as shown in Figure 26.2.

The ideal is to have all four of these elements highly integrated in the ad so that they mutually reinforce each other. However, this is all too rarely achieved and 'different elements of the ad compete with each other for the attentional resources available'.[3] Even some integration is better than none. The Volkswagen ad, for example, goes part way in that the visual execution reinforces the verbal message ('Volkswagen puts safety first').

Similarly, the visual execution of the Dairy Soft ad (Figure 26.1) dramatically reinforces its verbal message—'easier to spread'. Here, two of the elements (the execution and the message) are highly integrated and work very effectively to reinforce each other. To remember the execution is almost certainly to remember the message and vice versa. Compare this with the Minute Maid fruit juice ad, which has much less integration. Few ads manage to have all four elements highly integrated. The more integration there is the higher the chances of the ad's success.

The most common problem in advertising is, without doubt, registering the (correct) brand in memory. It is staggering how much advertising fails

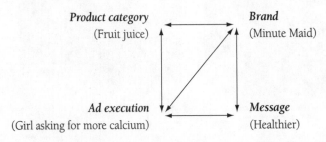

Note: Four elements need to be represented in memory and bound by connections

Figure 26.2
An ad experience memory network

because it doesn't successfully connect up everything else with the (correct) brand in memory.[4] Back in Chapter 20 we showed how to use 'constants' to help in this task of binding the brand into the memory network. It is a real advantage if you can use elements that are strongly and uniquely associated with that brand because they act as effective retrieval cues for the brand over and above the brand name itself. For example, when you see a health ad with Fergie (the Duchess of York), chances are you think of Weight Watchers. Or if you see a fast food ad with a Chihuahua dog, you think 'Taco Bell'. You don't have to see the brand but you get the brand all the same.

Looking at this another way: when your memory network is activated at two points simultaneously (i.e. the product category and an execution fragment like Fergie), the activation speading from those two points and activating any other strong connections should trigger the brand. This is epitomised in some of the Nike commercials that are able to 'sign off' with the 'Swoosh' and nowhere in the ad is there any explicit mention of the brand 'Nike'.

One point that can be strongly connected to the brand is the ad execution (e.g. Fergie and Weight Watchers). Another is the message (e.g. 'Don't leave home without it' and American Express). If the brand has a unique message that has remained constant for some time, just the message itself should trigger the brand. For example 'Where's the beef?' and 'Just do it'. These are unique retrieval cues that immediately communicate their respective brands (Wendy's and Nike) even without any explicit mention of the brand name.

Ad effect measures

In the past, some advertisers placed great store on people being able to recall their ad. Others did not believe in ad recall but thought it important that people be able to indicate they had seen the ad by at least recognising it. Some advertisers have put the focus on communication of the message rather than people remembering the ad itself, while others have argued that consumers' ability to parrot back a message is not relevant to the ad's sales effectiveness. There is a resolution to all this. To arrive at it we must first understand that *the effect of an ad is a process*, and that evaluating the effectiveness of an ad using continuous tracking data is also a process.

The process of evaluating an ad

Suppose that an ad like the Minute Maid ad, when first exposed, is not showing clear and obvious effects on changing behavior (as measured by sales, market share, or other behavior measures such as trial, repeat buying, etc). The first part of any doctor's diagnosis is to determine whether there is a *real* problem and, if there is, to locate the source of it.

As has been made clear in earlier chapters, advertising does not just make us 'run out and buy'. In order to capture its intermediate effects we need indicators of its impact on more than just behavior. For each strategic point in this attempted influencing process, we should aim to have an appropriate measure to indicate what is happening. When sales and market share movements as well as other behavior measures do not react immediately to advertising, the advertiser needs urgently to diagnose what is happening. It is at this point that the other measures assume center stage, because it is necessary to trace back through the intermediate effects to see where the ad is having an impact and where it is not, so as to make a judgment about what to do.

In the last chapter we touched briefly on the four important brand measures—brand behavior, brand attitude, brand awareness and brand image. Now it is time to extend this and look at the full range of measures, including ad-focused measures.

The main measures

The second set of measures (see Table 26.1) focuses on the ad itself—ad recognition, ad recall, message take-out, and liking and believability of the

Table 26.1
Measures of advertising effectiveness

Brand-focused	Ad-focused
Brand-purchasing behavior	Ad recognition
Brand attitudes/purchase intentions	Ad recall
Brand awareness	Correct branding
Brand image	Message take-out
	Ad liking
	Ad believability

ad. These measures fit together with the brand-focused measures in the total picture of advertising evaluation because they are used in a process of elimination to try to assess, first, whether the ad is working and, if it is not, to isolate what is going wrong. The questions that are asked about the effectiveness of an ad (e.g. the Minute Maid ad) will call for information derived not only from the brand-focused measures but also from the ad-focused measures.

The crucial difference is that having all these measures enables the pursuit of a full diagnostic interpretation.

Use of the brand-focused measures

The brand-focused measures that we met in the last chapter are primary. The questions they answer are shown again in Table 26.2.

We need to elaborate a little more on these four brand-focused measures.

1. *Are more buyers purchasing it?* (Or are the same people buying more of it?) The earlier it is in the campaign, the less likely that *purchase-behavior* evidence will show clear, unequivocal evidence of movement, especially for products such as durables where the purchase cycle may be months or years, and movements cannot be expected instantly.
2. *Is the ad showing any signs of affecting people's overall attitude to the brand or, in other words, their disposition towards purchasing it?* (Another way to

Table 26.2
Brand-focused measures

1. Are more buyers purchasing it?	Measure **brand behavior**
2. If not, are they more predisposed to purchase it? (but perhaps being prevented by something like a competitor's cut-price promotion)	Measure **brand attitudes or intentions**
3. What is the likelihood they think of or notice the brand? (If they don't think of it at the appropriate time this can prevent them buying it.)	Measure **spontaneous brandawareness**
4. When they do notice or think of the brand, what is the likelihood that the (image) information from the ad is activated?	Measure **brand–image association**

think about it is in terms of their attitudinal commitment or loyalty to it.) The answer can be provided by brand-attitude (or purchase-intention) measurement. It can often be revealing to see how much brand attitudes are changing even though behavior itself may not (yet) have changed. Note, though, that the earlier it is in the campaign the more likely that the evidence from this too may be 'fuzzy' and inconclusive because the effect may (as yet) be only small.[5]

So, especially during the early period, the next level of diagnostic measure comes into play, requiring information from the next two brand-focused measures. When, initially, there is only fuzzy information on changes in the behavior and attitude measures, these next two, somewhat more sensitive, measures provide 'early-warning' indicators as to whether the ad has a *likely* problem.

3. *Is spontaneous (category-cued) brand awareness increasing?* The one thing that is almost always in our minds when we are about to buy something from a particular product category is the name of the product category itself. So the product category (e.g. fruit juice, cars, computers, margarine, beer) is almost always an important retrieval cue that should bring the brand to mind in the purchase situation. When market researchers measure spontaneous brand awareness, they ask people what brands in the product category they can name. Which ones can they easily bring to mind? This is a gauge of the degree to which the product category acts as a retrieval cue in bringing the brand to mind; it indicates how closely the brand is connected to the product category. An increase in spontaneous brand awareness therefore provides an indicator of a strengthening in the connection between the product category (as retrieval cue) and the brand[6] (shown as connection *a* in Figure 26.3).

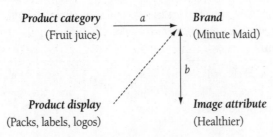

Note: The two key memory connections, and how product display may act as a supplementary retrieval cue.

Figure 26.3
Associative mental network connections

If spontaneous brand awareness is increasing, the ad is achieving at least that part of its aim. But if it isn't, then it signals the need to explore why the ad seems to be failing to produce this part of its effect.

4. *Is brand image association strengthening?* The brand's association with the key image attribute featured in the advertising (e.g. 'healthy') should also be showing signs of strengthening. If the image attribute association is strengthening (connection *b* in Figure 26.3) then the ad is doing this part of its job. But if it is not, it signals the need to explore why the ad does not seem to be achieving this part of its intended effect.

Pinpointing where an ad is breaking down

Establishing that either (3) (the category-brand association) or (4) (the brand-image association) is not strengthening will raise the question *why?* It is in order to explore the 'where and why' of something breaking down that we need the ad-focused measures. The ad-focused measures are diagnostic supplements. As we said, ad recognition, ad recall, message take-out and ad liking do not substitute for brand-focused measures but complement them. They assist in pinpointing which components of the ad are not performing and which ones are. They also indicate something about the nature of the remedial action(s) that might be taken to redress these problems.

For example, suppose we found that the connection (in Figure 26.3) between the retrieval cue—the category (fruit juice)—and the brand (Minute Maid) was not being strengthened. In other words, spontaneous (category-cued) brand awareness was not increasing. Naturally, the advertiser wants to know why. There are two possible reasons.

First, as we saw in Chapter 24, the ad may not be achieving 'mental reach'. It may simply not be capturing attention. Alternatively, the ad may be capturing attention and being seen but it may be weak in communicating the link between the product category (fruit juice) and the brand (Minute Maid), perhaps because people remember the ad but don't remember the brand. To take remedial action, the advertiser needs to know whether it is the attention-getting characteristics of the ad that need to be changed or the communication content itself. At this point, the ad-focused measures assume center stage and allow us to trace back through the cognitive effects to see exactly where the ad may be falling down.

Episodic memory and knowledge memory

When we store experiences such as ads as events in episodic (autobiographical) memory, we can learn from the experience. A non-advertising example illustrates this nicely. If a fox terrier bites us we remember the episode but we also learn that this cute type of dog can be fierce and to be more cautious of it next time. In other words, the events in our episodic memory feed into our 'knowledge' memory, as represented in Figure 26.4.

The experience may be one of being bitten by a dog. Or it may be an experience with a brand (such as enjoying a cold glass of Minute Maid fruit juice after school). Or it may be an experience with an ad for that brand (such as seeing the Minute Maid ad in a magazine we read last night).

So there are:

- memory networks that represent *brand experiences,* and
- memory networks that represent *ad experiences,*
  both of which feed into
- *'knowledge memory'* networks.

Ad experiences and brand experiences also percolate through to affect the strength of the various connections in our 'knowledge memory' network. We don't know *exactly* how these two types of networks interact and affect each other but we do know that activating two items simultaneously in one network, affects the other. For example, strengthening the connection between the category (e.g. fruit juice) and the brand (e.g. Minute Maid) in our memory for the ad experience, as represented in Figure 26.3, also strengthens the corresponding connection between the same two items in our 'knowledge memory' (Figure 26.4). The 'spreading activation' primes or strengthens that connection as well as any other closely associated connections.

Armed with our newly acquired perspective on the modern view of memory, we can now resume our examination of how the ad-focused measures

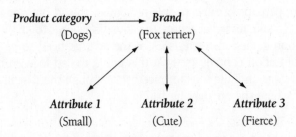

Note: The fox terrier part of the network affected by experience.

Figure 26.4
Dogs' knowledge memory network

perform as diagnostic aids. It is time to examine, one by one, the more common measures that focus on the ad itself and outline the role of each, how it is used, its strengths and weaknesses, and where it fits into the overall diagnostic armory.

Ad recognition

We visited ad recognition in Chapter 24. 'Ad recognition' is the conventional name for this measure but, in line with our modern view of memory, it should really be called 'execution-cued ad awareness' because it is recall that is prompted by the ad execution. Whatever we choose to call it, however, it is measured by showing people the ad execution (or describing the execution)[7] and asking if they recognize having seen it before.

For example, people may be shown the ad for Volkswagen which shows the man's horribly scarred face (Figure 26.1). When asked whether they have seen the ad, and they say 'no', this has a clear implication. Either they have not been exposed to it or, if they have, it has failed to command enough attention to get noticed. As a result it will almost certainly fail to show any observable effects on behavior, or on any other measure. As discussed in Chapter 24, this is a good measure of 'mental reach' and indicates whether the ad is at least being noticed.[8]

It is not a very demanding test but is useful because it provides an indication of the proportion of the audience that has been 'mentally reached' by the ad. The Thorsen and Zhao laboratory research referred to in Chapter 24 indicates that when a TV ad is aired once, we can expect about 60 per cent of the people who have their eyes on the screen to be able later to recognize having seen it before.[9] When people are given multiple 'opportunities to see' an ad, as happens in campaigns of several weeks, tracking results indicate that 70 per cent is the absolute minimum figure this should reach and it should preferably be much more. Note that this is among those who have had an opportunity to see it—this, of course, must be quantified by the cumulative reach media figures for the ad that pertain up to that point (see Chapter 24).

It is in cases where recognition turns out to be low that this measure is especially helpful for diagnosis. If people don't recognize the ad after a few weeks on air, the advertiser can be certain there is something very wrong—because it is such an 'easy' test. The question is, is there something wrong with the ad or with the media schedule? We can eliminate the possibility of it being a media scheduling problem by checking on the media figures that show what the cumulative reach of the ad has been (the percentage of people who have actually had at least one opportunity to see it). If cumulative reach is okay, then the low recognition figure reveals that this ad is 'wallpaper'—that is, it does not capture enough attention to get noticed.

In reality you will find that low recognition figures and 'wallpaper' ads like this are rare—for TV at least. Most often, 70 to 90 per cent of people who have been exposed to an ad a number of times in a TV campaign do recognize they have seen it—unless there is something very wrong with the ad. A high figure shows that the ad is capturing enough attention to get noticed and may give the advertiser warm feelings—but keep it in perspective. It is important to emphasize that this reveals nothing about the *strength* of any mental connections that have been established. This is because ad recognition is, in a sense, an 'easy' test, merely testing that a connection is there. It confirms that the ad execution does have some representation in consumers' memory networks. It has been seen. Establishing this is one thing. Measuring the *strength* of the mental connections within the network is another.

This difference can be demonstrated with old ads—but it applies to new ones as well. As pointed out earlier, those of us who are old enough will recognize that we still have a mental connection between Karl Malden and American Express. We remember that Karl Malden was the presenter for many years of the original American Express 'Don't leave home without it' commercials. That is, we can remember when prompted, so the connection is there in our minds, but ask yourself how many years it is since that memory saw the light of day. How long is it since it was last activated in your mind? In the same way, those of us who remember the famous commercial 'I'd like to buy the world a Coke' rarely, if ever, think of that song or that ad when we encounter Coke today. The connections still exist but they have become so weakened by lack of use they don't work of their own accord. The connections are dormant.

So the recognition measure can tell us that the connections exist but tells us nothing about their current strength or the likelihood that these connections will be activated by everyday events, especially at the point of purchase. The fact is that there are many, many connections in our minds that lie dormant and never influence us because they are never spontaneously reactivated. Even though we may recognize an ad, it reveals nothing about the likelihood that the right connections will be activated in the purchase situation. Ad recognition (execution-cued ad awareness) is therefore a diagnostic measure to check whether the ad has been seen—nothing more. In saying that, let us not take away from the fact that it is a very valuable measure for that purpose and consequently needs to be included.

But, in addition to it, we need to provide diagnostic indicators as to the strengthening of the connections that the ad is attempting to influence.

Spontaneous ad recall (category-cued ad recall)

Suppose, as a consumer, you are asked to describe any ads for 'cars' that you have seen recently. You describe an ad showing a man's horribly scarred face. This provides evidence of a mental connection between the product category and the ad execution in your mind—one that is strong enough to be triggered by the product category as a retrieval cue. This is conventionally known as 'spontaneous ad recall' but, in the modern view of memory, it is more accurate to call it 'category-cued ad recall' as it is recall prompted by the product category. (Remember that the more appropriate label for recognition is 'execution-cued ad recall' because it is prompted by the ad execution.)

After you have described the ad, you are asked which brand was being advertised and you answer correctly 'Volkswagen'. This is 'ad execution-brand association'. It provides the evidence that the execution is connected up to the correct brand in your memory.[10]

When you are asked to recall and describe ads for product categories like this, which ones do you describe? Those which are activated in your memory by the 'spreading activation' moving outwards from the two points in the network that have been activated (i.e. from the product category 'cars') and from a point representing the general notion of advertising.[11] The ads you describe are those that have the strongest memory connections to the product category at that point in time. These will be ads with already high activation (e.g. those exposed very recently) and ads that have established high strength (those that have been exposed more frequently).

When consumers are cued only by the product category and they spontaneously recall an ad along with the correct brand and the correct message, it tells advertisers more about the likely strength of the connections in their memories than if they are merely able to recognize the ad. It requires a stronger connection for us to be able to recall details like this rather than simply being able to recognize the ad.

If, in response to the product-category cue, a respondent can recall and describe the ad execution and also correctly recall the brand, an advertiser can deduce two things. First, the ad has undoubtedly been seen.[12] Second, it is strengthening the interconnections in memory between the product category, the brand and the execution.

Advertising tracking has demonstrated that increases in category-cued ad awareness almost always lead to increases in spontaneous (category-cued) brand awareness (unless the memory of the ad is not being linked up with the correct brand.[13] This is because activation spreads out in all directions from the initial point of activation and reinforces or strengthens any other close connections to it. Spontaneous (category-cued) ad recall is therefore a check to see that the ad is doing this part of its job—strengthening the connection between the brand's ad and the product category (the purchase-situation retrieval cue). (We consider some other, supplementary retrieval cues at the end of this chapter.)

Ad-brand association

The strength of the connection between the ad execution and the brand is revealed in the answer to the second part of the questioning procedure outlined above—namely, what brand was being advertised? This measure of correct brand association with the ad is important because it is perfectly possible for us to recall and describe an ad in detail but have it mistakenly connected in our memory with the wrong brand. When this happens, some other brand (e.g. Volvo) may be benefiting from a brand like Volkswagen's advertising.

This is not an uncommon cause of 'leakage' in the effectiveness of many ads. It means that everything is working except that the advertised brand (in this case Volkswagen) is not being successfully connected to the memory network. Consequently, its association with the product category ('cars') or the attribute ('safety') is therefore not being strengthened. Some other competitive brand (Volvo) may be connecting to the memory network instead and getting the benefit of the advertising.

Failure to connect up the (correct) brand in the memory network is an all too frequent problem. A check on ad-brand association is therefore a crucially important procedure in the total armory of diagnostic checks.

Message take-out

Let's look at the Minute Maid ad again (Figure 25.3) and assume the ad is

- being seen (as revealed by execution-cued ad awareness), and that
- the connections between the product category and the ad and the brand are all strengthening (as revealed by category-cued ad awareness and correct ad-brand association).

Suppose Minute Maid discovered that its ad did not strengthen the association between the brand and the attribute 'healthier'. We would expect it to strengthen because this is an objective of the ad. What else could be going wrong? We know that the ad-brand association is okay so there is little if any brand 'leakage', so why isn't Minute Maid increasing its association with the attribute 'healthier'?

The problem may lie with the quality, or clarity, of the message and this is where 'message take-out' assumes center stage to determine whether this is the problem. *Message take-out* is usually measured by asking, 'What was the main message that the ad was trying to communicate to you?' Suppose consumers answer, 'It is healthier because it has calcium and kids ask for it/like it'. This tells us that the message take-out is in line with the objective of the ad, and would effectively eliminate this as the source of the problem. Note how these measures are used as part of a process of elimination to close in on 'causes'. If we had found that people were seeing the ad and associating it with the correct brand but that the message take-out did not conform to what we intended, this would reveal the ad's weak link. But in this case we assume that the message take-out is okay.

If message take-out is okay and the communication is successful, what could possibly be causing the failure of Minute Maid to strengthen its association with the attribute 'healthier'?

Believability

Failure to strengthen the brand's image on the attribute can happen if people have cause to disbelieve the message. For example, what happens if people saw a *Reader's Digest*-type article about calcium that says its health benefits are overrated and that it can cause unwanted health problems in itself? (We are making this up merely to illustrate the point.) These people may still recall the message of the ad but it will be much less likely to translate into a strengthening of the connection between Minute Maid and the attribute 'healthier'.

A direct inconsistency between two ideas is a signal for our minds to stop and examine the ideas and decide which one is correct. The consistency of the message with what is already in our minds is crucially important (see Chapter 10). If the ad or its message is inconsistent with what is already in our minds, if there is motivation for our minds not to accept what is being said, then simply remembering the message will not necessarily influence our underlying 'knowledge' network. This is where a measure of believability of the ad is a helpful aid to detect whether this is the problem.

Message recall can be neutralised by our minds' actively rejecting the proposition. It is therefore imperative to keep the diagnostic nature of message take-out in clear perspective. Many people have argued over the years, and much evidence has been presented, that recall is unrelated to advertising effectiveness. The fact is that in many cases it is related—but recalling the message of an ad does not in itself mean the ad is effective. It is perfectly possible for us to parrot back the message that the ad is trying to communicate even though the strength of the connection between the brand (Minute Maid) and the attribute ('healthier') remains unaffected.

We can now see why so many people have been led to argue that no relationship exists between ad recall and ad effectiveness.[14] To hear and remember something is not necessarily to accept it and build it into our network of underlying 'knowledge'. Message recall is only one component of the process. Cognitive consistency is another.

Message recall is nevertheless a valuable diagnostic tool to have in the advertiser's armory because, when an ad is going wrong, it can help the advertiser to analyze why or how. Like other measures, it may be limited in what it reveals but it can, nevertheless, be particularly revealing at times of where and how the ad is falling down. Specifically, if an ad is not working, message recall can help answer these questions:

- Is it because the ad failed entirely to communicate the message that was intended?
- Or did it communicate the message but was just not accepted? (Ad believability helps to sort this out.) A third possibility also exists:
- The attribute (e.g. healthier) may not be relevant.

The message may be successfully communicated and accepted, and strengthen the brand's connection with the attribute. But if the attribute itself is not relevant to the consumer's decision-making processes, then the ad still won't affect behavior. So the degree to which the attribute is relevant is also important.

Attribute importance

Which attribute does the advertiser choose to emphasize? Clearly, different brands put their faith in different attributes. In the beer market, for example, one beer might rely on forging a connection with the attribute of 'reward for a hard-earned thirst' by showing people consuming the brand in a variety of thirst-raising, physical exertion situations. In contrast, another brand may rely on creating connections with 'natural brewed'—a very different attribute. And still another brand may focus on communicating the fact that their beer is 'less filling'.

Like the Minute Maid ad, these try to connect the brand with an attribute that the manufacturer thinks will be important or at least relevant to the consumer's decision-making process. If it is relevant, then the advertising maximizes its chance of being successful. If it is not relevant, then even if the ad successfully breaks through the clutter and communicates the message and the message is accepted, the advertising may still be ineffective in influencing behavior.

If the message is not right, if the attribute is not relevant to the consumer, then effectiveness may be limited or non-existent. To have any effect at all in that situation, the ad will be totally reliant on increasing the salience of the brand in people's minds (i.e. strengthening the connection of the brand with the product category). Just creating greater salience of the brand may not be a big enough feather in itself to tip the beam-balance and lead to sales increases for the brand. Much depends on whether the opposition brands that are ranged up against it are seen as otherwise equal (see Chapter 1).

Attribute relevance, or attribute importance, is or at least should be researched up front as part of the 'message engineering' at the time an ad campaign is being developed. The aim is to convey a message that has some relevance to the consumer, or one that has some chance of influencing the choice decision. (The relative importance of attributes may also be tracked by asking people to rank, or rate, how important each attribute is to them in their purchasing of that particular product category.)

Ad liking

In a substantial number of product categories where transformational advertising is the norm, liking the ad is critical to making people feel good about the brand—especially where there is not much else to differentiate it from other brands.[15]

This is the last of the ad-focused measures and simply asks people if they liked or disliked the ad. On the beam-balance of choice, if everything else is equal, liking for the brand's advertising can tip the balance. As was made clear earlier, a brand's advertising is similar to its packaging in that it is part of the brand's personality wardrobe. A brand's advertising attire can make a brand more attractive and make the essential difference when everything else is equal. With certain types of products and certain types of advertising, ad liking can be an important diagnostic aid.[16]

Supplements to the category retrieval cue

Before concluding, let us round out the picture by considering the notion of supplementary retrieval cues. The main retrieval cue we have looked at is the product category itself. This is why category-cued brand awareness provides an important diagnostic measure of advertising effect. However, smarter advertisers also build other retrieval cues into their advertising which may need to be considered in the measurement of that advertising's effectiveness.

To illustrate, during the work day or some other extended activity many of us have said, 'Have a break' or 'Give me a break'. If we weren't aware that we were feeling 'snackish' before we said this, we probably would be afterwards. Drinks and snacks are closely connected in the mental network to the notion of taking a break. 'Have a break' or in some countries 'Time for a break' and/or 'Gimme a break' are retrieval cues that not only remind us we might be hungry but, as a result of advertising, also activate a particular brand that has become closely connected to the expression. That brand is, of course, Kit Kat. 'Have a break. Have a...Kit Kat'. 'Time for a break. Have a...Kit Kat'. 'Gimme a break. Have a...Kit Kat'.

Another way of thinking about this is to be aware that a brand can tie itself to some connection, some retrieval cue, that helps it break through the mental or visual point-of-sale clutter and pop into mind, especially at the point of sale or point of consumption. The clutter that it has to fight against may be just mental clutter or it may also include the visual clutter that is presented by a product display crowded with brands and assorted variants. The brand wants to 'own' the occasion, or the moment or the feeling. Motorola wants to own the feeling of having accomplished something by having a cell phone handy. NutriGrain breakfast bars wants to own those hectic mornings when you're running too late for breakfast. Kit Kat wants to own the moment when you have a break.

Figure 26.5
'Have a break. Have a...Kit Kat'

The advertiser wants the advertised brand to be more strongly connected with something that is likely to be in our mind or in the product display at the time of purchase—something that will remind us of the brand or help it to be noticed for long enough to gain our consideration.

The main retrieval cue is the product category (name) because, almost by definition, this is in our minds when we are about to make a purchase. However, there are other cues—especially those that are likely to be encountered near or at the point of purchase (or sometimes consumption). These supplementary cues can be visual or verbal. The important thing is that something is included in the advertising that is also likely to be encountered at the point of purchase. Signs that tie in with the advertising, or a distinctive logo, pack shape or designer label that are included in (or tie in with) the advertising can all function in this way.

As an example of a visual cue let us cite one very convincing experiment. A brand of breakfast cereal took a single-frame shot from its TV commercial and incorporated it prominently on the pack. This acted as an effective retrieval cue connecting the pack and the brand to what was in people's minds about the ad. It gave it a boost that helped that cereal break through the shelf-display clutter.[17]

Advertisers who have built strong supplementary retrieval cues into their advertising rely correspondingly less on the connection between the product category and the brand to do all the work. 'Spreading activation' can bring the brand to mind by spreading out from the product category or the supplementary retrieval cue or both. This has implications for measuring the strength of not just one but all of these connections to the brand. In the evaluation of Kit Kat's advertising, for example, monitoring the strength of the association between the expression (e.g. 'Have a break') and Kit Kat is important as well as the association of Kit Kat with the product category itself.

Summary

This and the previous chapter have covered the main measures of ad effectiveness. This coverage is not completely exhaustive. There are other, less used ad measures but the main measures have been covered.

As we said at the outset, advertisers can get understandably confused about measures of ad effect. In the end it is behavior that they want to influence and therefore measures of behavior such as sales and market share are what they want to see moving. However desirable, changes in sales and market share are rarely sensitive enough and rarely *sufficient* in themselves to measure ad effectiveness. To capture advertising's immediate effects, it is necessary to have indicators of cognitive impact as well as behavioral impact. For each strategic point in this attempted influencing process an appropriate measure is needed that can indicate what is happening.

Behavioral measures can't diagnose why an ad works or why it doesn't. Without mental measures, advertisers can develop very little understanding of this buy-ology of mind and the real effects of advertising. These measures provide diagnostic tools that are all-important if advertisers are to translate the knowledge that something worked into a wider learning experience that generalizes to help formulate new effective advertising for the brand. Unless a brand is tracked on a wide range of mental measures it is difficult, if not impossible, to say how and why it worked and to use that knowledge to design better advertising in the future.

27

Conclusion

When we die we will have spent an estimated one and a half years just watching TV commercials. No matter which way you look at it, advertising today takes up a significant chunk of our lives. For that reason, if for no other, advertising is an important phenomenon in our society.

As children we wonder about how car engines work, how aeroplanes fly or how it is possible to transmit voices invisibly through the air. We also wonder about advertising as we are growing up—but for a quite different reason. Unlike cars and aeroplanes, ads seem deceptively simple—indeed, so blatant and so transparent that it is difficult to understand how they could really persuade anybody. What really puzzles us, then, is why such advertising continues to survive. Is there some secret that advertisers are not telling us? It seems irrefutable that advertising must be doing something to somebody—but what, how and to whom?

This is the traditional view of advertising that has held sway in our society for as long as we can remember. It is a view that has been based on intuition and introspection and which gets fanned from time to time by books alluding to 'the secret' in terms of hidden persuaders or subliminal seductions. This book has tried to present a fuller understanding of the subtleties and complexities of advertising as revealed through the systematic, continuous tracking of advertising campaigns as well as by scientific developments in psychological research into memory and behavior.

This book has tried to demystify advertising by developing an understanding of some of the real psychological mechanisms underlying it. Not all the mystery is solved because, as we have seen, advertising, far from being simple, turns out to be more complex than the traditional view suggests.

To some extent this complexity reflects simplicity in disguise. If you bolt together enough simple things, you get something that appears complex. So the way to begin to understand such seemingly complex things as radios or car engines or advertising is to start breaking them down into their simpler components and functions and looking at them at a micro level before moving up to the macro perspective. Understanding how advertising works on a macro level comes from understanding how all these micro-bits fit and function together.

We readily embraced the opportunity to track the effects of advertising over the years because it provided a window through which we could observe first-hand the effects of one of the childhood 'mysteries'. Looking at advertising through this window has led us to several conclusions:

1. Advertising works on people just like you and me—not just on those other 'more gullible' people out there.
2. The typical world of advertising that we may have envisaged where advertisers always knew exactly what their advertising was doing turned out to be very far from the truth.
3. The reality is that there are more ads that fail than ads that are outstandingly successful. The great majority of ads are at best mediocre in their effect.
4. The fourth realisation was that much of the myth and mystique of advertising has come from the 'tribal' agencies—many of which know less than they would like us to think about how or why advertising works. As with medicine men, their powers and methods have seemed all the greater because of the mystery that surrounds them. By imputing witch-doctor-like powers to advertising agencies, books like *The Hidden Persuaders* and *Subliminal Seduction* helped to enshrine and perpetuate this mythology.
5. The fifth realisation is that persuasion per se is a mechanism that is rarely involved in advertising. If it were, this book might have been called *The Not-So-Hidden Persuaders*.
6. Finally the real mechanisms underlying advertising effects turn out to be more subtle than they are mystical.

This book, in revealing the much more benign nature of these so-called 'unconscious' effects of advertising, has we hope dispelled many of the myths and much of the overclaiming that have been associated with advertising. At the same time, it has tried not to downplay the subtlety of these influences, or their potential effect on the success or failure of one brand over another *especially when everything else is equal.*

In fact, the advertiser and the consumer have been closer bedfellows than they knew. Both have been frustrated by not knowing more about the effects of advertising. All too often advertisers have known little more than consumers about how, why or when their advertising was working. This is beginning to change with new tracking and research techniques but, again, as our understanding of the mechanisms of advertising grows, so too does greater recognition of its limitations as well as its effects. This knowledge probably lessens rather than heightens the anxieties people may have about advertising having unbridled power.

There is one message that both consumers and advertisers can take from this book: the fact that advertising doesn't *seem* to be working doesn't necessarily mean that it isn't working. It takes sensitive measurement to gauge the often small and subtle but cumulative effects. At the same time, any fears that we may have had of being exploited by wholesale subliminal manipulation are way off the mark. The reality is that advertising has most impact on us in those areas that we care least about—where we are otherwise disinterested in the choice between alternatives.

Individual advertisers who have felt for a long time that they don't know enough about what their advertising is doing should be prompted by this book to stiffen their resolve to overcome this. In an era that is now coming to an end, where ad agencies enjoyed and exploited their mystique as the wise medicine men, the state of knowledge remained primitive. But, increasingly, the better agencies are coming to realise that, like modern-day doctors, they must be accountable. Appeals to faith or mysticism only work on people who are in a primitive state of knowledge. Effectiveness today has to be proven and established by observation and careful measurement. Mysticism eventually gives way to scientific reality.

By continuously tracking their advertising over time advertisers are coming to understand much more about what works, what doesn't and why. Accordingly, they are much better placed to brief their ad agencies. In being better equipped to articulate exactly what they want from their advertising, they are in a position to demand and confidently expect advertising that is successfully directed towards faithful implementation of their communication strategy.

The message of this book to both consumer and advertiser is that it is time to forget the mystique and focus on the real effects. Human beings have the ability to see the same thing in different ways, depending on the frame of reference that we bring to it. This book represents a frame of reference that will allow us to see advertising in a different perspective. For consumers, this perspective should be a more balanced and less fearful one. Understanding advertising and its real effects should make us less suspicious of it.

Advertisers, on the other hand, should take the attitude that it is indeed possible to know what works, and what doesn't and why. As a result they can confidently reject attempts to obscure their inquiries or fob off their concerns about whether their advertising is working. Belief in the exclusive power and province of the tribal medicine man belongs to an era that has passed. Accordingly, advertisers should be able to get much more effectiveness out of their advertising budget and out of working with their advertising agency. And consumers should be able to accept, without necessarily feeling threatened, that advertising does influence which brands they choose, especially when it doesn't matter to them personally which brands they choose.

APPENDIX

How to prompt ad awareness

In this Appendix we address the ways that ad awareness questions can be asked and clarify some of the confusion that abounds about exactly what is being measured. It provides an understanding of how different ways of asking the question may result in different figures. It explains why that is and indicates which questions are best for your purpose.

What is the cue?

Every ad awareness question has a prompt or what is more technically called a *cue*. Sometimes, people mistakenly use the term *unprompted* ad awareness. There is no such thing! There *always* has to be some kind of prompt in a question to tell people what it is you want them to try to remember. It would be absurd simply to ask 'Do you remember?' Remember what?

You have to tell them something about what it is you want them to remember. You have to prompt them with some kind of a retrieval *cue*. So the issue is not whether you use a cue but exactly which cue you use. Should you use:

- the ad execution,
- the brand, or
- the category?

Using Diners Club advertising as an example, there are three broad questioning options available:

1. **Execution-cued**. Have you seen an ad telling you about a brand of charge card where you receive 1.5 Airline Frequent Flyer points for every dollar spent on the card? (In face-to-face interviews photo-stills of the execution are shown.)
2. **Brand-cued**. Have you seen any advertising for Diners Club on TV recently?
3. **Category-cued**. Describe for me any advertising you have seen for *charge cards* on TV recently.

Figure A.1
Three types of questions to choose from

Figure A.1 gives full definitions and illustrative question wordings for each of these.

Questions like those in Figure A.1 are designed to trigger the memory in some way. Like giving an actor a cue from offstage, the cue in the question is designed to act as a starter that jogs the memory. Any ad-awareness question has to have some kind of cue built in. The various forms that the question can take, therefore, amount mostly to variations in the type and richness of the cue that is used.

Practicality

For most product categories it is impractical to use the ad execution as the cue *for all ads*. It would require you to show or describe the ad execution for *every* ad and *every* brand. There can be dozens of brands and an impossible multitude of ads. Consider the huge number of brands and ads in categories like financial services, shampoos or computers, for example. If you used execution-cued ad awareness, these questions would fill up the whole questionnaire, overly tax the respondents and leave no room for the many other important things you need to cover.

For the purpose of measuring awareness of *your own* ad(s) as an indicator of their mental reach, execution-cued ad awareness is a highly valuable measure and is most appropriate for this purpose (see Chapter 23).

While it is very useful if you can do it, comparing the mental reach of your ads with that of your competitors' ads is rarely practicable.

The other two forms of cueing are by category or by brand. As discussed in Chapter 25, these also give some idea of the strength of associative connection. However, as we shall see, only one of these two lends itself to complete coverage of all ads and all brands in the market.

Brand vs category cueing

For comparative purposes, then, which question is best to use—the one with the category cue or the one that uses the brand cue (Figure. A.2)?

One prominent company has always favored brand cueing and has long been critical of category cueing.[1] Others take strong issue with their unsupported assertions on this, pointing out that their claims are not based on empirical evidence.[2] Let us look a little more closely at the two.

When the two are compared, you will find that the brand-cued advertising awareness figure is usually *higher* than when the question is category-cued. In other words more people claim awareness when the question is cued by the brand. This is apparent in the case examples in Figures A.3 and A.4. In case 1, the brand-cued ad awareness figure averages 33 per cent compared with a category-cued figure of 18 per cent. In case 2, brand-cued is 46 per cent and category-cued 22 per cent. Such differences are reasonably typical.

So, why is the brand-cued figure generally higher? Is it just that brand cueing focuses the memory on a more specific question that people find easier to wrap their minds around (i.e. 'Have you seen any advertising for Diners Club on TV recently?')? Or is there more to it than that?

> 1. **Category-cued**. Describe for me any advertising you have seen for *credit cards* on TV recently.
> 2. **Brand-cued**. Have you seen any advertising for Diners Club on TV recently?

Figure A.2
The controversial alternatives

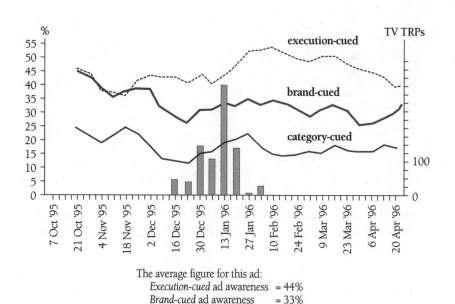

The average figure for this ad:
Execution-cued ad awareness = 44%
Brand-cued ad awareness = 33%
Category-cued ad awareness = 18%

Figure A.3
Case 1 Category- vs brand-cued advertising recall. *Source*: NFO MarketMind

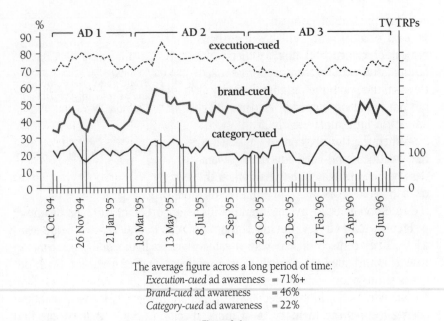

The average figure across a long period of time:
Execution-cued ad awareness = 71%+
Brand-cued ad awareness   = 46%
Category-cued ad awareness   = 22%

Figure A.4
Case 2 Category- vs brand-cued advertising recall. *Source*: NFO MarketMind

The nature of the output

There is indeed more to it than that. Note that there is a difference in *expected output* from the two types of questions. Category cueing ('Please describe any advertising you have seen for charge cards on TV recently') expects people to recall *and describe* what happened in the ad. Compare this with brand cueing where you provide the advertiser's name (or pack or logo) and ask: 'Have you seen any advertising for Diners Club on TV recently?'

> A simple yes/no is recorded for each brand, hence this measure is also known as *claimed TV ad awareness*, as the respondent does not have to prove or describe an execution.[3]

Now, think about this for a moment. If the respondent 'does not have to prove or describe an execution', what does it mean if, for example, 46 per cent of people say 'yes' to the question 'Have you seen any advertising for Diners Club recently?' What does the figure tell you about the current Diners Club ad?

Ad awareness

Not until respondents are asked a follow-up question like 'Describe the ad (you have seen recently for Diners Club)' can you begin to uncover how this claimed (brand-cued) 'advertising awareness' is made up. When you question further, you will find that it invariably reveals that those claimed advertising recalls are made up of not one thing but at least *four* things. These include false recalls, old ads and ads where they can remember only the brand (Figure A.5). Typically, if you have, say, a 46 per cent level of (brand-cued) advertising awareness then maybe half or less are valid recalls of the current (Diners' 'frequent flyer points') ad.

This should make it crystal clear that—when using the brand-cueing type of question—you must also apply the follow-up request and ask people to describe the ad. Only in this way can you quantify the level of ad awareness of the current ad. Using the information gathered from the follow-up question, you can subtract from the claimed awareness those claims that are not valid recalls of the current ad. This will lower the result which is now more likely to resemble the figure you would have obtained had you category-cued the question instead of brand-cueing it. This is because the figure represents a measure of *ad* awareness now that you have subtracted all extraneous items. Before you modified the figure, it represented claimed *advertising* awareness.

Asking people to describe the ad they claim to have seen for the brand will reveal that claimed advertising recalls are made up of at least four things:

1. *Current ad.* Valid recalls of the current ad (e.g. 'I remember the ad that said Diners earns you 1.5 frequent flyer points for every dollar spent').
2. *Past ads.* Recalls of past ads (for Diners Club) that are mistakenly remembered as being on air recently.
3. *False recalls.*
   (a) Brand 'slippage'. These are recalls or descriptions of competitors' ads (like American Express, MasterCard or Citibank) mistakenly recalled as being ads for Diners Club (e.g. 'I remember the ad where Jerry Seinfeld tells us to use Diners Club').
   (b) Category 'slippage'. These are recalls of advertising from another product category, mistakenly recalled here (e.g. an ad for an airline club (like Admirals Club) might co-brand its membership card with Diners Club card).
4. *'Don't knows'.* 'I can't describe the ad but I know it was for Diners Club.' (But is this correct? And, if it is, is it a past ad or the current ad? There is no way of knowing.)

Figure A.5
Components of advertising recalls

Ad awareness vs *advertising* awareness

Too often people use the terms '*ad* awareness' and '*advertising* awareness' interchangeably. If 46 per cent of people claim to have the perception or belief that they have seen a Diners Club ad recently, this is *advertising* awareness. It simply means that the brand has an image, among 46 per cent of people, of having advertised recently. *Advertising* awareness is an image in the person's mind. It is not *ad* awareness. It is not a measure of awareness of any specific ad or campaign.

Ad awareness and advertising awareness are not the same. One is an image dimension of the brand. The other is the level of ad recall for a specific ad (or campaign). One quantifies the brand's perceived advertising presence. The other helps you diagnose how people are processing the *current ad* (inferred from the questions on content, message, branding, etc—see Chapter 25).

The bottom line

The bottom line is: If you want to use ad awareness as a measure, if you want to use it to help diagnose what's working and what's not in your current ad (or campaign), then you have to ask people to describe the ad anyway, whether you ask them to do this using a question that is:

- **Category-cued:** '*Describe for me any ads you have seen recently on TV for charge cards.*'
  or
- **Brand-cued:** '*Have you seen any advertising for Diners Club on TV recently?*' making sure that it is followed by '*If yes, describe the ad you saw*'.

Debating which *way* you ask this (category-cued or brand-cued) is something of a red herring. It is not as material as making sure that you *do* ask it and therefore making sure you get a measure of *ad* awareness, not just an image measure of *advertising* awareness.

So this is a key reason why brand-cued *advertising* awareness figures almost always *appear to be* higher than category-cued ad awareness figures. They have all that extraneous material in them.

Evaluating ads

Let us emphasize yet again that, in evaluating ads, awareness is a *diagnostic* measure. Ads should not be judged on whether they can obtain high ad awareness but on their ability to change behavior and attitudes (see Chapters 24 and 25). It is therefore important always to keep in mind exactly what the diagnostic objective is of including ad awareness in the measures.

It is a perfectly valid objective to want to *quantify the brand's perceived advertising presence* (see Chapter 4, 'Conformity: the popular thing to do'). For this specific purpose, brand-cued advertising awareness does the job well, although it would be more helpful if it were called 'perceived advertising presence' instead. This is because it is roughly equivalent to asking in an image bank a question like this: 'As I read out each brand please tell me for each brand if you think it is...'

- recently advertised on TV   yes/no
- good value for money   yes/no
- often on promotion   yes/no
- etc

But for the objective of evaluating the *ad* itself and diagnosing why it is or is not working, you cannot escape asking people to describe the ad and the message they took from it—whether you begin with category cueing or brand cueing.

Three measures move together?

At the risk of too broad a generalization, it is our experience that all three measures of ad awareness (category-cued, brand-cued and execution-cued) tend to *move* in a similar way, more often than not. The graphs shown in Figures A.3 (page 293) and A.4 (page 294) illustrate this and show how they tend to move together.

But note that there is a major difference in their *absolute* values (as discussed on pages 294–5).

While more often than not the measures do tend to move together, it would not be true to say that they *always* do, or that they *necessarily* do. They *don't*, and there are very good reasons for this.

Let's look closely at the three measures in turn.

Recognition

Why is the ad awareness figure highest when this type of recognition cueing is used? It is because it is a richer cue than the other two.

It is a well established principle in psychology that memory is most effectively triggered if the cues at time of retrieval are identical to those at the time of exposure.[4] What this means is that in an ideal world we would show the video of the ad and ask whether respondents recognize it and have seen it recently.

As we have pointed out, in the real world of survey research, cueing memory by using the ad itself in this way is both difficult and expensive. You would never be able to use telephone interviewing and interviewers would have to carry video equipment to play the ad. (However, developing technology now makes it possible to play ads to respondents over the Internet.)

If it is impractical to play a video of the ad, the alternative is to trigger the memory with a surrogate, substitute cue. The more this cue approximates the full ad itself, the more likely that it will effectively trigger the person's memory.

Showing photo-stills from the ad execution, or describing the ad verbally, is the next best thing to playing the ad. This is called *execution-cued ad awareness*, as we have already discussed. While it is rarely practical for use with *all* brands and *all* ads in a market, it *is* valuable to use for your own ad(s). There are some important things to note about exactly how it is measured.

Execution-cued ad recall

For telephone interviewing execution-cued ad awareness usually goes something like this: 'Have you seen an ad telling you about a brand of charge card where you receive 1.5 frequent flyer points for every dollar spent on the card?'

For most ads the ad execution may be described to the respondent in words. Clearly, however, there are some executions—some ads—that are so complex they defy verbal description. Fortunately, these are the exception (and as researchers we just have to grapple with them the best way we can in the particular circumstance—one way round it is face-to-face interviewing).

For face-to-face interviewing, execution-cued ad awareness is most often measured by showing photo-stills from the ad *which should always have some of the words from the audio track underneath*. Let us repeat: you *must* provide cues taken from the audio track as well as cues taken from the video. It is amazing how often this is overlooked and yet it makes a huge difference to the level of recall.

When you show photo-stills or describe the ad, strictly speaking this should not be referred to as recognition. Even though people are being asked if they recognize having seen the ad previously, it is not the full ad that they are being exposed to but a surrogate—a representation of it. So to avoid possible confusion it is better to refer to this as execution-cued ad awareness (though admittedly it does not trip off the tongue so easily).[5]

Execution-cued is usually highest

In the graphs in Figures A.3 and A.4, note that execution-cued ad awareness produces the highest ad awareness figure of all three measures of ad awareness.[6] This is not surprising since this measure usually provides the richest set of cues. If the objective is to find out what percentage of the target population has been mentally reached by the ad, then this is the best measure of the three to use. It gives the best estimate. (As discussed earlier, it is mainly the practicalities that get in the road of using it for brands other than your own.)

This measure—execution-cued ad awareness—establishes whether there is *any evidence* that the person has been *mentally exposed* to the ad. This is irrespective of whether respondents can spontaneously retrieve the ad, what details they can remember, and whether they paid it scant or great attention. It addresses the question: in what percentage of the target market does the ad appear to have any 'mental reach'?

Problem with the media or the ad?

As discussed in Chapter 23, this percentage figure needs to be compared against the percentage of people who have had the 'opportunity to see' the ad according to the cumulative reach in the media schedule.

This cumulative reach figure from the media schedule for the client's ad sets the ceiling that you can expect for execution-cued ad awareness. The degree to which the execution-cued ad awareness falls short of it quantifies something meaningful.

Large gaps between the level of execution-cued ad awareness and the cumulative reach indicate either:

- *a media schedule problem*—people without an 'opportunity to see' the ad; or
- *an ad problem*—people who had an 'opportunity to see' it, but who failed to notice it—at least enough to recognize it again.[7,8,9] Advertising that people have been exposed to but don't recognize having seen is like advertising they have never actually been exposed to.[10]

As part of the diagnostic process of elimination you have to rule out the possibility that the media schedule is the problem *before* you can start concluding that the ad is a problem. The execution-cued ad awareness measure is immensely valuable for this for your own ad(s).

When an ad doesn't track well on this measure (i.e. there is a large gap between it and the cumulative reach), our experience is that it most often identifies a problem with the media schedule (i.e. that it is not delivering on its cumulative reach objective). It is much rarer that it turns out to be a problem with the ad itself (i.e. the ad being just 'wallpaper' and not being noticed—especially after multiple exposures).

Include the execution-cued measure before the ad goes to air

The execution-cued ad awareness measure must go into field before the ad goes to air, for two reasons:

1. Sometimes, when a new ad is very similar to other ads in the category, people can indicate they recognize having seen it even before it goes on air.[11] This problem of 'generic content' is an important reason why, *when execution-cued ad awareness is used, the question should be put into the tracking before the ad goes to air* so that the degree of false claiming can be quantified. When false claiming like this occurs, it almost certainly indicates that the ad is *not* going to be successful (except for promoting the category itself).[12]
2. There is one other circumstance where false claiming can occur. That is when the ad is a sequel or it contains elements similar to the brand's previous advertising—such as the same presenter, character, verbal expression, scenes, etc. This type of continuity can be a positive so some small degree of false claiming in this situation is tolerable and not necessarily negative. But it should not be large and again *it needs to be quantified by incorporating the question in the tracking before the ad goes to air.*

Brand cueing

Brand cueing suffers from a similar limitation to execution-cued ad awareness. As we saw with execution-cued ad awareness it is mostly not possible to get complete coverage of all ads for all brands in the market. There are just too many for it to be practical. The same applies to *brand cueing,* although to a slightly lesser extent.

This limitation of rarely being able to get full coverage is reasonably apparent when you think about it but it is rarely drawn to advertisers' attention. To use brand cueing, there is a need to ask specifically about *each* brand. This means a separate question for every brand. *'Have you seen any TV advertising for Brand X recently?'* This can mean a lot of questions.

The situation worsens when we remember the need to follow up each question by two further questions:

- *Describe the ad.*
- *What message was it trying to communicate?*

So unless yours is a market with a very limited number of brands it will be impossible to ask about *every* brand in the market if you use brand cueing. If you use brand cueing you will have no choice but to use a *subset* of brands, which means yet again that the tracking compromises on getting coverage of the full competitive ad spectrum. (Category cueing, which does not suffer from this problem, therefore usually represents a more attractive alternative.)

Ads for new brands and new variants

There is another important point to note with brand cueing—if a new competitor enters the market, you will miss out on its advertising because any new brand or variant will not be specifically included in the list of brands that the interviewer has to ask about. You only become aware of this omission *after* the new advertising has been launched. And then you have to decide whether the brand is going to be important enough to warrant putting it into the questionnaire. This is a difficult decision: if the new brand is going to have substantial impact, then the answer is yes; if it is not, the answer is no. But predicting this is exactly why you want to capture the ad awareness in the first place. You want it to act as an early warning system to indicate to you how much impact its advertising is likely to have.

With category cueing, on the other hand, if the new brand's advertising is salient enough, it will be recalled and automatically picked up by the category-cued question—without any need to intervene manually and change the questionnaire. So category cueing, as well as offering full brand coverage, also has the advantage of this automatic capture of new brand advertising by the questionnaire.

Category cueing

It should be apparent that, in most cases, using category cueing is about the *only* practical way to get coverage of the full competitive spectrum in the ad awareness question. Hence it is generally the recommended choice for that reason as well as the automatic capture of new brand advertising.

There are, however, some limitations of category cueing that you need to watch out for. One difficulty with category cueing is definition of the category. There can be contention over whether the category is best described one way or some other way. (For example, in our earlier example of Diners Club, would it be better to describe the category as 'charge cards' or 'credit cards'? This is a fairly trivial example but it helps to make the point.)

Some categories are easier to define than others. Categories like banks, shampoo and cookies are fairly clear-cut. Others are not—sometimes because they are at a higher level of aggregation and sometimes because they are not well formed as categories in people's minds. For example, consider the following:

- financial services;
- hair treatment products;
- snacks.

What exactly does each of these mean? Categories like financial services, hair treatment products and snacks are at a much higher level of aggregation than banks, shampoo and cookies and are consequently less well formed as categories in people's minds. It is not entirely clear exactly what falls into each category. For example, is an ice cream a snack? Is an insurance company a financial service? Is a hair dryer a hair treatment product?

When categories are specified like this at a high level of aggregation, it is more difficult to define the category and on some occasions it may be impossible. Fortunately, this tends to be more the exception than the rule. But there are times when category cueing will have its limitations. In particular, it will have problems with ill formed categories and possibly miss out on some low-salience ads, but on balance the positives of category cueing more often outweigh the negatives.

The positives of category cueing can be summarised as follows:

- It allows complete coverage of the ads for all brands—not just a subset of brands.
- It does not miss out on ads for new brands or variants that inevitably come on the market.
- It is clearly the easiest to manage from a questionnaire point of view and avoids the problem of the questionnaire getting out of date by new product/variant entries.

Recommendations

Where the category is relatively *well defined* (e.g. banks, shampoo, cookies) there is strong argument to use category cueing rather than brand cueing. This measures strength of connection of the brand to the product category (see Chapters 24 and 25).

With categories that are *less well defined* (e.g. financial services, hair care and hair treatment products), where you don't feel completely comfortable with category cueing and especially if there is only a small number of brands, then brand cueing may be preferable in that minority of cases. *But be sure to include the follow-up question asking people to describe the ads they claim to have seen so that you can come up with a measure of ad awareness and not just an image measure of advertising awareness.*

In addition, it is important to include a measure of execution-cued ad awareness for your own ad(s) in order to be able to quantify the absolute level of 'mental reach'. It tells you nothing about the strength of any connections but will tell you if your ad is not capturing enough attention and how many people it has 'mentally reached' (see Chapter 23).

Notes

PART A—INTRODUCTION

1. David Ogilvy, *Confessions of an Advertising Man*, Atheneum, NY, 1963 and 1984, p. 96.
2. Variously attributed to John Wanamaker in the USA and to Lord Lever-Hulme in the UK.
3. John Philip Jones, *When Ads Work: New Proof that Advertising Triggers Sales*, Lexington, NY, 1995, p. 28.
4. *Wall Street Journal*, August 12, 1998, p. 9.
5. William Lutz, *Doublespeak*, Harper Perennial, NY, 1990, p. 70.
6. William Lutz, op. cit., p. 74, quoting estimates by author and TV critic Dr Jean Kilbourne.
7. Vance Packard, *The Hidden Persuaders*, Mackay, NY, 1957.
8. Alec Benn, *The 27 Most Common Mistakes in Advertising*, Amacom, NY, 1978, p. 5.
9. As Kover has pointed out: 'Copywriters have a "reputation" in the folklore of the advertising business. They are charged with defending their work and its integrity against any change, no matter how small. They do this against account management, against their own creative department managers, and often in opposition to research findings and the urging of clients.' Arthur Kover, 'Copywriters' implicit theories of communication: an exploration', *Journal of Consumer Research*, vol. 21, March 1995, p. 604.
10. Jones 1995, op. cit., p. 27.
11. John Rossiter and Larry Perty, *Advertising and Promotions Management*, McGraw-Hill, NY, 1987, p. 558.

Chapter 1—Influencing people: myths and mechanisms

1. Referring to this effect as a feather is not meant to deprecate its importance. On the contrary, it is meant to give consumers an intuitive *feel* for why we often find it difficult to introspect on how advertising affects us. We don't feel the effect because it is below the JND (just noticeable difference), but that doesn't mean that feathers aren't important or effective. They are! If an ad has real news to convey, it can become a very big feather, in which case we don't need an explanation of the effect. Mostly, however, they are much smaller feathers.

2. John Deighton, 'The interaction of advertising and evidence', *Journal of Consumer Research*, vol. 11, no. 3, December 1984, pp. 763–70.

3. Scott Hawkins and Stephen Hoch, 'Low involvement learning: memory without evaluation', *Journal of Consumer Research*, 19 September 1992, pp. 212–25.

4. Scott Hawkins, Joan Meyers-Levy and Stephen Hoch, 'Low involvement learning: Repetition and coherence in familiarity and belief', *Advances in Consumer Research*, vol. vxxii, 1995, p. 63. Even though it may be small, a single reinforcement/reminder exposure can have substantial effects on short-term sales and market share for well established brands with established ad campaigns. See the pioneering work by John Philip Jones, *When Ads Work: New Proof that Advertising Triggers Sales*, Lexington, NY, 1995; and Colin McDonald, 'From "Frequency" to "Continuity"—Is It a New Dawn?', *Journal of Advertising Research*, July/August 1997, pp. 21–5.

5. M. Von Gonten and J. Donius, 'Advertising exposure and advertising effects: new panel-based findings', *Journal of Advertising Research*, July/August 1997, p. 59.

6. S. Shapiro, D. Macinnis and S. Heckler, 'The effects of incidental ad exposure on the formation of consideration sets', *Journal of Consumer Research*, vol. 24, June 1997, pp. 94–101.

7. M. Sutherland and J. Galloway, 'The implications of agenda setting for advertising research', *Journal of Advertising Research*, 1981, Sept. 1983, pp. 52–6.

8. Food Marketing Institute, as reported in *Businessweek* 7/1/96.

9. Andrew Ehrenberg, Neil Barnard and John Scriven, 'Differentiation or salience', *Journal of Advertising Research*, Nov./Dec. 1997, pp. 7–14.

10. M. Sutherland and S. Holden, 'Slipstream marketing', *Journal of Brand Management*, June 1997.

11. R. Fazio, P. Herr and M. Powell, 'On the development and strength of category-brand associations in memory: the case of mystery ads', *Journal of Consumer Psychology*, 1992, vol. I (1), pp. 1–13.

12. P. Dickson and A. Sawyer, 'The price knowledge and search of supermarket shoppers', *Journal of Marketing*, July 1990, pp. 42–53.

13. W. Wells and L. Losciuto, 'Direct observation of purchasing behaviour', *Journal of Marketing Research*, Aug. 1966, p. 227.

14. M. Sutherland and T. Davies, 'Supermarket shopping behavior: An observational study', Caulfield Institute of Technology Psychology and Marketing Series no. 1, Aug. 1978.

15. NFO MarketMind proprietary market research tracking for a new brand introduction, 1991.

16. Giusberti et al. 1992 as reported in C. Cornaldi et al., *Stretching the Imagination: Representation and Transformation in Mental Imagery*, Oxford University Press, NY, 1996.

Chapter 2—Image and reality: seeing things in different ways

1. Duck/rabbit figure as used in various psychology experiments such as Chambers and Reisberg 1985.

2. I.P. Levin and G.J. Gaeth, 'How consumers are affected by the frame of attribute information before and after consuming the product', *Journal of Consumer Research*, vol. 15, 1988, pp. 374–8.

3. G. Hughes, *Words in Time*, Blackwell, Cambridge, 1988, p. 174.

4. Scott MacKenzie, 'The role of attention in mediating the effect of advertising on attribute importance', *Journal of Consumer Research*, vol. 13, no. 2, Sept. 1986, pp. 174–95.

5. Meryl P. Gardener, 'Advertising effects on attribute recalled and criteria used for brand evaluations', *Journal of Consumer Research*, vol. 10, no. 3, Dec. 1983, pp. 310–18.

6. The Greenland Saga, as reported in Hughes, *Words in Time*, p. 155.

7. Stephen Fox, *The Mirror Makers: A History of American Advertising and its Creators*, William Morrow, NY, 1984, p. 16.

Chapter 3—Subliminal advertising: the biggest myth of all

1. Andrew Ehrenberg, 'Repetitive advertising and the consumer', *Journal of Advertising Research*, vol. 1, Sept. 1982, pp. 70–9.
2. A. Pratkanis and E. Aronson, *Age of Propaganda*, W.H. Freeman, NY, 1991, p. 201.
3. W. Weir, 'Another look at subliminal "facts"', *Advertising Age*, 15 October 1984, p. 46.
4. Pratkanis and Aronson, *Age of Propaganda*, p. 203.
5. Wilson Bryan Key, *Subliminal Seduction*, Signet, NY, 1972.
6. Roy Greenslade, *Maxwell's Fall*, Simon & Schuster, London, 1992, p. 99.
7. John R. Anderson, *Cognitive Psychology and its Implications*, Freeman, NY, 1990, pp. 183–8.
8. Giep Franzen, *Advertising Effectiveness: Findings from Empirical Research*, NTC Publications, Oxfordshire, 1994, p. 45.
9. HBS case: 9–392–032, 'The Body Shop International', Harvard Business School, Cambridge, MA, 1991, p. 2.
10. Alan Hirsch, 'Nostalgia: a neuropyschiatric understanding', *Association for Consumer Research Annual Conference*, Oct. 1991.
11. Gerald Gorn, 'The effects of music in advertising on choice behavior: a classical conditioning approach', *Journal of Marketing*, vol. 46, pp. 94–101.
12. William J. Ruth, H.S. Mosatche and A. Kramer, 'Theoretical considerations and an empirical test in advertising', *Psychological Reports*, vol. 60 (2), 1989, pp. 1131–9.
13. James Keflaris and Anthony Cox, 'The effects of background music in advertising: a reassessment', *Journal of Consumer Research*, 16 June 1989, pp. 113–18.
14. W. Moran, 'Brand presence and the perceptual time frame', *Journal of Advertising Research*, Oct/Nov 1990, pp. 9–16.

Chapter 4—Conformity: the popular thing to do

1. Lee Iacocca, *Iacocca: An Autobiography*, Bantam, NY, 1984, p. 286.
2. D.L. Altheide and J.M. Johnson, 'Counting souls: a study of counselling at evangelical crusades', *Pacific Sociological Review*, 20 (1977), pp. 323–48.
3. Robert Cialdini, *Influence: the new psychology of modern persuasion*, Quill, NY, 1984, p. 118.
4. L. Urdang et al., *Every Bite a Delight and Other Slogans*, Visible Ink Press, 1992, p. 50.
5. Merely hearing a new, hypothetical brand name is sufficient to increase the probability of that same name being mistakenly judged as an established, known brand 24 hours later. See S. Holden and M. Vanhuele, 'Out of mind influence: incidental and implicit effects on memory', Association for Consumer Research Annual Conference, 1996, Tucson, AZ. And as referred to in a summary prepared by M.T. Pham (1997), 'Really low-involvement consumer learning', *Advances in Consumer Research*, vol. 24, pp. 121–2, Provo, UT: ACR.
6. L.L. Jacoby, C. Kelley, J. Brown and J. Jasechko, 1989, 'Becoming famous overnight: limits on the ability to avoid unconscious influences of the past', *Journal of Personality and Social Psychology*, vol. 56 (3), pp. 326–38.
7. Unpublished survey conducted by Caulfield Institute of Technology students, Melbourne, 1978.
8. W. Moran, 1990, ibid.
9. S. Shapiro, D. Macinnis and S. Heckler, 'The effects of incidental ad exposure on the formation of consideration sets', *Journal of Consumer Research*, vol. 24, June 1997, pp. 94–104.
10. Nigel Hollis, 'They said my brand was popular—so what?', *Proceedings of the Advertising Research Foundation 1996 Advertising and Brand Tracking Workshop*, pp. 105–22.
11. A. Rindfleish and J. Inman, 'Explaining the familiarity–liking relationship: mere exposure, information availability, or social desirability?', *Marketing Letters* 9:1, 1998, pp. 5–19.
12. Irving Rein, Philip Kotler and Martin Stofier, *High Visibility*, Dodd, Mead, NY, 1987.

Chapter 5—The advertising message: oblique and indirect

1. Herbert Krugman, 'The impact of television advertising: learning without involvement', *Public Opinion Quarterly*, vol. 29, 1965, pp. 349–56.

2. D.L. Schacter, *Searching for Memory*, Basic Books, NY, 1996, ch. 6, pp. 161–91.
3. L. Postman and R. Garrett, 'An experimental analysis of learning without awareness', *American Journal of Psychology*, vol. 65, 1952, pp. 244–55. E. Philbrick and L. Postman, 'A further analysis of learning without awareness', *American Journal of Psychology*, vol. 68, 1955, pp. 417–24. F. Di Vesta and K. Brake, 'The effects of instructional "sets" on learning and transfer', *American Journal of Psychology*, vol. 72, 1959, pp. 57–67. B.D. Cohen et al., 'Experimental bases of verbal behavior', *Journal of Experimental Psychology*, vol. 47, 1954, pp. 106–10.
4. Leon Festinger, *A Theory of Cognitive Dissonance*, Stanford University Press, Stanford, California, 1957.
5. L. Postman, 'Short-term memory and incidental learning' in A. Melton (ed.), *Categories of Human Learning*, Academic Press, NY, 1964.
6. Russell Fazio, Martha Powell and Carol Williams, 'The role of attitude accessibility in the attitude-to-behavior process, *Journal of Consumer Research*, vol. 16, no. 3, Dec. 1989, pp. 280–8.
7. Charles Osgood, G. Suci and P. Tannenbaum, *The Measurement of Meaning*, University of Illinois Press, Urbana, Ill., 1957.
8. It is necessary to be wary of simple 'halo' effects in such cases. That is, when a brand is advertised it is frequently seen in a more haloed light generally (i.e. across a wide range of attributes). This happens simply because it is advertised. What needs to be shown is that there is greater movement on the target dimension than is evident in all the other more peripheral 'halo' dimensions.
9. John Grinder and Richard Bandler, *The Structure of Magic*, Science and Behavior Books, Palo Alto, California, 1976.
10. Kevin Keller, 'Memory factors in advertising: the effect of advertising retrieval cues on brand evaluations', *Journal of Consumer Research*, vol. 14, Dec. 1987, pp. 316–33.

Chapter 6—Silent symbols and badges of identity

1. R.B. Cialdini et al., 'Basking in reflected glory: three field studies', *Journal of Personality and Social Psychology*, 1976, vol. 36, pp. 463–76.
2. A. Pratkanis and E. Aronson, *Age of Propaganda*, op. cit., p. 168.
3. H. Tajfel, *Human Groups and Social Categories*, Cambridge University Press, Cambridge, 1981.
4. A. Bandura, J. Grusec and F. Menlove, 'Vicarious extinction of avoidance behavior', *Journal of Personality and Social Psychology*, vol. 5, 1967, pp. 16–23.
5. Nicolas Humphrey, *A History of the Mind*, Harper Perennial, 1993, p. 119.
6. R. Brasch, *How Did It Begin?*, Fontana Collins, 1985, p. 28.
7. R. Brasch, *How Did It Begin?*, p. 273.

Chapter 7—Vicarious experience and virtual reality

1. Robert Pirsig, *Lila: An Inquiry Into Morals*, Bantam Press, London, 1991, p. 364.
2. Morton Heilig, as quoted in Howard Rheingold, *Virtual Reality*, Secker & Warburg, London, 1991, p. 56.
3. Gregory Boller and Jerry Olsen, 'Experiencing ad meanings: Aspects of narrative/drama processing', *Advances in Consumer Research*, vol. 18, Association for Consumer Research Annual Conference, 1990, pp. 172–5.
4. C. Scheibe, Character portrayals and values in network TV commercials, unpublished Master's thesis, Cornell University, Ithaca, NY, 1983, as cited in John Condry, *The Psychology of Television*, Lawrence.
5. Erlbaum Associates, Hillsdale, NJ, 1989.
6. Pirsig, *Lila: An Inquiry Into Morals*, p. 364.
7. D. Anderson, L. Alwitt, E. Lorch and S. Levin, 'Watching children watch television', in G. Hale and M. Lewis (eds), *Attention and The Development of Cognitive Skills*, Plenum, NY, 1979, pp. 331–61.

Chapter 8—Messages, reminders and rewards: how ads speak to us

1. *Advertising Research for Bottom Line Results,* Proceedings of the ARF Key Issues Workshop, November 1991, Advertising Research Foundation.
2. Larry Bisno, 'News, news and more news', Breakthrough Marketplace Advertising Research for Bottom Line Results, Proceedings of the ARF Key Issues Workshop, November 1991, Advertising Research Foundation, p. 75.
3. See Rossiter and Percy, ibid., 1997, pp. 120–2, for clarification of the terms 'informational' and 'transformational' motives in advertising.
4. John Philip Jones, *When Ads Work: New Proof that Advertising Triggers Sales,* Lexington, NY, 1995, pp. 66, 225, 229.
5. See, for example, E. McQuarrie and D. Mick, 'Figures of Rhetoric in Advertising Language', *Journal of Consumer Research,* 1996 (March), vol. 22, pp. 424–38.
6. Elsewhere John Rossiter following Werner Kroeber-Riel has conceptualized this in terms of RAM-Conveyor Theory in Forschungsgruppe Konsum und Verhalten, Konsumentenforschung, Munich: Vahlen, 1994.
7. In a study of 87 print ads tested against a pure 'no information' ad, it was revealed that only about one third of the ads were substantially more effective than the pure brand reinforcement ad. Eric Marder, *The Laws of Choice,* Free Press, NY, 1997, pp. 308–9.
8. E. McQuarrie and D. Mick, op. cit., 1996.
9. E. Loftus, *Eyewitness Testimony,* Harvard University Press, Cambridge, 1979; E. Loftus, 'The Maleability of Memory', *American Scientist,* 1979, vol. 67, pp. 312–20.

Chapter 9—What's this I'm watching? The elements that make up an ad

1. We are indebted to the insightful work of McQuarrie and Mick in this section. See E. McQuarrie and David Mick, 'On resonance: A critical pluralistic inquiry into advertising rhetoric', *Journal of Consumer Research,* vol. 19, Sept. 1992.
2. Giep Franzen, *Advertising Effectiveness: Findings from Empirical Research,* NTC Publications, Oxon, 1994, p. 35.
3. Ibid., p. 35.
4. Terence Shimp, *Advertising, Promotion and Supplementary Aspects of Integrated Marketing Communications,* 4th edn, Dryden Press, Orlando, Fl., 1997, p. 299.
5. J. Severn, G. Belk and M. Belk, 'The effects of sexual and non-sexual advertising appeals and information level on cognitive processing and communication effectiveness', *Journal of Advertising,* vol. 19, no. 1, 1990, pp. 14–22.
6. Shimp, op. cit.
7. Thanks to Simon Anholt for some of the examples used in this section.
8. John Rossiter and Larry Percy, *Advertising Communications and Promotions Management,* 2nd edn, McGraw-Hill, NY, 1997, p. 288.
9. Ibid., pp. 242, 288.
10. Ibid., pp. 285, 295.
11. Franzen, op. cit., p. 189.
12. G.E. Belch and M.A. Belch, *Advertising and Promotion: An Integrated Marketing Communications Perspective,* 4th edn, Irwin McGraw-Hill, Boston, MA, 1998, p. 287.
13. Rossiter and Percy, op. cit., p. 282.
14. Franzen, op. cit., p. 64.
15. E. Walster and Leon Festinger, 'The effectiveness of "overheard" persuasive communications', *Journal of Abnormal and Social Psychology,* vol. 65, 1962, pp. 395–402.
16. 'New Animation', *Marketing News,* American Marketing Association, 6 August 1990.
17. James Wahlberg, Celluloid Studios, Denver US, as reported in *Marketing News,* American Marketing Association, 6 August 1990.
18. Laurence Gibson, 'What can one exposure do?', *Journal of Advertising Research,* April/May 1996.

Chapter 10—The limits of advertising

1. A. Benn, *The 27 Most Common Mistakes in Advertising*, Amacom, NY, 1978, p. 94.
2. P. Kotler, *Marketing Management*, 9th edn, Prentice Hall, New Jersey, 1997, p. 309.
3. Alan Hirsch, 'Nostalgia: a neuropsychiatric understanding', *Association for Consumer Research Annual Conference*, October 1991.
4. Leon Festinger, *A Theory of Cognitive Dissonance*, Stanford University Press, Stanford, 1957.
5. This quality positioning line is actually used very successfully in Australia for the brand John West.
6. A.S.C. Ehrenberg, 'Repetitive advertising and the consumer', *Journal of Advertising Research*, vol. 1, Sept. 1982, pp. 70–9.
7. M. Schlinger, 'A profile of responses to commercials', *Journal of Advertising Research*, 1979, vol. 1, no. 2.
8. E. Walster and Leon Festinger, 'The effectiveness of "overheard" persuasive communications', ibid., pp. 395–402.
9. John Deighton and Robert Schindler, 'Can advertising influence experience?', *Psychology & Marketing*, vol. 5, no. 2, Summer 1988, pp. 103–15. John Deighton, D. Romer and J. McQueen, 'Using drama to persuade', *Journal of Consumer Research*, vol. 16, no. 2, Dec. 1989, pp. 335–43.
10. Raymond Bauer, *Advertising in America*, The Graduate School of Harvard, Massachusetts, 1968, p. 290.

PART B—INTRODUCTION

1. Note that this is merely the average frequency figure. The fact is that some people will have seen it only once, others will have seen it twice and still others will have seen it three or more times. The overall average for the number of times seen is, however, a single figure and this figure is known as *average frequency*. The more astute advertisers today are demanding that their media plans and media schedules be looked at in more than this simplistic way. They are demanding information on the full frequency distribution of these figures rather than the simple overall average, so that they can see exactly how many people were exposed once, twice, three times, etc, rather than having just a single overall average figure.
2. See note 1.

Chapter 11—Continuous tracking: are you being followed?

1. John Philip Jones, *When Ads Work: New Proof that Advertising Triggers Sales*, Lexington, NY, 1995.
2. Richard Morris, *Behind the Oval Office*, Random House, NY, 1997.

Chapter 12—New product launches: don't pull the plug too early

1. Alice Sylvester, 'What Works, What Doesn't. Practical applications of Adworks Material', *Admap*, March 1992.

Chapter 13—Planning campaign strategy around consumers' mental filing cabinets

1. Raymond Burke and Thomas Srull, 'Competitive interference and consumer memory for advertising', *Journal of Consumer Research*, vol. 15, June 1988, pp. 55–68.
2. Alan Baddeley, *Your Memory*, Prion, London, 1996, pp. 141–3.
3. Michael Anderson and James Neely, 'Interference and inhibition in memory retrieval', Chap. 8 in Elizabeth Bjork and Robert Bjork (eds), *Memory*, Academic Press, San Diego, 1996, pp. 237–313.

4. John Anderson, *Cognitive Psychology and its Implications*, 3rd edn, W.H. Freeman, NY, 1990, pp. 164–70.
5. Such data are available in most developed countries. For example in US through Monitor Plus database from the Nielsen Media Research Company New York; in UK from Media Expenditure Analysis Limited, London; and in Australia from AIM Data Media Monitoring Service, Sydney.
6. Giep Franzen, *Advertising Effectiveness*, NTC, Oxfordshire, 1994, p. 20.
7. Under conditions of forced attention it is not uncommon to find research that appears to contradict this and supports multiple executions but this is very different from the normal low involvement conditions. See, for example, H. Rao Unnava and Robert Burn Grant, 'Effects of repeating varied ad executions on brand name and memory', *Journal of Marketing Research*, vol. xxviii, Nov. 1991, pp 40–1.
8. Burke and Srull 1998 suggest that 'competitive advertising would have the strongest inhibitory effect on the memory of consumers who are not in the market for a product, or who do not have the ability and/or the motivation to process ads in a manner that will enhance information retrievability', p. 65.
9. Max Sutherland, 'To build a brand, use something old as a link to something new', *Journal of Brand Management*, vol. 3, no. 5, April 1996, pp. 284–6.

Chapter 14—What happens when you stop advertising?

1. 'Advertising as an anti-recession tool', *Harvard Business Review*, Jan–Feb, 1980.
2. William Moran, 'Relating the product line to market needs and wants', *Handbook of Marketing*, 2nd edn, McGraw-Hill, NY, 1986.
3. Ibid.
4. Kenneth Longman, 'To build brand equity, it pays to advertise', *Journal of Brand Management*, vol. 5, no. 5, 1998, p. 366.

Chapter 15—The effectiveness of funny ads: what a laugh!

1. We are grateful to Simon Anholdt (Worldwriters) for some of the international ad examples used in this chapter.
2. John Rossiter and Larry Percy, *Advertising Communications & Promotion Management*, McGraw-Hill, NY, 1997.
3. Marc Weinberger and H. Spotts, 'Humor in U.S. versus U.K. TV advertising', *Journal of Advertising*, vol. 18, no. 2, 1989, pp. 39–44.
4. As Charles Gruner points out, wit deals more often with real events while humor more usually deals with fantasy. (Charles R. Gruner, *Understanding Laughter: the workings of wit and humor*, Nelson-Hall, Chicago, 1978.)
5. See Tony Chapman and Hugh Foot (eds), *Humor and Laughter: theory, research and applications*, Wiley, London, 1976.
6. Eric Smith, *An Accidental History of Words*, Bay Books, p. 83.
7. Chapman and Foot, 1976, p. 1.
8. A study of highly successful comedy script writers in the USA found that humorists were not able to provide much in the way of conscious insights about their technique. Most 'showed a charming and convincing naiveté about humor theory per se'. Chapman and Foot, 1976, p. 251.
9. Adapted partly from P. McGhee, 'Development of the humor response—a review of the literature', *Psychological Bulletin*, vol. 76, 328–48.
10. Arthur Koestler, *The Act of Creation*, 1964.
11. D. Schacter, *Searching for Memory*, Basic Books, NY, p. 210.
12. G.E. Belch and M.A. Belk, 'An investigation of the effects of repetition on cognitive and affective reactions to humorous and serious television commercials', *Advances in Consumer Research*, vol. 11, 1984, pp. 4–10.

13. McCollum/Spielman research report, 1978. Also B. Gelb and G. Zinkhan, *Journal of Advertising*, vol. 14, 1985, pp. 13–20.
14. Belch and Belk, 1984.
15. G. Zinkhan and B. Gelb, *Advances in Consumer Research*, 1990, vol. 17, p. 440.
16. Ibid.

Chapter 16—Learning to use 15-second TV commercials

1. D'Arcy, Masius, Benton and Bowles, 'Advertising in Japan: keeping the message short and sweet', *The Business Brief*, Melbourne, Nov./Dec. 1991.
2. Lee Weinblatt, 'People meters for print', *Print Media Magazine*, March 1990, pp. 35–7.
3. *Improved Marketing Productivity or Advertising's Vietnam?*, Association of National Advertisers, NY, 1990.
4. Analysis of the distribution of Day-After-Recall scores revealed that a majority of all 15s scored at the low end of the DAR scale. J. Walter Thompson publication: *A Closer Look at 15-second Commercials in the Nineties*.
5. M. Von Gonten and J. Donius, 'Advertising exposure and advertising effects: new panel-based findings', *Journal of Advertising Research*, July/August 1997, p. 59.
6. L. Jacoby and M. Dallas, 'On the relationship between autobiographical memory and perceptual learning', *Journal of Experimental Psychology: General*, vol. 110, 1981, pp. 306–40.
7. The technical term for this effect is 'backward masking'. For formal definition of it, see M. Eagle, 'The effects of subliminal stimuli of aggressive content upon conscious cognition', *Journal of Personality*, vol. 27, 1959, pp. 578–600.
8. L. Jacoby and C. Kelley, 'Unconscious influences of memory for a prior event', *Personality and Social Psychology Bulletin*, vol. 13, pp. 314–36.

Chapter 18—Underweight advertising: execution anorexia

1. Two writers have suggested independently 50 TRPs per week as the minimum threshold. See John Philip Jones, op. cit., 1995 and M. Von Gonten and J. Donius, op. cit., 1997. (50 TRPs means that at best only half the target has an opportunity to see the ad during that week.)
2. 150 TRPs could mean 100 per cent of people exposed on average 1.5 times. In this case it was more like 93 per cent of people exposed on average about 1.6 times in the week.
3. Note that laboratory research using *forced attention* is quite different from natural-viewing, low-involvement conditions (see E. McQuarrie, 'Have laboratory experiments become detached from advertiser goals? A meta-analysis). Not infrequently laboratory forced-attention studies produce findings that might *appear* to support the use of multiple executions. We believe these are applicable only to high-involvement conditions. See, for example, H. Rao Unnava and Robert Burnkrant, 'Effects of repeating varied ad executions on brand name memory', *Journal of Marketing Research*, vol. XXVIII, Nov. 1991, pp. 401–17. Also S. Hawkins, S. Hoch and J. Meyers-Levy, 'Low-involvement learning: repetition and coherence in familiarity and belief', *Journal of Consumer Psychology*, forthcoming.
4. It is important to note that brand buyers are relatively more involved with that brand than non-buyers of it. By implication, brands with low market shares have a communication 'handicap' compared with brand leaders—especially if the brand leader is talking to its own buyers. For empirical evidence of this, see B. Rice and R. Bennett, 'The relationship between band usage and advertising tracking measurements: international findings', *Journal of Advertising Research*, vol. 38, no. 3, May/June 1998, pp. 58–66.

Chapter 19—Why radio ads aren't recalled

1. John Rossiter and Larry Percy, *Advertising and Promotion Management*, McGraw-Hill, NY, 1987, p. 447.

Chapter 20—Maximizing ad effectiveness: develop a unique and consistent style

1. David Aaker, 'Resisting temptations to change a brand position/execution: the power of consistency over time', *Journal of Brand Management*, vol. 3, no. 4, Feb. 1996, pp. 251–8.

Chapter 21—Sequels

1. Max Sutherland, 'To build a brand, use something old as a link to something new', *Journal of Brand Management*, vol. 3, no. 5, April 1996, pp. 284–6.

Chapter 22—Corporate tracking of image and issues

1. Jagdish Agrawal and W. Kamakura, 'The economic worth of celebrity endorsers', *Journal of Marketing*, vol. 59, July 1995, pp. 56–62.
2. Alan Cleland and Albert Bruno, *The Market Value Process: Bridging Customer and Shareholder Value*, Jossey-Bass, San Francisco, 1996.
3. When seen in the context of the numbers 16, 17, 10, 12, 83 per cent of people see this stimulus as the number 13. When seen in the context of the letters L, M, Y, A, 92 per cent see it as the letter B. Jerome Bruner and L. Minturn, 1951, as reported in J. Grivas, R. Down and L. Carter, *Psychology*, Macmillan Education, South Melbourne, Australia, 1996, p. 128.

Chapter 23—The Web: advertising in a new age

1. L. Maddox and D. Mehta, 'The role and effect of web addresses in advertising', *Journal of Advertising Research*, vol. 37, no. 2, March/April 1997, pp. 47–59.
2. Scott McDonald, 'The once and future web', *Journal of Advertising Research*, vol. 37, no. 2, March/April 1997, p. 25.
3. B. Hilliard, 'Beyond click-through: the Internet as an advertising medium and more'. Paper presented to the American Academy of Advertising Conference, Albuquerque, New Mexico, March 1999, accessible at **www.utexas.edu/coc/admedium**
4. R. Briggs, 'A road map for online marketing strategy', *Admap*, March 1998, pp. 27–30.
5. John Leckenby and Jongpil Hong, 'Using reach/frequency for web media planning', *Journal of Advertising Research*, vol. 38, no. 1, Jan./Feb. 1998, pp. 7–20.
6. Jongpil Hong and John Leckenby, 'Audience duplication issues in worldwide web reach/frequency estimation'. Paper presented to the American Academy of Advertising Conference, Albuquerque, New Mexico, March 1999, accessible at **www.utexas.edu/coc/admedium**
7. Like telephone in the early days, the Web does not have everybody online. However, any skew in samples will diminish as more and more of the population get hooked up to the Internet.
8. See, for example, **www.nfow.com/nforesearch/products.asp**
9. Scott McDonald, 1997, p. 26.
10. It is important to realize that even when the percentage gets smaller the absolute numbers clicking through may be increasing because of the sheer growth in the total number of people on the Web and hence so many more people being exposed.
11. M. Sutherland and T. Davies, 'Supermarket shopping behavior: an observational study', Caulfield Institute of Technology Psychology & Marketing Series, no. 1, Aug. 1978.
12. Steve Edwards, 'Telepresence in media and advertising'. Paper presented to the American Academy of Advertising Conference, Albuquerque, New Mexico, March 1999, accessible at **www.utexas.edu/coc/admedium**
13. Stephen Masiclat and Fritz Cropp, 'Designing online advertising: the search for useful alternatives to the banner ad'. Proceedings of the 1999 Conference of the American Academy of Advertising, M. Roberts, ed., p. 272.

Chapter 24—'Mental reach': they see your ad but does it get through?

1. Giep Franzen, *Advertising Effectiveness: Findings from empirical research*, NTC, Oxfordshire, UK, 1994, p. 20.
2. Zapping happens most frequently in the first five minutes and the last five minutes of a program and during the first five seconds of commercials. See Giep Franzen, ibid.
3. Franzen, ibid.
4. Ulric Neisser as quoted by D. Schacter, *Searching for Memory*, Basic Books, NY, 1996, p. 22.
5. Esther Thorsen and Xinshu Zhao, 'Television viewing behaviour as an index of commercial effectiveness', Association for Consumer Research Advertising and Psychology Conference, 1994.
6. Source NAB 1990 as cited by Franzen, op. cit., p. 14.
7. John Philip Jones, *When Ads Work*, Lexington Books, NY, 1995.

Chapter 25—Measurement of advertising effects in memory

1. This is referred to in the USA as 'message take-away' but in other parts of the world it is more commonly known as 'message take-out'.
2. Of the various ways that purchase behavior can be measured (i.e. sales figures, market share figures or self-report) a distinct advantage of self-report (e.g. the last time you bought margarine which brand did you buy?) is that particular purchases can be identified with particular individuals—something which sales and market share measures have traditionally lacked. Developments in computer technology and electronic scanning in the last 20 years now make it possible to identify individuals and link their purchases via an identity code which they present at the point of sale and which can be scanned along with the purchased items. With household grocery purchases an alternative is to recruit a household panel of people who agree to scan their own purchases when they get them home and whose behavior is then 'self-reported', and transmitted electronically. (See Rossiter and Percy, op. cit., 1997, p. 507 and Jones, op. cit., 1995, for explication of scanner measurement of purchase behavior.)
3. Wilder Penfield, *The Mystery of the Mind: A Critical Study of Consciousness and the Human Brain*, Princeton University Press, Princeton, New Jersey, 1975.
4. The question of whether these 'experiences' are memories of actual incidents or mere fantasies or hallucinations has been raised by Daniel L. Schacter, *Searching for Memory*, Basic Books, NY, 1996, p. 77.
5. For an excellent account of 'spreading activation' theory, see John R. Anderson, *Cognitive Psychology and its Implications*, 3rd edn, Freeman, NY, 1990, pp. 150–209.
6. Daniel L. Schacter, 1996, op. cit., p. 77.
7. D. Schacter, K. Norman and Wilma Koutstaal, 'The cognitive neuroscience of constructive memory', *Annual Review of Psychology, 1998*, vol. 49, p. 291, Annual Reviews, Palo Alto, CA.
8. Technically this is known as 'content addressability'.
9. Daniel L. Schacter, op. cit., p. 103.
10. Brain-imaging technology reveals that things that have high connection strength do not necessarily have to be physically close but are often widely distributed throughout the brain. See, for example, Schacter et al., 1998.
11. Milk or calcium may also act as retrieval cues. So seeing the milk display may also remind some people of Minute Maid as a substitute for milk. (For purposes of illustration we keep the analysis simple here and keep the focus on just the one mechanism.)

Chapter 26—The buy-ology of mind

1. For an excellent account of episodic memory, see Mark H. Ashcroft, *Human Memory and Cognition*, Scott Foresman, NY, 1989.
2. An emerging view is that the residue of repeated information from similar episodes forms semantic (knowledge) memory. See Francis Bellezza, 'Mnemonic Methods for Storage and Retrieval', in Bjork and Bjork (eds), *Memory*, Academic Press, San Diego, 1996, pp. 356–7.

3. Scott MacKenzie, 'The role of attention in mediating the effect of advertising on attribute importance', *Journal of Consumer Research*, vol. 13, no. 2, Sept. 1986, p. 178.

4. This is based on our NFO MarketMind experience over more than a decade of tracking numerous campaigns and more recently is strongly supported by the publication of the work of Eric Marder, *The Laws of Choice*, Free Press, NY, 1997.

5. Extensive studies by Marder (ibid.) indicate that the effect attributable to a *single* placement of a print ad is small and below the order of magnitude that can be detected in many research sample designs (p. 287). However, with TV the average effect, while still small, is many magnitudes (8 or 9 times) greater (p. 319).

6. R. Fazio, P. Herr and M. Powell, 'On the development and strength of category-brand associations in memory: the case of mystery ads', *Journal of Consumer Psychology,* 1992, vol. I (1), pp. 1–3.

7. For example, people may be questioned about the Volkswagen ad by asking whether they have seen an ad for cars that showed a close-up of a man's face that is badly scarred.

8. Ad recognition (execution-cued ad awareness) can be a good measure of 'mental reach' only if precautions are first taken to set benchmarks and control for the tendency towards 'yeah'-saying. A new ad can look or feel familiar even when people have not actually seen it before—particularly if the new ad is generically similar to other ads. We have observed as many as 43 per cent of people in benchmark periods claiming to have seen an ad, before it even went to air. It is amazing how many market research companies ignore this and fail to benchmark these types of measures.

9. Esther Thorsen and Xinshu Zhao, 'Television viewing behavior as an index of commercial effectiveness', Association for Consumer Research Advertising & Psychology Conference, 1994.

10. It is possible to do this an alternative way, by asking people if they have seen any advertising for the brand and, if they have, to describe the ad. This is known as brand-cued ad recall. This is discussed in more detail in the Appendix.

11. In fact, people are more likely to recall TV ads than print ads like this but we have used the print example for clarity of illustration.

12. Note that this is not a good estimate of the percentage of people who have seen and noticed the ad which will be significantly greater and more appropriately indicated by the execution cued (recognition measure). Movements in the two measures are usually correlated (see Appendix). Here, what is being indicated is the percentage of people for whom the connection has not only been established but is strong enough to be triggered into mind spontaneously by the product category.

13. There is also some tendency for the reverse to be true. Increasing brand recall can also lead to an increase to some extent in advertising recall for that brand. If more people become involved with that brand they may be more likely to notice its advertising. But this relationship is much weaker and not a necessary one at all.

14. Jack B. Haskins, 'Factual recall as a measure of advertising effectiveness', *Journal of Advertising Research*, 1964, vol. 4, March, pp. 2–28.

15. Advertising that is not designed to solve a problem or remove a dissatisfaction but depicts consumption of the brand as a source of reward in its own right. For a fuller understanding of tranformational advertising, see John Rossiter and Larry Percy, 1997, op. cit., p. 121.

16. It is important to recognize that brand users are usually more favorable to that brand's advertising than non-users of it. This needs to be borne in mind especially when comparing one brand's ads with another smaller brand's ads. See B. Rice and R. Bennett, 1998, op. cit.

17. Kevin Keller, 'Memory factors in advertising: the effect of ad retrieval cues on brand evaluations', *Journal of Consumer Research*, Dec. 1987.

Appendix: How to prompt ad awareness

1. Graham Staplehurst, 'Effective research for effective campaign results'. Paper presented to Australian Market Research Society 1996 Annual Conference.

2. See, for example, Frank Simper, 'A response to "Effective research for effective campaign results"'. Paper presented to Australian Market Research Society Annual Conference 1997.
3. Staplehurst, 1996, p. 12.
4. This is known as the encoding specificity principle: see E. Tulving, E. and D. Thomson, 'Encoding specificity and retrieval processes in episodic memory', *Psychological Review*, vol. 80, 1973, pp. 352–73.
5. Frequently, the brand will be masked out of the photo-stills and the description—in which case it is called 'masked, execution-cued ad awareness'.
6. A study by Stapel provides evidence that all recall comes from the much larger group of people who recognize the advertising. J. Stapel, 'Recall and recognition: a very close relationship', *Journal of Advertising Research*, vol. 38, no. 4, July/Aug. 1998, pp. 41–5.
7. When consumers look at your advertising communications what do they think about? Some are daydreaming—staring while their minds are 'off elsewhere'. An hour later 40 per cent or more won't even recognize having seen it. See Esther Thorsen and Xinshu Zhao, 'Television viewing behaviour as an index of commercial effectiveness'. Paper presented at 7th Annual Advertising and Consumer Psychology Conference, Minneapolis, 1994.
8. Doing something else at the same time as watching TV reduces our ability to recall advertising. Contributing to lower advertising recall is the trend to viewers doing something else while they are watching TV. The main things include talking to other people, eating dinner, reading, using the phone, handicrafts, napping, ironing, playing with kids and pets, etc. The following US figures tell this story:

	1965	1974	1981	1986	1990
Only watches TV	72%	53%	59%	61%	50%
Does something else at the same time	28%	47%	40%	39%	50%

Source: NAB 1990 (as cited by Franzen, op. cit.)

9. Also, incidental viewing seems to be an ever growing problem. In 1980, in the US about 10 per cent of people in the room were there by chance, that is, they were *not* there to watch TV. By 1990 this figure had increased to 25%. About half of the other 75% in the room watching TV are also doing something else at the same time (as reported by Franzen, op. cit.).
10. We are assuming here that the question is well designed. A gap can reflect a poorly designed ad description or poor selection of photo-stills—especially if you don't include cues from the audio track as well as the video. Remember the photo-stills or the ad descriptions have to be realistic surrogates for the ad.
11. One complication is that when an ad is very similar to other ads in the category it is possible for people to say they recognize having seen it before it goes to air. This usually signals that it is a problem ad because it is not distinctive enough—its content or style is too 'generic'. It is crucial to quantify this level of 'false claiming' by including the question in the tracking *before the ad goes to air*. This then becomes a diagnostic in its own right.
12. See Chapter 20: 'Maximising ad effectiveness: develop a unique and consistent style.'

Index

Absolut vodka, 90, 210fig, 227
actions, as advertising constant, 214
ad awareness, 144fig, 252–4, 277–9,
    295–6; versus advertising awareness,
    296; barriers to, 253; as diagnostic
    measure, 296–7; questions to elicit,
    291–303; techniques for measuring,
    157–8, 291–303; *see also* ad recall;
    ad recognition; awareness
ad believability, 272, 281–2
ad-brand association, 280
ad effectiveness: ad-focused, 266, 272–3,
    275, 277–83, 296–7; audience
    involvement and, 160; brand-focused,
    271–5; of competing advertisements,
    157–9; constraints on, 121–35; creative
    elements in, 85–98; of disliked
    advertisements, 86–7; factors
    influencing, 160; of 15-second TV
    commercials, 179–90; flighting and,
    160; indicators, 157–8; of 'lecture-style'
    advertisements, 86–7, 103–4, 106–10;
    limits on, 121–35; measurement,
    255–86 *passim;* of negative
    advertisements, 118–19; of 'news'
    advertisements, 86–7; reach and, 160;
    techniques for, 262–6, 291–303;
    through celebrity presenters, 108;
    through humor, 102–3, 172–8; through
    liking an ad, 88, 176; through music,
    105–6; through testimonials, 103–4

ad execution, 269; and advertising
    effectiveness, 160, 174–6, 269–70;
    audience involvement, 199–202; as cue
    for ad recall, 291–2, 298–300, 303;
    defined, 139; elements of, 99–100;
    integration of brand with, 174–5,
    175fig; level of exposure, 197–202;
    optimum number, 198–9; risk of
    underweight advertising, 197–202
ad experience, 269–70, 276; elements of,
    269; memory network of, 270fig
ad hoc surveys, 143, 146
ad liking, *see* liking for an advertisement
ad recall, 163–4, 223–4, 224fig, 249–50,
    252–3, 255, 268, 271–2, 272, 277–9,
    279–80, 295; brand-cued, 292–7,
    300–1, 303; category-cued, 279–80,
    292–4, 296, 301–2, 303; claimed
    versus actual, 295, 297; conditions for,
    90; execution-cued, 277–8, 291–2,
    298–300, 303; false, 280, 295, 300;
    spontaneous, 279–80; through
    constancy in style, 226–8; through
    sequels, 224–6; *see also* ad awareness;
    ad recognition; salience
ad recognition, 249–50, 252, 255, 271,
    277–9; barriers to, 253; *see also* ad
    recall; mental reach; salience
ADM (Archer Daniels Midland), 233
advertisement execution, *see* ad execution

316